THE
FALL
OF
JAPAN

THE
FALL
OF
JAPAN

The Final Weeks of
World War II in the Pacific

WILLIAM CRAIG

OPEN ROAD

INTEGRATED MEDIA

NEW YORK

Copyright © 1967 by William Craig

Cover design by Mimi Bark

Cover image © Omikran Omikran/Getty Images

ISBN: 978-1-5040-4689-3

This edition published in 2017 by Open Road Integrated Media, Inc.
180 Maiden Lane
New York, NY 10038
www.openroadmedia.com

To my wife, Eleanor

CONTENTS

CONTENTS

THE
FALL
OF
JAPAN

PROLOGUE

In September of 1931, the U.S. Secretary of State, Henry Stimson, wrote in his diary: "Trouble has flared up again in Manchuria. The Japanese, apparently their military elements, have suddenly made a coup." Stimson's entry was prophetic. The coup initiated a period of almost fifteen years during which Japan's militarists controlled her foreign policy, and the spirit of militarism—with all its extremist passion, its brutality, its frenzy of determination—infected the Japanese Empire like a plague.

The 1931 Manchurian "trouble" was instigated by Army officers who wanted to wage a war of conquest and prove themselves more powerful than the Japanese Cabinet. Both of these goals were realized. By the end of 1931 the Japanese Army, overriding the protests of stunned officials in Tokyo, had taken over Manchuria.

Increasingly thereafter, the Imperial Army shaped the destiny of the nation. In 1937, the Army invaded China and perpetrated atrocities on the people of Nanking which repelled the rest of the world. Japan joined the Axis in September 1940; and by 1941 the Army had occupied French Indo-China—after France had fallen to Nazi Germany and could no longer protect her interest in Asia. Inexorably, Japan was building toward a confrontation with the West.

One of the chief architects of this design was a man about five feet four inches tall, bald, with a scraggly moustache, round eyeglasses and nicotine-stained fingers. His name was General Hideki Tojo, and his nickname was "The Razor." Strong man of the Army, Tojo had worked diligently to achieve his preeminent position. He had earned a reputation as a brilliant administrator, skilled organizer and scrupulous executor of the Emperor's orders. He was a man of huge personal ambition, drive and dedication. In 1937 he had become chief of staff of the elite Kwantung Army in Manchuria. A major spokesman for the military, he held that Japan's war with China was a "defensive" action designed to contain a hostile neighbor. In 1938 he had gone to Tokyo as Vice-Minister of War; two years later, immediately after Japan joined forces with Germany and Italy, he had become Minister of War. During the year that followed, the Imperial forces continued to move southward on the Asian mainland, thus projecting themselves into an area that directly pertained to American, British and Dutch interests. In the summer of 1941 when these nations finally refused to allow Japanese importation of vital oil from the Dutch East Indies, Tojo and his army felt that sufficient proof had been given that the Western allies intended to encircle and destroy Japan.

The American Secretary of State, Cordell Hull, demanded that Japan withdraw from the Chinese mainland and Indo-China. In answer, on September 6, the Imperial policy makers made a tentative decision to go to war if negotiations failed. In October 1941, Hideki Tojo was asked to form a new cabinet to solve the deepening crisis with the United States. He was now Premier of Japan. Most Americans would think of him as a dictator equivalent to Hitler or Mussolini; he was, rather, a bureaucrat—a militarist at the head of a militarist ruling faction. Narrow-minded, with an almost paranoid distrust of American intentions, Tojo could not envision any policy but a firm stand against outside "encroachment."

When statesmen and even supra-belligerent Navy officers hesitated to take such a drastic step as attacking the West, it was

Tojo who stiffened their resolve. Dissident voices were stilled by threats of violence. The Commander in Chief of the Imperial Navy, Isoroku Yamamoto, was openly condemned when he told his admirals that Japan could not defeat the United States in a long war. Deeply disturbed at the prospect of disaster, Yamamoto conceived an operation designed to immobilize the United States Fleet for one year, and so give the Japanese time to win a sizable number of victories before attempting a negotiated settlement. This operation was the bombing of Pearl Harbor. Pearl Harbor was Yamamoto's solution to the dilemma posed by his less practical colleagues.

The Army and Navy won the victories he had predicted. For six months, Japanese arms ruled the Pacific. Singapore, Bataan and Corregidor fell. Then at Midway, America turned the tide. Aided by the fact that Japanese codes had been broken and deciphered by American cryptoanalysts, the United States fleet inflicted an enormous defeat on Yamamoto's task force, which had sailed out intending to annihilate the remnants of Admiral Nimitz' battle line.

Yamamoto retreated to his cabin on the battleship *Yamato* and did not come out until she docked in Japan. After he left his flagship, wounded crewmen were furtively taken to isolation wards of hospitals. Survivors of the stricken warships were warned not to mention anything about the Battle of Midway. Until the end of the war, few military men in Japan knew, as Admiral Yamamoto did, that in June of 1942 the Japanese Navy had been irreparably damaged and the Empire had suffered a fatal wound.

After Midway, some admirals in the Imperial Fleet began to think of a negotiated peace. In the Imperial Army such thoughts were rarely entertained. Only in the Navy was there a sizable nucleus of officers willing to discuss it. In the summer of 1943, one of them, Admiral Sokichi Takagi, was summoned to Tokyo by the Naval Ministry to conduct a survey of the war. He pored over available information and concluded that if the Americans succeeded in winning the Solomons, Japan must sue for peace.

By the end of 1943 the Solomons fell, but Takagi still dared not circulate his conclusions in writing lest he be accused of defeatism—or worse, treason. Instead, he chose to approach top officials one by one, hoping to impress them individually with his country's desperate situation. When he did, each man in turn was afraid to act on the warning.

The first break within Japan's ruling circle did not occur until after the Americans landed on Saipan in June 1944. In countless engagements since Midway—Guadalcanal, New Guinea, Tarawa, Kwajalein—Imperial soldiers and marines had been dying by the thousands. With the invasion of Saipan, and with his vaunted army in serious straits, Premier Tojo was at last confronted by his opposition.

The *jushin*, a group of elder statesmen serving in an advisory capacity to the Emperor, decided that Tojo had to resign. Though officially powerless, the jushin exerted a subtle influence on Government policy. All its members were former Premiers. In July, when Tojo's fortunes were at a low ebb and he was trying to reorganize his cabinet, the jushin imposed several conditions designed to inhibit his power. They not only forced Tojo to relinquish his concurrent post as Chief of Staff of the Army, and to oust Navy Minister Shimada, a Tojo ally; they also insisted on having several senior statesmen of their own choosing included in any new cabinet. This last issue led directly to Tojo's downfall: the Premier could neither induce some of his own supporters to resign, nor persuade jushin men to join the cabinet under his leadership. With his cabinet in disarray, Hideki Tojo had no choice but to resign.

At this time, Japanese control of the Pacific was shrinking visibly. As the Imperial forces found themselves being pushed back to their Home Islands, they fought with increasingly suicidal desperation. Tojo went home to his wife and garden and left his successors to preside over the fall of Japan.

ONE

The Tactics of Despair

By the autumn of 1944, many of the Japanese officers responsible for the day-to-day prosecution of the war against the Allies knew that the likelihood of victory was becoming remote. One of these men was Admiral Takijiro Onishi, a headstrong, arrogant commander who exuded a masculinity and drive contagious to the younger men who served with him. A cult of junior officers worshipped Onishi much as Americans had adored Teddy Roosevelt in his Rough Rider days. On the other hand, many officers equal or superior in rank to Onishi detested his aggressive, showy manners, his bluntness, his condescending attitude toward those who disagreed with him. Onishi was a zealot who impressed his own ideas upon others with unwavering self-confidence.

In 1941 Onishi had been instrumental in drawing up the Yamamoto plan for the attack on Pearl Harbor. Immediately after the attack he ordered the devastating assault on Clark Field, outside Manila, which virtually eliminated American air capability in the Far East. Onishi had given this order despite the considered opinion of his staff, who felt that weather conditions were bad enough to force a cancellation of the mission. The admiral, however, was not about to lose the initiative—he saw any opportunity to destroy the enemy as precious. The mission was effected despite the weather. Such boldness commanded fierce loyalty.

In October 1944, an American armada appeared near the eastern Philippines. Since the Americans had many aircraft carriers off Leyte, some way had to be found to immobilize these ships while Japanese battleships and cruisers closed in to deal with the outgunned enemy.

The situation was of desperate importance. If the Philippines went under, the Empire would be cut in two and its supply lifelines ripped away. Onishi was sent from Tokyo to Manila to take command of Japan's First Air Fleet, now reduced to less than one hundred effective planes. His job was to remedy the tactical situation by whatever means available.

To the Japanese naval mind, carriers had always been the biggest menace in the war. Onishi concentrated on them with ferocious intensity. In so doing, he typified the blind spot that Admiral Weneker, the German attaché in Tokyo during the war, noted: "The Japanese admirals always thought of the U.S. carriers. They talked about how many were being built and how many were in the Pacific, and said that these must be sunk . . . their mission was at all times the American carriers." Instead of devoting increased efforts to intercepting American supply lines, to attacking merchantmen and transports, the Japanese concentrated on the dreaded carriers.

Admiral Onishi was thinking of carriers on the evening of October 19, 1944, as he drove up to the main headquarters at Mabalacat Airfield on Luzon. Two men met him—Asaichi Tamai, executive officer at the base, and Commander Rikihei Inoguchi, senior staff officer of the First Air Fleet.

Onishi soberly outlined his plan: "As you know, the war situation is grave. The appearance of strong American forces in Leyte Gulf has been confirmed. . . . Our surface forces are already in motion . . . we must hit the enemy's carriers and keep them neutralized for at least one week." After this preamble Onishi broached a momentous idea: "In my opinion, there is only one way of assuring that our meager strength will be effective to a maximum degree. That is to organize suicide attack units composed of Zero fighters armed with 250-kilogram bombs, with each plane to crash-dive into an American carrier. . . . What do you think?" There it was, the bold desperate plan to stem the tide, to perform a miracle! It was worthy of an Onishi, a violent man given to violent solutions.

He struck the right nerve with his men. Stunned by the magnitude of this savage answer to the enemy's power, his staff leaped at the opportunity to implement his strategy.

Four special attack units were formed immediately on Luzon. They waited for four days, then five, to strike at the enemy. Finally, a scout plane radioed back the sighting of a large American carrier force.

On October 25, at 7:25 A.M., nine planes rose from Mabalacat and headed east over the vast and lonely Pacific. The men in the aircraft were hoping, in fact eager, to die for their admiral and the Emperor. All wore white scarfs around their necks. Their helmets fitted snugly about their heads, almost concealing the white cloth each man had wrapped around his forehead. This was the *hachimaki*, a cloth worn centuries earlier by the samurai warriors of feudal Japan who used it to absorb perspiration and to keep their long hair from falling into their eyes. In 1944, the white cloth became the ceremonial emblem of the Special Attack Corps—the kamikazes.

Five of the nine planes were suicide craft. The other four went along to protect them from American interference. Lieutenant Yukio Seki led the mission.

At 10:45 A.M., the unsuspecting carrier force was sighted. It was a group of escorts protecting the beachhead at Leyte. The Japanese came at the perfect psychological moment. For hours the American fleet had been running before the brute power of Admiral Kurita's force, which had burst out of San Bernardino Straits and turned south to destroy the fleet off Leyte. The carriers and destroyers had fought a tremendous delaying action against

Kurita. It was only within the hour that the Japanese had turned and gone back, fearing a trap by other American units somewhere in the general area.

The *St. Lo* and her sister carriers had secured from general quarters at 10:10, and the crews were relaxing after the terribly close rendezvous with extinction. When Seki and his formation sighted them, the Americans had their guard down.

The Japanese bored in low. At 10:50, a warning went out to the carriers: "Enemy aircraft coming in fast from overlying haze." At 10:53, a plane roared in over the *St. Lo's* ramp, then went into a steep dive and crashed on the flight deck near the center line.

At 10:56, the gas below decks ignited. Two minutes later, a violent explosion rocked the ship. A huge section of the flight deck was gone. Flames roared up one thousand feet. By 11:04, the *St. Lo* was a mass of flames.

She sank twenty-one minutes later.

While the *St. Lo* burned, the other suicide planes banked and screamed straight into their targets. Not one missed. The *Kitkun Bay*, the *Kalinin Bay* and the *White Plains* were torn by explosions as steel smashed into steel at hundreds of miles per hour. Five planes had hit four ships. One carrier was sunk, the others badly damaged. This kamikaze mission was successful, as was another launched from Mindanao earlier that day. Onishi formed new units immediately.

During the next several months, the United States Navy became increasingly aware of the murderous suicide planes. In January 1945, when MacArthur sent an invasion fleet to Lingayen Gulf on Luzon, nearly forty warships were damaged by the new squadrons. Though the landings of General Krueger's Sixth Army were successful, worried American admirals hoped the kamikazes were just a temporary expedient, not to be repeated on a wide scale. They did not know Admiral Onishi's Special Attack Corps by name or organization. They did not know that equipment and personnel had been deployed to multiply its strength many times.

In March 1945, as Japanese intelligence sources reported increased enemy interest in the area around Okinawa, only 350 miles from Japan, Onishi had the satisfaction of having his Corps integrated into the defense plan of this island. Indeed, at the highest levels in Tokyo, Army and Navy staff officers were convincing themselves that the suicide planes could change the course of the war.

For some months after Saipan fell in July of 1944, American strategists had looked for the next most strategically desirable islands to invade on the way to Japan. Following the Honolulu conference that summer, MacArthur had carried out the occupation of Leyte in October. He now stood on Luzon. Once Iwo Jima was taken, Admiral Nimitz had wanted to invade Formosa—but Formosa was eventually ignored in favor of Okinawa. Sixty miles long and the largest of the Ryukyu Islands, Okinawa could be used by the United States both as a jumping-off point for the invasion of Japan and as a base for intensive bombings of the Home Islands of Kyushu and Honshu.

Fresh troops of the newly formed Tenth Army were to mount the assault on Easter Sunday, April 1, 1945. Under the command of Simon Bolivar Buckner, the son of a Confederate general, the Tenth was composed of veteran outfits molded in the jungles of other waystops to Japan. Its divisions were already hallowed: the First Marines from Guadalcanal, New Britain and Peleliu; the Second Marines, as reserve, from Tarawa and Saipan; the Seventh from Attu and Leyte; the Seventy-seventh from Guam and Leyte; the Ninety-sixth from Leyte; the Twenty-seventh from the Marshalls and Saipan; the newly formed Sixth Marines made up of men from Eniwetok, Guam and Saipan. The soldiers and Marines, elite troops of the Pacific, would need the experience gained in countless confrontations with the Japanese; for even as they clambered into transports for the pitching ride to the shores of Okinawa, other Americans were suffering from the newly revised defense tactics of the Japanese on Iwo Jima.

The Imperial General Staff in Tokyo had decided that the tactic of the banzai charge was too costly, and the "meet them at the beach" theory was replaced on Iwo by "let the enemy come to us." On that island, the Japanese stayed in caves and poured fire down on the heads of the Marines, who had trouble even getting a glimpse of them. Heavy artillery was used as an integral part of Japanese weaponry, and the corpse-strewn beaches of Iwo showed that for the first time in the long island-hopping trail to Tokyo, the Japanese were literally tearing the Americans to bits.

The same tactics awaited the Tenth Army at Okinawa, where General Mitsuru Ushijima, a tall, stocky veteran of the war in Burma and, most recently, superintendent of the military school at Zama, was in command. A realist, Ushijima understood the power that would be brought against him. Not wanting to squander his resources, he planned a bitter end defense on the southern part of the island. Japanese last-ditch strategy for Okinawa included kamikazes at maximum strength. Ushijima would wait to spring his trap until the kamikazes had come down from the Home Islands and destroyed the hundreds of ships standing offshore. With American land forces cut off from their apparently endless supply of manpower and material, Ushijima could attack and win a crushing Japanese victory. The kamikazes were the key. If they failed, Ushijima was as good as dead.

The general watched passively as United States Army combat teams occupied the offshore Kerama atolls in late March. He watched passively as the first soldiers strolled onto Okinawan beaches on April 1.

Forty-eight hours later, the American Ninety-sixth Division crossed the waist of the island and reached the eastern shore. Then, while the Sixth Marines wheeled north, other units moved south toward the capital city, Naha.

On April 5, the bulk of the Tenth Army ran headlong into General Ushijima's concealed defenses. He unleashed his personal surprise, the largest concentration of artillery assembled by a Japanese army in one place during the whole war. Two hundred and eight-seven heavy fieldpieces began to fire at American soldiers burrowing frantically into shallow foxholes. The advance to the south stopped abruptly. The dying began.

On April 6, Onishi's kamikazes came in great strength. From Oita and Kanoya, from airfields scattered throughout the island of Kyushu, hundreds of men lifted their airplanes into the sky for a final sortie against the enemy. Their foreheads were girdled with the white hachimaki; their farewell letters had been mailed to their families.

The first American units to detect the presence of suicide craft were picket boats, destroyers placed to the north of the invasion beaches. These graceful gray warships slipped through the calm seas, their crews listening carefully to electronic equipment on board or searching the skies for the telltale specks.

The destroyers were both guardians and sacrificial lambs. While alerting the main line of ships to the south, they would offer themselves as targets to the kamikazes in order to keep them away from the huge capital ships hovering about the beaches.

The Japanese came singly, in pairs and in large groups. Most of them concentrated on the small picket ships. A few drove farther toward the beaches. During the morning, the pickets suffered badly as the Divine Wind blew across their bows. The sky was filled with black clouds of flak and the sea was laced with white necklaces of pom-pom fire as the destroyers blasted the oncoming planes. Though the Japanese incurred severe losses, the destroyers too showed effects of the combat. At least fifteen ships received gaping wounds from hurtling aircraft.

The U.S.S. *Bush* was not one of those struck on the morning of April 6. Well into the afternoon, she and her complement of more than three hundred men had escaped any physical damage. Only the men's nerves showed strain. Exhausted by hours at battle stations, they were forced to keep a constant, nerve-wracking vigil.

Then, at thirteen minutes after three, a single-engined kamikaze was sighted dead ahead and low on the water, headed straight for the *Bush* at Picket Station One.

The enemy craft was employing evasive tactics to upset the aim of the ship's gunners. It dipped and rose, sometimes coming within ten feet of the ocean. Tracer bullets reached for it in vain. It bored in at the *Bush*, which twisted desperately to avoid a collision.

At 3:15 the kamikaze smashed into the destroyer at deck level between Number One and Number Two stacks, demolishing the galley, laundry, sick bay and repair locker, and rendering the automatic-firing guns inoperative. Although the *Bush* caught fire, it seemed possible to save her. Another destroyer, the *Colhoun*, moved closer to offer help.

For over an hour the stricken *Bush* labored in the swells as her crew sought to repair the damage. The dead were removed from the shambles. The wounded were treated as quickly and efficiently as possible. The *Bush* continued to ride the ocean in a reasonable state of seaworthiness. Knotted lines were hung over the side so that sailors could escape enemy planes coming directly for their positions. In this way, the affected crew members could avoid both machine gun attacks and an ultimate crash dive on their particular position. The captain hoped to spare lives by this unusual expedient.

At 4:35, the crew of the *Bush* was horrified to see American air cover disappear to the south without any prior warning. Crippled and exposed, the ship lay helpless as the kamikaze attack intensified. Ten to fifteen fighters approached from the north. They circled the destroyers below, then veered off. One headed unerringly toward the *Bush*, its guns blazing. It smashed into the port side, nearly cutting the destroyer in two. The *Bush* was now a derelict, both sides gaping, wreckage and death inside her hull. Just before twilight a single plane flew over at mast height and soared away to the port side. Then it wheeled slowly and began a last run, holding a level course just above the water. The men on deck were paralyzed at the sight. It tore into the middle section of the *Bush*. Her back broken by violent collisions with three aircraft, she settled lower in the water. The ship was finished. Sailors began to abandon her. The forward and aft sections of the picket each pointed toward the sky. As water rushed into the jagged tear amidships, the battered destroyer slid slowly beneath the sea.

In the twilight, survivors of the slaughter dotted the ocean. The grueling and ferocious struggle with a fanatical enemy had taken its toll among them. One after the other, officers and men were seen hysterically stripping off their life preservers. In a frenzy, they swam off to some imagined haven, some refuge from the maddening horror of the kamikazes. Thirty-three men struck out for safety without their life jackets, without any real hope. One by one they sank beneath the waves.

Others waited quietly for rescue ships to pick them up. As destroyers moved among them, the last tragedy of the *Bush* was enacted. Reaching out for lines, for a helping hand, several men smashed their heads against the hulls and sank in silence. Others were swept by waves into the screws of ship propellers and disappeared in a froth of blood. Ten sailors died in these last moments, bringing to a total of eighty-seven the men lost aboard the U.S.S. *Bush*.

Altogether, twenty-four ships were sunk or damaged by the kamikazes that day. Though the suicide planes had not succeeded in penetrating to the beaches, the cost to the United States Navy had been high. And April 6 was only a prelude to mounting terror in the seas off Okinawa.

Onishi's planes were not the only expedient by which the Japanese Navy hoped to turn Okinawa into a victory for the Emperor. From Tokuyama on the Inland Sea, the colossal battleship *Yamato*, displacing 72,909 tons, sped toward the Bungo Suido, between Kyushu and Shikoku. She was accompanied by two cruisers and six destroyers. Her destination was Okinawa. Her goal was the destruction of American transports and disruption of the beachhead. Since the *Yamato* carried only enough oil to take her to the island, she would have to be beached after firing her nine massive batteries of eighteen-inch guns at the American fleet. She had been sent out as floating suicide ship *sui generis*.

Shortly after five o'clock on the afternoon of April 6, the commanders of the submarines *Threadfin and Hackleback* watched in fascination as the monstrous *Yamato* moved across their periscopes. They noted her direction and signaled back to American carriers and heavy capital ships that nine ships were apparently headed south toward Okinawa. As darkness closed around the Japanese warships, they churned westward in a course designed to keep them away from American airpower as long as possible. The Japanese themselves had no protective cover in the skies.

Like chess players, the Americans maneuvered to thwart the enemy. Carriers and battleships moved up to intercept the *Yamato* at the first light of day. On the *Yamato*, nearly three thousand men waited tensely for the dawn and the ultimate confrontation.

At 8:22 A.M., a plane from the carrier *Essex* picked up the group, churning ahead at twenty-two knots. For the next four hours, Catalina flying boats hovered over the Japanese convoy as it ran due south toward Okinawa. Shortly after noon, massed carrier attacks began. Flying out of low clouds and rain, the American planes harried the *Yamato* and her escorts for over two hours. Repeated bomb and torpedo hits reduced the flagship to a shambles, yet she stayed afloat, firing continually at her tormentors.

When at last she was listing heavily, her captain ordered his men to abandon ship. Despite repeated protests from his aides, Captain Ariga refused to leave with them. Instead he had himself lashed to a support with heavy cord. Survivors recall one seaman remaining behind with him. From his pocket the seaman took a handful of biscuits, broke one, and held a piece up to the captain's lips. Ariga looked at the man, then at the biscuit, smiled, and opened his mouth. The *Yamato* began to go under. Bound to his ship, Captain Ariga and his crewman died with her at 2:23 on the afternoon of April 7.

The last suicidal surface attack by the Japanese Imperial Navy had been a complete failure. Only four destroyers got back to Japan to report the loss of the most powerful battleship in the world.

In terms of overall strategy, the battle for Okinawa—the last land campaign of the Pacific war—was over before it began. American superiority was a foregone conclusion. But to the American Marines and soldiers struggling for survival there, it seemed that the Japanese had never fought as fiercely or as effectively. The land war was a savage killing match, fought on terrain which uniquely resembled Japan itself—familiar to the enemy, thus all the more alien to the Americans.

As April passed, the ruthless ferocity of the island war was evidenced on any given day. Marines running through gullies toward a rise called Wana Draw were attacked from the flanks by guns, pistols and mortars that fired and fired till all the men in the open had ceased to move. American flamethrowing tanks seared hillsides with gallons of liquid fuel, roasting hundreds of Japanese hiding in caves. As survivors ran out, waiting infantrymen fired clip after clip into them. Japanese shellfire was incessant, night and day, as never before in the Pacific war.

Ushijima's heavy guns fired ceaselessly, searching out the Americans cowering in shallow depressions in the ground. Under the constant whine and roar of gunfire, sleep was fitful for the Marines and soldiers, and physical and mental exhaustion became commonplace. Cases of combat fatigue grew alarmingly, to a point where, before the campaign was over, thirteen thousand Americans had been brought to the edge of collapse.

Once a quiet haven for farmers, Okinawa soon stank of cordite and decaying corpses. The fields were torn, the roads pocked with holes. On both sides of the line, men crouched, waiting for the enemy to show himself and then rising up to beat him or shoot him or stab him again and again—until the next appeared. They lived in holes in the ground that were filled with water from the constant rain. Their clothes were continually soaked. Their boots and socks rotted. Their morale disintegrated and their minds were consumed with hatred and fear of the enemy just across the ravine or beyond the trees. Japanese and Americans alike wallowed in filth.

Out on the seas the immense American fleet continued to stand by. Here too nerves stretched beyond endurance as the Japanese pressed the kamikaze attacks throughout the month of April. Over a hundred American ships were damaged or destroyed. Nearly a thousand Japanese planes were lost in this period. But still Ushijima's dream of routing the fleet and isolating the enemy on land remained unrealized.

Despite this disappointment, the kamikazes figured heavily in one last all-out effort undertaken by the Japanese command on May 3. The new strategy came into being painfully, born of bickering and bitterness among Ushijima's staff. In headquarters one hundred feet below the ground, under the stronghold of Shuri Castle, an increasingly belligerent group of officers had tired of remaining on the defensive and were urging a massive counterattack. One of the radical leaders was Colonel Naomichi Jin, a staff officer who was disgusted at the conservative elements around Ushijima. As casualties mounted and the Americans inched down the island, Jin and his followers openly threatened the life of Colonel Yahara, chief proponent of a defensive strategy. General Ushijima faced a rebellion within his own ranks.

The inevitable showdown occurred in an acrimonious meeting in which General Isamu Cho, a man who for years had been an extreme rightist in army affairs in Japan, hotly argued for a strong attack on American fortifications. Hard-pressed by the shouts and threats of Cho, Jin and other diehards, Ushijima relented and gave weary approval to a massive offensive beginning May 4. The objective was to destroy the American Twenty-fourth Corps and to force back the entire American line. Arrangements were made with Admiral Onishi's air arm for an intensive new kamikaze assault on the ships offshore to begin on the evening of May 3. Once more the Japanese hoped to effect a complete rupture of naval support to the army on the island.

Onishi's squadrons came down from airfields in Kyushu as planned and managed to put eighteen ships out of action. One of them, the destroyer *Aaron Ward*, took five kamikaze dives, lost ninety-eight men killed or wounded, yet stayed miraculously afloat. But the vast bulk of American ships remained undamaged.

The land fighting that began at dawn on May 4 was chaotic, costly, and for the Japanese, hopeless. A thunderous initial bombardment by Japanese artillery was followed by the confusion of close-quarter fighting, where friend and foe passed each other in the fluid battle zones without realizing it. An entire squad of Japanese soldiers marched in close order right into the automatic rifles of the Seventy-seventh Infantry Division and was annihilated on the spot. A column of American soldiers, smoking and talking, their rifles loosely slung, walked toward the front lines under the eyes of Japanese infiltrators and were all killed in seconds. One Japanese advance late in the afternoon of May 4 succeeded in penetrating over a mile behind American positions. It was quickly blunted by superior firepower.

This action of May 4–5 represented the full extent of the last Imperial Army offensive in World War II. Japanese resources could not sustain another. On the next day General Ushijima ordered his badly beaten forces back into their caves and bunkers, and his army resumed a defensive posture. The influence of Cho and Jin and their supporters broke against the hard facts of reality.

In the deep shelter under Shuri Castle, General Ushijima tried without much hope to encourage his aides. On the other side of the lines, General Simon Bolivar Buckner ordered his forces to go over to the offensive. By May 8, V-E Day, the initiative had passed forever to the Americans.

The Japanese situation deteriorated steadily through May and the early part of June as American forces slowly pushed into the southernmost area of the island. General Ushijima's forces were unable to withstand the relentless pressure of superior firepower. When Shuri Castle, the last bastion, fell on May 31, the battle was nearly over.

American infantrymen walking into that former headquarters of Ushijima's Thirty-second Army witnessed a scene of utter devastation. Heavy shells and bombs had torn apart the town which ringed the castle grounds. Only a Methodist church and a two-story concrete building still stood. Shuri Castle itself was demolished. In this fortress from which former kings of Okinawa had ruled, nothing lived. The Japanese had left their dead and retreated to the south. The last center of organized resistance had dissolved.

In the next three weeks, the retreating General Ushijima managed to perform a minor miracle by organizing another zone of defense, but he knew it could hold only a short time. The end was close.

By now even Japanese soldiers knew it. Bombarded by millions of leaflets which assured them of fair treatment, they considered the idea of laying down their arms. Many decided against it and instead committed suicide. But for the first time in the war, hundreds of tattered and dirty soldiers came out of caves and walked toward American lines with hands held high over their heads. Eventually over seven thousand Japanese surrendered.

Inside a cave under Hill 89, General Ushijima read Allied surrender leaflets and laughed. His assistant, General Cho, relaxed with a bottle of Scotch as he listened to late reports coming in from the scattered units in the field. The front line had disintegrated. Japanese troops had become a disorganized rabble, skulking in holes and trenches, wandering through the countryside looking for food and water. They were without hope.

In an open field near Kadena Airbase more than a hundred shrouded bodies lay in neat rows on the grass. All of them were American sailors washed ashore from the wreckage of ships blown to pieces by kamikazes. Soldiers passing by paused, many of them aware for the first time of the price paid by the Navy in supporting the foot soldier at the beaches.

A huge cave inside the Japanese lines was serving as a field hospital where three hundred badly wounded Japanese Marines were being treated. Their commander, Admiral Ota, feared that the enemy would pour fire and gasoline into the cave before asking questions. He ordered the senior doctor to make sure that the patients did not suffer further, that they had an honorable death.

The doctor and his assistants readied hypodermic needles and walked through long rows of sick men. With tears rolling down their cheeks, they methodically squeezed syringes into three hundred outstretched arms. Finally there was no sound in the hospital except the sobbing of the medical staff.

Another Japanese doctor, named Maehara, had given up trying to cope with the mounting disaster and had sought refuge among Okinawan natives who were prowling through the battlefields. Maehara fell in with a group of men and women living in a series of caves gouged from the side of a hill. In these close quarters, he fell in love and shared his bed with a small, bright-faced native girl. In the midst of death, they clung together and spoke of an uncertain future.

In the third week of June, the Americans surrounded the hill. Maehara and the girl planned to escape by one of the several tunnels burrowed through the hillside to open ground hundreds of yards away. Fearful, they delayed leaving. American soldiers stalking the enemy came eventually to the mouth of the cave and threw in satchel charges of dynamite. Maehara retreated into the deepest recesses. The girl followed. When a flamethrower shot a burst into the entrance, the Japanese doctor shouted for the girl to follow him out through one of the escape hatches. Scrambling, twisting, he reached the cooling breezes outside. Behind him, nothing stirred. Shocked, Maehara retraced his steps into the blackness and came upon a crumpled form. The girl had been caught by the searing heat of the flamethrower and died in the dirt. Maehara wandered dazedly out of the cave and surrendered to the enemy. He was beyond caring.

On the eighteenth of June, General Simon Bolivar Buckner came to the forward positions to oversee the mop-up. Standing in an observation post, he watched the battle for the caves. Suddenly, a Japanese dual-purpose gun fired a shell which struck a rock formation above him. A jagged piece of coral flew down and hit Buckner in the chest. He died within minutes.

On the evening of the twenty-first of June, Generals Ushijima and Cho sat down to a sumptuous meal in their home under Hill 89. Overhead the Americans walked on top of the escarpment, where Japanese soldiers continued to resist them by fighting for every rock and tree.

The generals ate quietly. As their aides offered toasts, the two leaders drank to each other with dregs of whiskey preserved for this moment. A full moon shone on the white coral ledges of Hill 89 as a final tribute rang through the cave: "Long live the Emperor."

At 4:00 A.M. on the morning of the twenty-second, Ushijima, cooling himself with a bamboo fan, walked with Cho between lines of crying subordinates to the mouth of the cave. There Cho turned to his superior and said, "I will lead the way." The two generals emerged into the moonlight. They were followed by several staff officers.

Outside the entrance a quilt had been laid on top of a mattress. Loud firing sounded on all sides as American infantrymen, no more than fifty feet away, sensed movement. Ushijima proceeded to sit down and pray. Cho did the same.

Ignoring the guns and grenades, Ushijima bowed low toward the ground. His adjutant handed him a knife. The general held it briefly in front of his body, then ripped it across his abdomen. Immediately his adjutant raised a jeweled sword and brought it down across his neck. Ushijima's head toppled onto the quilt and blood spattered the onlookers. Within seconds, General Cho died the same way.

The battle of Okinawa had ended. Over 12,000 Americans and more than 100,000 Japanese were dead. The American flag flew only 350 miles from Japan.

TWO

Meetinghouse

If General Ushijima hoped that by destroying the Americans at Okinawa he would spare his homeland the horrors of war, then the Thirty-second Imperial Army's furious defense of the island was an exercise in mass futility. Even as the fighting raged on Okinawa, the cities of Japan were burning. In the wreckage of thousands of homes, men and women sobbed the names of loved ones, buried in the debris left by Bi-ni-ju-ku, the dreaded B-29 bomber.

Squadrons of these beautiful silver planes had come with increasing frequency from the south to terrorize the people of Japan. When they appeared over a metropolitan center, the next hours were filled with suffering for the humanity massed below. It had been that way for several months, since March, when General Curtis Lemay, commander of the Twenty-first Bomber Command in the Mariana Islands, discovered the strategy needed to knock down the cities of Japan.

When he first inherited his job in January 1945, Lemay was faced with a paradox: the B-29, a superior weapon, available in sufficient numbers to perform the most ambitious kinds of missions against the Home Islands, was not working out as it should have. Something was wrong with the way the machine was being used by aerial tacticians. Doctrines established in the air war over Europe were not succeeding in Asia. Lemay had come to remedy the situation.

At thirty-eight, he was a strategic bombing specialist, a "hard-nose," a soldier dedicated to the belief that the heavy bomber could effect the destruction of any nation. A veteran of the Army Air Force, he had first joined the fledgling service in the budget-poor days of 1928. After graduation from Ohio State, Lemay became a lieutenant in an army that boasted precious little in the way of an air arm. He lived through the pioneer days, times when men feared for their lives every time they went up in rickety machines. Then he gravitated to the bombardment section of the tiny service and built up impressive experience in the primitive art of attacking an enemy with long-range aircraft.

When the United States entered World War II, Curtis Lemay began to implement his theoretical training. From England, he flew against the German Luftwaffe and quickly learned the rude facts of modern air strategy. Forced to improvise tactics in daily combat, Lemay proved a brilliant, resourceful commander, whose bomber squadrons always penetrated German defenses to hit their targets. In spite of constant attack, the B-17's of the English Air Force gradually began to hurt Germany's capacity to wage war. Curtis Lemay, as leader of the Third Bombardment Division, was known as a hard-driving taskmaster, a ruthlessly efficient exponent of aerial bombardment. On the basis of this impressive record, General Hap Arnold saw him as a natural choice to tackle the problems surrounding a new bomber which had just begun to operate in the Pacific, and in June of 1944 he recalled Lemay to the States.

The B-29 itself was an awesome weapon, capable of nearly twice the performance of the time-tested B-17 being used in Europe. Built by Boeing, the silver-painted four-engine aircraft was 99 feet long, 27 feet 9 inches high, with a wing span of slightly over 141 feet. Its armament included twelve 50-caliber machine guns and a 20-millimeter cannon in the tail. The B-29 could operate at 38,000 feet and cruise at over 350 miles per hour. It could fly 3,500 miles with four tons of bombs. It was the answer to the Army Air Force's search for a Very Long Range bomber. It could reach across the Pacific from great distances and strike at the enemy's industries. It could, in short, alter the balance of the war. But so far the efforts to use it effectively in the Pacific had brought nothing but frustration.

Lemay spent the summer familiarizing himself with the big bomber and learning to fly it. In the fall he was sent to China, where he took command of B-29 raiding missions from airfields around Chengtu. His job there was almost impossible.

Chengtu was the wrong place for such an operation. The basic problem was one of logistics. All supplies for the raiders had to be flown in over the Hump, that formidable barrier of mountains otherwise known as the Himalayas. Gas, oil, bombs, bullets, food, incidental supplies, were brought to China by transport planes. Though more and more tonnage was moved each month by this means, it was never enough to mount a massive offensive. Rarely did more than one hundred bombers take off together on a mission. Lemay was frustrated by the failure of his planes to evidence their destructive capability. Washington, also disillusioned by the Chengtu situation, gradually began to shift emphasis away from that area, and at the turn of the year Lemay was moved to Guam. There in the Marianas, shorter supply lines would eliminate the most vexing problems of the China operation.

Chengtu could not be called a complete failure, however. Roosevelt and Churchill had paid a political debt to Chiang Kai-shek by stationing the big bombers in his country. Disillusioned at the apparent lack of interest in his cause, the Generalissimo had been considerably heartened by the decision to mount an attack on the enemy from China. His war-weary people also were cheered by the sight of the B-29's flying toward the Japanese homeland. From a practical standpoint, too, the China experience had value. Chengtu was a proving ground, a training base for both crew members and commanders of the new bombardment force.

Lessons learned there were remembered in the Marianas as the Twenty-first Bomber Command started to fly to Japan.

During the first two months of 1945 Lemay sent missions out to prove his theory that he could level the enemy. By March, he had accomplished almost nothing. The enemy had not been hurt badly. In fact, the morale of civilians in Japan rose markedly as they found their patterns of daily life unchanged. Even some of the Japanese leaders regained confidence as they noted that the national war machine still functioned at a high rate. So far the B-29 had not performed well, and Curtis Lemay knew it.

Several factors combined to thwart the bombing efforts. Weather was paramount. Between the Marianas and Japan it was atrocious. Jet streams blew at two hundred miles an hour across the skies. Heavy cloud cover enveloped targets repeatedly. Bombs dropped from thirty thousand feet were scattered by the winds. In the first six weeks after Lemay arrived on Guam, only one opportunity arose for visual sighting on a city. All other raids had to be accomplished by means of radar, which was still unreliable and so caused frequent misses on aiming points. Eleven priority targets in the Home Islands were virtually undamaged despite repeated attacks. One, the Mushashino aircraft-engine plant in Tokyo, was functioning at ninety-six percent of capacity though the B-29's had gone after it several times.

The big planes themselves were beginning to malfunction at an alarming rate as the strain of flying at over thirty thousand feet for long distances caused engine breakdowns. The tremendous burden of climbing to rarified altitudes was showing in daily operations reports listing aborted missions, in which disabled aircraft were unable to reach targets in Japan. As March began, Lemay surveyed his domain and wondered just what he could do to effect a miracle.

For several weeks he had had a bold plan in mind, conceived from his own observations and in conferences with other B-29 commanders in the Marianas. It was a daring thrust, a gamble for the big prize—the destruction of Japanese war production.

He felt that percentages favored its success. Yet, not sure of what reaction it would receive, he chose not to mention it to General Hap Arnold, Air Corps Chief of Staff. He simply went ahead with his operation.

Orders were cut on March 7 for implementation on March 9. Three wings, the 73rd, the 313th and the 314th, would fly the mission. The target was the northeast urban section of Tokyo, code-named Meetinghouse. Bombing runs would commence on the city just after midnight. Bombs would be released at altitudes between five thousand and nine thousand feet. *All* guns would be removed from the B-29's. Only incendiary bombs would be used on the congested wooden homes of Meetinghouse.

To crew members on the flight, the idea of flying over the most heavily defended city in Japan at five thousand feet without guns was shocking. Intelligence experts on Guam estimated that the enemy had massed 331 heavy-caliber guns, 307 automatic-firing weapons, 312 single-engine fighters and 105 twin-engine interceptors around Tokyo. Yet Lemay intended to challenge this defensive arsenal by going in low, at night and without ammunition.

His reasoning was quite sound. The key ingredients in his plan were the night attack and the low altitude. Both struck at the Japanese in their most vulnerable spots. Japan had so far failed to develop an adequate night fighter which could shoot down the B-29. Neither had it converted its antiaircraft weapons to radar control. Thus the low-level assault would tend to confuse the manually controlled weapons surrounding Meetinghouse.

If these suppositions were correct, Lemay had eliminated the need for guns in his own planes. By so doing, he also reduced the weight of the bombers and allowed for increased bombloads. Other bonuses followed.

Because the B-29's did not have to fly at great heights, less gas was needed, permitting a further increase in bombload. The lower altitude also reduced strain on the engines and decreased the probability of malfunction during and after the mission.

Buoyed up by these positive factors, General Lemay hoped to drop over two thousand tons of incendiary bombs on the people of Tokyo and incinerate part of the Japanese factory system, which had been decentralized and flourished inside the private homes of the city.

One danger was apparent. The Japanese might just adjust to his unorthodox tactics in time to inflict horrible losses on the defenseless bombers. If they did, the Marianas would be a land of the bereaved and Curtis Lemay proved a fool.

The Meetinghouse flight went ahead as planned.

On March 9, at twilight, thirteen hundred motors turned over and roared into the night as 325 massive B-29's left their hardstands and formed a continuing line of bombers moving toward the ends of runways. One by one they lifted into the sky. Since the flight plan had eliminated the need for rendezvous, the B-29's moved singly to the north, gaining altitude as they went.

The first twelve aircraft in each wing were pathfinders. Their mission was to mark the target area in Meetinghouse by sowing their incendiaries in a huge X across the congested section. Hundreds of magnesium, napalm and phosphorus canisters would ignite and spread like a beckoning torch.

The long line of planes droned toward the mainland. Over the island of Chichi Jima, in the Bonins, the Japanese sent up sporadic antiaircraft fire but found no victims.

In the darkness, the B-29's made landfall by radar, using checkpoints on the Bose Peninsula, southeast of Tokyo, and moving toward them for the turns to a final approach on the unsuspecting mass of humanity.

As midnight arrived, lights were mostly out in the thousands of homes jammed into the neighborhood around the Sumida River, several miles northeast of the Imperial Palace. The moon shone coldly on the waters of Tokyo Bay. A chill, twenty-eight-mile-an-hour wind tossed paper through narrow streets.

Though many civilians had heard on the radio that B-29's were active that night, it appeared that they were well east of Tokyo and heading away to the north.

The pathfinders turned west and roared in low and fast. They slipped across the darkened city and loosed a series of E-46 bombs, each of which exploded at twenty-five hundred feet and scattered thirty-eight more pipe-like canisters into the wind. The two-foot-long projectiles fell into the middle of wooden homes and began to burn ferociously.

As frightened civilians moved into the open streets, the pathfinders fled swiftly to the south. Behind them a blazing X marked the target for more onrushing B-29's with their loads of incendiaries. The airplanes came individually and spewed their cargoes into a spreading sea of red and white flame. To the first crews over the target it was obvious that Tokyo would burn badly that night. "It looked like a forest fire," one man reported. In thirty minutes the blaze was completely out of control. There was no way to stop it. It roared upward for hundreds of feet and moved rapidly outward in many directions. The high winds threw burning embers across firebreaks and pushed a solid mass of flame before them. And still the planes came in, dropping cluster upon cluster of magnesium, phosphorus and napalm. Tracer bullets arched up toward the gleaming underbellies of the bombers. Antiaircraft shells exploded among them. The sky became an unbelievable panorama of light, noise and movement.

As the fires expanded and intensified, bombers coming in over the target began to have trouble. Violent updrafts from the whirling storm in the city tore at the fuselages and threatened to rip them apart. Instead of worrying about the antiaircraft guns, the pilots struggled to control their ponderous planes. Turbulence tossed the B-29's several thousand feet in seconds and they went straight up or down at dizzying rates. In some ships terrified crew members crawled on their hands and knees and shouted, "Let's get the hell out of here!" as M-47 and M-69 canisters fell out of bomb bays toward the inferno below. Battered B-29's got out as quickly as they could.

Above them, one plane circled the target area for a long time. It carried General Tom Power, Lemay's Chief of Staff, Eager to observe the results of the raid, Power stayed and stayed over the awesome sight. The target sector of the city was dying beneath his feet. As artists sketched the scene, Power radioed back to Guam that the gamble had worked. Lemay had revolutionized bombing technique.

Power's plane finally left for home, but on the streets of Tokyo there was no place to go. Frenzy mounted as the heat rose. People ran and fell to the ground, the breath pulled from their lungs. Some died standing up in the close-packed, airless shelters. Inside the Meiji-za Theatre, bodies were stacked eight feet high. Those who chose to go outside again fought each other savagely to escape. Many stood waist-deep in streams and pools, to sink beneath the surface as the fire sucked away oxygen. Everywhere people clawed their throats but found no air to breathe. Police and fire officials were trampled by rioting crowds. Fire-fighting equipment—ninety-nine pieces in all—was destroyed in the intense heat.

The only possible exits were the bridges spanning the Sumida River. Across the river, in the blackness of the wholly untouched portions of the city, victims could see safety. Thousands ran in that direction while screaming and tearing at each other. Men and women were pushed into the river to drown. Faces were smashed in, fingers, arms, legs and genitals battered and torn from bodies. The bridges across the Sumida became a battlefield of panic. Hundreds of bodies lay in mounds, just a short way from freedom.

From his shelter in the suburb of Arakawa, a young boy named Wakabayashi came out to see the extent of the damage. A B-29 dropped a shower of magnesium canisters, one of which broke open and sprayed him. His hand was badly burned but he was not otherwise hurt. He helped his neighbors put out some of the small fires with "hitataki," bamboo poles tipped with cotton cloth and soaked in water. But there were too many canisters plunging from the sky. Wakabayashi and the others left the area, which was rapidly becoming an inferno of crackling fire. They went to a river and saw hundreds of people standing up in the water, packed against each other. They were all dead. Wakabayashi stumbled on, away from the silent victims.

By three o'clock in the morning the last B-29 swept low over the city and scattered its seven tons into the billowing fire. Then the noise of motors trailed off to the south. Of the mission's 325 bombers, 279 had gotten to the target. Antiaircraft fire, which had weakened as the flames intensified, ceased as the planes disappeared. The crackle of wildfire mingling with cries in the night remained as witness to the efficiency of the intruders, who formed a long, erratic line toward the south and the Marianas.

In the rear planes, men attempted to drive away the most lingering memory of the mission. Almost all were nauseated because their nostrils were filled with an awful, stomach-wrenching stench that could never be forgotten—the odor of burned human flesh. Some airmen vomited onto the cabin floors and onto their clothes as the foul breezes wafted into the B-29's. Only then did a sense of the enormity of the disaster reach its perpetrators. As they rode the peaceful skies back to their home bases, they still smelled the remains of charred bodies.

At six o'clock in the morning of March 10, a Japanese student stood on her roof four miles west of Meetinghouse. She saw a glow in the eastern sky and called her family to see the beautiful sunrise. It was not a sunrise they saw, but the funeral pyre for over 100,000 souls, slaughtered in the most ferocious holocaust ever visited on a civilized community.

Almost sixteen square miles of Tokyo was now flat, scorched and still smoldering. In certain places, one could stand and see for miles. Nearly two thousand tons of incendiary bombs had been dropped into the most densely populated region in the world. Over 250,000 buildings had crumbled under flames which had reached an intensity of 2,000 degrees.

Rescue teams that morning were visibly overwhelmed as they were confronted by mountains of their dead countrymen. Despite the gauze masks the living wore, they retched helplessly as they lifted and separated the remains. Many of the victims were charred; almost all had suffocated.

In the rest of the city, a subdued population went to work. As details of the bombing spread through offices and factories, the people of Tokyo knew that the B-29 had, for the first time, assumed mastery over their lives.

On Guam, senior officers of the Twenty-first Bomber Command scanned photographs and reports of the raid. Curtis Lemay, who had staked his career on success and whose bold gamble had been proven sound, knew that he had found the necessary tactic to reduce Japan to ashes. He had lost only 14 planes and 140 men in devastating the capital. He immediately ordered additional sorties, and in the next days the B-29's, loaded with incendiaries, set out for Nagoya, Osaka, Kobe and other industrial cities. In April and May, while the Japanese Thirty-second Army was dying on Okinawa, Lemay's crews killed many thousands of Japanese civilians. At night the skies there were reddened by smoldering factories and homes. During the day, civilians clogged the roads leading to the countryside. They had nothing left but the clothes on their backs. Behind them smoke hid the remains of their families and friends.

Much of Tokyo was now in ruins. After the first fire raid on March 9, the B-29's had come back three times. By the end of May, over fifty percent of the capital was destroyed. Several million people had been evacuated. Emperor Hirohito walked through the acres of devastation and tried to encourage survivors by his presence. They bowed reverently before his divinity and, for a moment, dried their tears.

The average civilian was willing to entrust his deliverance from terror to the abilities of statesmen and militarists. Beyond that he could not worry. His immediate needs were too painful.

THREE

The Diplomacy of Defeat

In the Summer of 1944 when the jushin, the elder statesmen of Japan, succeeded in removing Hideki Tojo as Premier, they did not in any way diminish the power of the militaristic policy he represented. The military faction remained as strong as ever in its power over the conduct of the war. Consequently Tojo's successor was a compromise candidate, General Kuniaki Koiso. He was the schism incarnate, a Premier who had no illusions about the eventual outcome of the war but was nevertheless convinced that the Americans would be much too harsh in discussing peace terms. The Imperial Army had agreed to his Premiership only because the generals had decided to ignore him when it came to making military strategy. The jushin had agreed to Koiso because they now had their own man, Admiral Yonai, the former Premier and an ardent end-the-war advocate, to stand behind the troubled Koiso and keep watch.

The new Premier had little chance to be effective. When MacArthur landed at Leyte in October 1944, Koiso broadcast the news that the forthcoming battle would be a "Tennosan," a decisive battle of the war, wherein Japan would be victorious. Thus out on a shaky limb, he was dumbfounded to learn that the Japanese Army had altered its plan and decided to wage its ultimate battle on Luzon.

As American forces spread to Luzon in January 1945, then to Iwo Jima in February, Premier Koiso became increasingly convinced that a drastic revision in command structure was necessary, because the Army continued to operate without telling him its plans. Koiso was left out of all strategy decisions. When he asked where the Americans would attack next, unanimous opinion centered on Formosa. When the Americans came instead to Okinawa on April 1, Koiso laughed in frustrated rage, for one day a lunatic had come to his office and told him quite seriously that Okinawa would be the next battlefield. Obviously, Koiso had gotten better advice from a madman than from experts in his own army.

On April 5, 1945, Koiso again demanded that the military structure be altered so that the Premier could share in the decision-making process. On the same day the generals and admirals refused to consider his proposal. Koiso could then do nothing but resign, which he did within hours.

An old man, retired Admiral Kantaro Suzuki, was Koiso's successor. The new Premier's ascendancy was sudden and surprising, at least to him. On April 5, Suzuki was summoned to a meeting of the jushin. On learning that he was their choice, the old man protested vehemently and tried to dissuade his supporters. The discussions continued over dinner. As the last course was being served, one man, Marquis Koichi Kido, approached the reluctant candidate and said, "Come here just a minute, Suzuki-san." He then led the old admiral to an adjoining room.

Kido was the Lord Keeper of the Privy Seal and the Emperor's closest confidant. A moustached, bespectacled aristocrat, Kido served as a buffer between Hirohito and the outside world. In his role as adviser to the Throne he exerted tremendous influence. He had made, and destroyed, many careers.

When he was alone with Suzuki, Kido explained, "Japan's situation is so critical that I, as Lord Keeper, must implore you to make a firm decision to save the nation." The intensity of these remarks struck Suzuki forcibly and he protested no more.

Several hours later, Suzuki was summoned to the Emperor to form a cabinet. Before he officially consented he felt obligated to remind the Emperor of his weaknesses, which included lack of political skill and advanced age. The Emperor retorted, "Your unfamiliarity with politics is of no concern, nor does it matter that you are hard of hearing." Hirohito wanted Suzuki to assume the office because he felt comfortable with him in charge of the nation's destiny. Once he had said of the old admiral, "To Suzuki I could pour my heart out." Now the Emperor was placing the country in the old admiral's hands. Though he did not specifically tell Suzuki that he wanted him to bring about surrender, Suzuki sensed what was on Hirohito's mind.

Suzuki became Premier while the fierce and bloody battle for Okinawa was raging 350 miles to the southwest. The Americans there had no idea that the Emperor of the Japanese people had just entrusted the nation to a man he hoped would strive for peace. For his part, Suzuki was not aware, as he took office, of the dimensions of the military disaster that confronted his country.

Ironically, not many days were to pass before the United States, too, would find itself with an untried leader. On April 12, President Franklin D. Roosevelt—who had been in office twelve years—died in Warm Springs, Georgia, and left a dazed Vice-President to conclude a global war and win a lasting peace.

Almost from the moment of his swearing in, President Harry S. Truman underwent intensive briefing sessions as his advisers prepared him for the awesome decisions that lay ahead.

On V-E day, May 8, 1945, Truman had been Chief Executive for only twenty-six days. Just the night before, he and his family had finally moved into the White House and slept there for the first time. In his office on the morning of May 8, he announced the capitulation of Germany to a hushed Washington Press Corps. "General Eisenhower informs me that the forces of Germany have surrendered to the United Nations. The flags of freedom fly all over Europe. . . . We can repay the debt which we owe to our God, to our dead, and to our children, only by work," he said. "If I could give you a single watchword for the coming months, that word is work, work, and more work. We must work to finish the war. Our victory is only half-over."

Truman was not exaggerating the issue. Indeed, the military and diplomatic problems which faced the United States were considerable. Truman had very quickly come to realize that relations between the United States and her wartime ally, Russia, were deteriorating. Nevertheless, he knew that his military advisers still hoped for Soviet involvement in the struggle against Japan. To that end, the late President Roosevelt had agreed at Yalta to give Premier Stalin territorial rights in the Far East. Yet the two top American diplomats in Moscow, Ambassador Averell Harriman and George F. Kennan, were urging a harder line toward the Russians. Dismayed by contradictory attitudes emanating from the Kremlin, the diplomats were fearful that the price of Soviet participation in the Pacific war was too high.

As for the Pacific war itself, there was no doubt in the President's mind of the outcome. Yet the cost in American lives was rising at an alarming rate. American casualties were growing tragically as enemy defensive tactics became more desperate. As Commander-in-Chief of all United States Forces, Mr. Truman found himself paying in dear coin for United States victories in the Pacific. Small wonder Truman's jubilance was modulated as he announced the end of the war in Europe.

While the new American President grappled with the problems of impending victory in the Pacific, and while the new Japanese Premier endeavored to construct some workable alternatives to absolute defeat, diplomatic and intelligence personnel of both nations were engaged in desperate, yet hopeful, schemes for ending the conflict quickly.

Toward the close of the war in Europe, when allied troops began to threaten Berlin, some members of the Japanese embassy staff had crossed the border into Switzerland and became attached to the Japanese legation in Berne. Among them was an obscure naval officer, Commander Yoshiro Fujimura. In Berne, the tall, soft-spoken Fujimura renewed an old friendship with an intensely pro-Japanese German national named Dr. Friedrich Hack.

Hack had many intimate friends in Japan. As early as 1910 he had been a businessman in the Far East where he had become friendly with some young officers in the Japanese Fleet. He cultivated those friendships over the years. Hack needed such connections in 1938 when he got into serious trouble in his own country, Nazi Germany.

As a long-time ally of Foreign Minister Joachim von Ribbentrop, Hack had been allowed into Hitler's inner circle. Unfortunately for him, he objected to various policies enunciated by the German Government and found himself *persona non grata*. Ribbentrop decided that Hack would have to be silenced. A false charge of sodomy was brought against him and he was sentenced to a concentration camp, presumably forever. Ribbentrop reckoned without the influence of the Japanese Navy. Hearing of Hack's plight, naval officers went to the Japanese ambassador to Germany and demanded that he be released. The Nazis, not wishing to upset the delicate harmony between Japan and Germany, freed Hack, who was then spirited to Tokyo for safekeeping.

Even there, the harassed refugee was in danger. Orders were given to the German legation in Japan to kill Hack at an appropriate time. The Japanese Navy, aware of the situation, once more protected its friend and sent Hack to Switzerland as an authorized agent purchasing strategic materials for the Empire. When Germany became embroiled in the war, the Nazis forgot about Hack, and he settled down to work for his adopted homeland.

Happy in Switzerland, Hack enjoyed doing whatever he could for his benefactors back in Japan. Belligerent actions on the part of the Japanese military between 1939 and 1941 alarmed him, and he wrote to his Navy friends in Tokyo urging caution in dealing with Far Eastern problems. When the Japanese attacked Pearl Harbor in December of 1941, he was disconsolate. Because he knew something of the strength of America, the victories of the Imperial Navy did not impress him. Just before Christmas he wrote a letter conveying his despondency to one of his friends in the Japanese embassy in Berlin—Commander Fujimura. In it he said that his beloved Japan had made a fatal blunder in attacking the United States.

Fujimura found the letter in his office when he returned from a pre-Christmas party given for the embassy staff. Free-flowing wine had added to the intoxicating effect of recent Japanese successes. Heady from the liquor, Fujimura was in a mellow mood as he opened the letter. His pleasure evaporated as he read it. What was the matter with Hack? Fujimura could not understand the dark pessimism from Berne. Hack was warning that Japan must get out of the struggle as soon as possible, that it must arrange a negotiated peace before American industrial power crushed the nation.

Fujimura put down the paper and stared out into the darkness of wintry Berlin. A sobering fear gripped him as he brooded on Hack's Christmas message. Could he be right? Was Japan doomed to ultimate defeat? Fujimura sat for hours behind his desk and slowly realized the logic of Hack's letter. America's industrial might *was* too much for Japan to challenge. A swiftly negotiated peace was the only sensible alternative.

As Hack's prophecy came true, the two men corresponded frequently. Midway, Guadalcanal, Saipan, Leyte; the names changed but the results were the same. Japan was being beaten to its knees. In Berlin, Fujimura was helpless to do anything but watch. In Berne, Hack read the newspapers and chafed at his inability to help his adopted homeland.

Fujimura stayed in the German capital as the Nazi war machine foundered. He endured frequent bombings and realized that the end was near in Europe for Japan's ally. He also became increasingly appalled at the brutality of the Hitler regime, the attempted extinction of the Jews, and he struck out at it in the only way he could. As a privileged member of a friendly embassy, he had access to black market food supplies. By plying Gestapo officials with choice cuts of steak and expensive coffees, he gained the confidence and loyalty of men who could help him in clandestine activities. Operating under his diplomatic cover, he managed to save seven Jews from the ultimate horror of the gas chamber by smuggling them out of the country.

As the end came for Germany in 1945, Fujimura himself crossed the border into Switzerland, determined to find a way to save his own nation. He quickly contacted his old friend Hack and the two began to plot Japan's exit from the war. Their obvious strategy was contact with America, and the means lay right in Berne. On quiet Herren Street, the Office of Strategic Services maintained an active center for clandestine activities in Europe.

This huge espionage organization had direct access to President Roosevelt, who was captivated by its leader, an imaginative ex-lawyer named General "Wild Bill" Donovan. Roosevelt allowed Donovan a free hand in mounting secret operations. OSS men and women infiltrated the entire European continent. Their successes were many, their failures sometimes spectacular. Their common bond was the challenge of the unusual assignments they undertook. One such venture had resulted in the surrender of the German Army in northern Italy. When the commanding Nazi general, Wolff, wanted to deliver his army to the Allies in order to save further bloodshed, the OSS arranged contacts with American and British military men, who worked out the details. Wolff was nearly caught by the Gestapo as he negotiated, but he survived because of helpful assistance from the American spies, who smoothed the complicated and treacherous path to peace.

Fujimura and Hack knew of this recent incident. Hack contacted the OSS and an informal meeting was arranged.

The chosen site was a restaurant lying at the foot of the Jungfrau. Fujimura and Hack entered and walked through to a balcony where they stood in the chilled air gazing out at the white mountain. Their breath freezing in the midday sunlight, they chatted for a while. Physically, the two men presented an odd contrast. The Japanese, ramrod straight, reflected his years of military training. Hack, a man addicted to tweeds, umbrella and bowler hat, lounged comfortably against the railing, very much the cultured European gentleman admiring the scenery. He bore a close resemblance to Britain's former prime minister, Neville Chamberlain.

Two men watched them silently from inside the restaurant, then moved out onto the balcony and stood nearby like another pair of tourists. The two groups struck up a conversation, then returned to the dining room and sat down together at a corner table. Lunch followed.

The Americans introduced themselves as Paul Blum and a Mr. White. They talked of trivial things. The war was never mentioned and the conversation seemed casual. Yet Fujimura was uncomfortably aware of an undercurrent of suspicion on the part of the men across the table as they weighed him, probed his personality, measured his worth. Though the atmosphere was innocuous, an evaluation was being made which might determine a country's fate.

The luncheon ended amid pleasantries, and the Americans departed without any indication that they were interested in further talks. Fujimura waited three days for a sign that the OSS cared to continue with him. Then one of the men called Hack and asked that further discussions be held.

It was on May 3, in broad daylight, that Hack walked to Herren Street and talked with Paul Blum. He presented a note which Blum read carefully:

Mr. Fujimura, Japanese Naval Attaché in Switzerland, wishing to do his best toward direct negotiations with the United States and Japan, is desirous to know American opinions on this question.

There was no mention of peace terms. Fujimura included a statement of his personal history which Blum knew was valid enough to warrant further conversation. He knew, too, that the State Department had told the OSS that information forwarded by them so far was interesting enough to explore further. Blum told Hack to contact Tokyo.

When Hack told Fujimura the results of his discussion with the Americans, the Japanese naval officer was elated. He spent several days composing an urgent cable in special code to be delivered only to the highest echelons at the Naval Ministry back home. On May 8, V-E Day, the note went to Admirals Toyoda and Yonai. It contained a lie. Rather than admit that he himself had instigated the talks, Fujimura clearly implied that the Americans had contacted him first. In the cable he included a brief description of Allen Dulles, head of the OSS European operations: "He is a leading political figure of America, who has long associated with Lippmann and Stettinius and especially enjoyed the confidence of President Roosevelt. . . ." In conclusion, the naval attaché begged: "Your instructions are requested immediately."

He was in a hurry, but others were not. Two days later, his cable unanswered, he sent another asking for direction from the Naval Ministry. No reply. The naval attaché frantically sent two more. In these, he catalogued American infantry units now boarding on ships in European ports for duty in the Far East. Still no answer from Tokyo.

On the sixteenth of May, Fujimura wrote about Allen Dulles' work in negotiating the surrender of German armies in Italy. Four days later, he followed that message with a description of Germany in ruins. The next day, the twenty-first of May, Tokyo finally responded.

The Bureau of Naval Affairs had been giving the matter careful consideration. The Navy was genuinely concerned about negotiations, but not in the way Fujimura envisioned. The admirals were suspicious. The telegram admitted that "the principal point of your negotiations with the OSS was fully understood, but there are certain points which are indicative of an enemy plot; therefore we advise you to be very cautious."

Fujimura was crushed. Behind the wording of the note, he saw the machinations of the conservative element in the Navy, led by Chief of Staff Admiral Soemu Toyoda. He was correct. Toyoda was afraid to give any young officers free rein in peace negotiations lest fanatical elements discover what was going on and rebel.

Fujimura kept trying. He sent back another cable: "As far as we can see, we are positive there is no plot." Tokyo ignored that message, and seven more sent from Berne.

As June arrived in Tokyo, so did Fujimura's sixteenth cable. He neither expected nor got an answer. He told Hack, "There is only one thing to do. I will go to Japan myself and plead in person with the admirals."

Hack once more went to the OSS and told them of Fujimura's difficulties. When Paul Blum heard what Fujimura planned, he suggested an alternative:

"The United States is fully aware of what is going on in Tokyo." Blum paused to let the words sink in. "Why doesn't Japan send a ranking statesman or a general or admiral to Switzerland? The United States will guarantee the air transportation from Japan to this country." The offer served a dual purpose. It would keep the naval attaché out of harm's way and also put the negotiations onto the highest diplomatic level.

Hack rushed back to the Japanese legation to tell Fujimura of Blum's proposal. The Naval attaché tried once more with Tokyo. After explaining the OSS proposition, he remarked: "In the light of our present plight, can the Navy Minister see any other course than peace with the United States?"

He got an answer within five days: "Your point is well understood. You are requested to take proper measures with the Minister to Switzerland and other persons concerned." The cable was signed "Yonai, Navy Minister."

Yonai had always been a cautious man. In the current situation, he wanted to send someone, anyone of high rank, to meet with the Americans, but he realized the power of the military extremists and he dared not. The designated man would certainly die before he left Tokyo. Yonai's judgment told him to sever this fragile link with the enemy and wait for another opportunity. He did so by passing the controversial Fujimura correspondence on to the Foreign Office for further study, in effect tabling it indefinitely.

Fujimura was consigned to oblivion. As the days passed, his dreams drifted away. He was contacted once by the Japanese Minister to Switzerland, Shunichi Kase, who asked for additional particulars in the matter. Commander Fujimura never heard from his government again.

After the war, Admiral Yonai apologized to him. He met the naval attaché in Tokyo and said: "I assume all responsibility for our failure successfully to guide the preparations for peace and peace negotiations with the Dulles agency. I have no words with which to apologize for it."

Fujimura had lost his battle, but an American naval officer, Captain Ellis Zacharias, continued to wage a similar one. Beginning at roughly the same time as Fujimura, Zacharias planned his tactics very carefully. One of the few men in the United States who had experience with the Japanese mind, he was convinced that the enemy would make peace if subjected to intense psychological assault. Under the supervision of the Office of War Information, Zacharias and his associates drew up a plan, code-named I-45, which proposed a bold thrust at the cabinet in Tokyo. It envisaged a series of propaganda broadcasts beamed from Washington to Japan.

The American naval officer had been observing the Japanese for twenty years. When Warren Harding was President, Zacharias was a language officer in Japan, studying the natives and learning the trade of espionage. Many years before Americans ever heard of Pearl Harbor, he spied on Japanese fleet maneuvers and, as Friedrich Hack had done, befriended future admirals of the Imperial Navy. Now, in the fourth year of the war, he drew upon a wealth of personal encounters with the foe as he outlined his strategy:

Careful observation of the Japanese under varying conditions and activities, such as conferences, military inspections, and crises, has led to the inevitable conclusion that no Japanese, regardless of rank or position, is so constituted that as an individual he is willing or able to assume responsibility for important decisions without the benefit of lengthy and repeated discussions sufficient to convince him that he does not carry the responsibility alone. This continued demonstration of individual inferiority, appearances to the contrary notwithstanding, is the Japanese weakness which must be exploited to the fullest.

His first broadcast, on May 8 (the same day that Fujimura first cabled his office about his contact with the OSS), told the Japanese that Germany had surrendered and that it was only a matter of time until Japan was destroyed. Speaking fluently in the enemy's tongue, Zacharias mentioned his relationships with Premier Suzuki, with Prince Takamatsu, brother to Hirohito, and finally, with Admiral Yonai. In this way he hoped to establish his credentials.

Within twenty-four hours, he found out that he had been recognized and acknowledged. In a most indirect manner, the Japanese Government spoke to him. The Domei News Agency included in its nightly broadcast an innocent-sounding item: "Prince Takamatsu has been designated to go to the Ise Shrine in the place of his brother, Emperor Hirohito." Zacharias caught the significance immediately. Mention of the obscure prince, almost forgotten by the people of Japan, was made to tell the American spokesman that his message had been received and the Japanese would listen to further speeches.

Two more broadcasts followed in which Zacharias elaborated on his message. In his fourth talk he struck hard at his target by naming generals responsible for the sorry state of the war. By making such personal attacks, he hoped to draw an official response. On May 27, he got his wish.

Dr. Isamu Inouye spoke for the Government from Tokyo. In highly camouflaged language, Inouye acknowledged that his nation was interested in some sort of general peace. The Japanese professor quoted a parable:

"The wind and the sun decided to make a man remove his coat. The wind blew harder and harder but the man held his coat tighter and tighter. The wind failed. The sun gently smiled and warmed the passerby with his sunbeams. The passerby shed his coat."

To Zacharias the implication was clear. The professor was warning that force would be met with continued resistance, but that reasonable conditions of surrender would bring cooperation from Japan.

At the end of his broadcast, Inouye said: "I should like to know what Zacharias-kun thinks of these words from Japan." *Kun* is a term used only between close friends.

Pay dirt. A direct line had been opened from Washington to Tokyo. The Government of Japan was listening to a relatively obscure naval captain in America as he probed the Japanese mind and tried to force it to do his bidding.

In early June, Zacharias pressed the campaign. The OSS in Switzerland had stolen a copy of a report filed by Jiro Taguchi, Domei News representative in Europe, to Minister Togo at the Foreign Ministry in Tokyo. Formerly a fanatical supporter of the war, Taguchi was now urging that Togo act quickly before the country suffered what Germany had. In his next broadcast Zacharias openly alluded to the report. He pointed out its obvious truth and reminded Japan that unconditional surrender would not mean enslavement.

By the middle of June 1945, Zacharias still manned an open line to the capital of the enemy. Over it he continued to talk to the highest echelons in the Japanese hierarchy. His approach seemed to be working.

Through July, Zacharias broadcast a new series of messages. He was joined in the attack by another military man, Colonel

Sidney Mashbir, who broadcast a weekly series of commentaries on the war from Manila. Mashbir, too, directed his remarks to the cabinet and old friends from prewar days.

Mashbir's background was similar to Zacharias'. Both men had worked together in Tokyo years before. Both men had spied for the United States Government. But Mashbir had gone further than his naval colleague. As an Army captain, he had tried to create an espionage network within the borders of the Japanese Home Islands against the day when America might be at war with Japan and need to have vital information at its disposal—this, early in the 1920's. In 1923, ostensibly annoyed by peacetime bureaucrats in the Army, Mashbir resigned his commission and tried, although unsuccessfully, to continue his undercover activities with Japanese "true patriots," as he later called them, whose names he has never revealed.

In World War II as a colonel on General MacArthur's staff, Mashbir supervised a huge team of translators, mostly Japanese-Americans, who decoded messages and interrogated prisoners. By radio from Manila in the summer of 1945, Mashbir's words began to echo and supplement Zacharias' radio barrage.

In Washington, Zacharias was becoming more explicit: "The leaders of Japan have been entrusted with the salvation and not the destruction of Japan. As I have said before, the Japanese leaders face two alternatives. One is the virtual destruction of Japan followed by a dictated peace. The other is unconditional surrender with its attendant benefits as laid down by the Atlantic Charter."

In addition to this radio message, he placed in the *Washington Post* an anonymous letter telling the Japanese that they had only to ask what the specific details of Allied surrender terms would be. His newspaper article was picked up by the Japanese ambassador to Switzerland, who forwarded its contents to Tokyo without comment.

His radio statement brought a swift response. On July 24, a Japanese spokesman, another Dr. Inoue (first name Kiyoshi), formerly a professor at the University of Southern California, answered in English from Tokyo: "Should America show any sincerity of putting into practice what she preaches, as for instance in the Atlantic Charter, excepting its (punitive) clause, the Japanese nation, in fact the Japanese military, would automatically, if not willingly, follow in the stopping of the conflict and then and then only will sabers cease to rattle both in the East and in the West."

This virtual admission of defeat and expression of a willingness to negotiate was the last Japanese statement in the extraordinary dialogue. Tokyo was to go no further. On the brink of success, Zacharias would hear only silence.

Though Captain Ellis Zacharias continued to broadcast from Washington to Tokyo, though Yoshiro Fujimura waited vainly in Berne for the chance to help his nation get out of the war, the ruling body in Japan chose Russian mediation as the most promising avenue to an acceptable settlement. It decided to entrust its hopes for peace to conversations with Moscow.

On June 22, within hours of General Ushijima's death on Okinawa, the Emperor had directed the Supreme War Direction Council—Japan's "inner cabinet"—to begin formal peace negotiations, if possible, through the "good offices" of Russia.

Because of prohibition by the Japanese military, direct conversations with the United States had been ruled out of the question. Statesmen in Tokyo suggested Russia as an alternative because it offered the Army two distinct advantages. Two months before, even as Suzuki was asked to form his own cabinet, Russian Foreign Minister Molotov had informed the Japanese Ambassador, Naosoke Sato, that the Soviet Union would not renew its Neutrality Pact with Japan. It would thus lapse automatically in one year. The implications were obvious. But if the Russians could be persuaded to mediate between Japan and the United States, they would probably stay out of the war. And if Japan at the outset offered Stalin certain Far Eastern territorial concessions, in exchange Japan might get raw materials needed to continue the war. No matter what the outcome of the negotiations in the coming months, Japanese Army leaders felt their strategic position would be improved by this ploy.

Direct action had become imperative. For several weeks prior to the Emperor's mandate, a former Premier, Koki Hirota, had tried informally to initiate contact with the Soviet Union through the Russian Ambassador to Japan, Jacob Malik. His deliberately casual approaches had failed to get anything but brusque rebuffs from Malik, who fully understood the implications of the Japanese maneuver. Now the Emperor was urging a high-level approach to Moscow.

Fifteen days later, on July 7, Hirohito called Premier Suzuki to the palace to ask what had been accomplished. When Suzuki admitted that he and others were still seeking the proper approach and presentation to the Soviets, the Emperor suggested: "How about dispatching a special envoy there with my personal message?"

Nearly a week later, Prince Fumimaro Konoye—an aristocrat of the first rank, and three times Premier in the past—met with the Emperor and accepted the special assignment. In Moscow the Japanese ambassador, Naosoke Sato, attempted to see Molotov within hours to inform him of the projected visit. The Russian Foreign Minister refused to see him, giving as a reason his imminent departure for the Potsdam Conference. Sato met with Alexander Lozovsky, the Vice-Minister, and stressed the importance of Konoye's intended mission. Lozavsky avoided a commitment, saying he would await Molotov's return from the Big Three meeting. Sato begged him to call Potsdam and make Molotov aware of the new development. Lozovsky promised to do so.

Several days passed. The Russians had other things on their minds. Stalin was making plans to enter the war against Japan, a move that would ensure, at relatively small cost to the Soviet Union, a favorable share of Far Eastern territories.

In July 1945, while Japanese diplomats strove to set up a viable procedure for peace negotiations through Russia, the Imperial

General Staff published a report dealing with the strength of the United States armed forces. The report listed in detail the Army and Marine divisions either in the Pacific or coming there from Europe. It catalogued the American air groups down to the individual unit. The estimate was neither pessimistic nor blindly optimistic. It merely pointed out the massive might of the enemy.

Another related paper was already in circulation in the offices of the Navy and Army general staffs. Called Ketsu-Go, it was the operational defense plan designed to obstruct an invasion of Japanese soil.

Ketsu-Go would go into effect when enemy troops attempted to seize either offshore islands such as Cheju-do, or the main islands of Shikoku, Honshu, or Kyushu.

It called for the all-out employment of every available weapon left in the arsenal. The Japanese had hoarded planes, boats, bullets and guns for one great battle. Five thousand two hundred and twenty-five aircraft were to be used as suicide planes. Many of them were hidden under trees or under camouflage nets. Their gas tanks held only enough fuel for one trip to an invasion beach. Their runways were narrow swaths cut through meadow grass. No provision had been made for landing again.

Japanese planners realized that only a single battle could be waged and that it must begin and end at the beach. The kamikaze planes would concentrate on the transports and landing barges. Unlike other invasions where aircraft carriers and warships had been singled out, the prime targets this time would be the soldiers and Marines coming in through the surf. The reasoning was simple: Kill as many men as possible and shatter American morale. Any hope of a negotiated peace rested on the infliction of enormous casualties. Beyond that the Ketsu-Go defense plan could promise nothing more. It was a desperate strategy, fashioned by men aware that Okinawa had been the last real opportunity to stop the Americans.

Japanese intelligence experts continually sifted all available data in forecasting both the time and place of attack.

Intelligence units listened to radio broadcasts and read newspaper reports for information about troop movements. Though many embassy channels had been closed to them as more and more nations ranged themselves against Japan, analysts in foreign countries interpreted enough material to form a fairly accurate picture of military movements and industrial production figures. Aided by these bits and pieces of data, the intelligence section of the Army General Staff in Tokyo set about predicting D-Day.

Radio monitors in Japan listened to merchant ships steaming in the Pacific from port to port. Most of these vessels spoke in clear language to each other and to authorities on shore. As unusually heavy traffic moved northward toward staging areas in the Okinawa region, as message volume picked up noticeably around the Philippines, the Japanese assumed that preparations were well under way for the move on Japan. Aware of the time patterns shown by the sequence of previous American assaults on Pacific islands, and mindful of the tremendous number of ships and men that would be employed in the ultimate invasion, the Japanese decided the Americans would land in Japan no later than November 1, 1945.

Though opinion was divided as to the actual point of the major thrust, it was finally agreed that Kyushu would receive the first blow. It would have to be seized before any attack on the main island, Honshu. From this vantage point, the Americans could utilize superior air power to cover most of Japan and limit any aerial interference with the main blow at the beaches around Tokyo itself.

In narrowing the choice of a first assault site to Kyushu, the defense strategists realized that they must have troops already in place when the attack came.

The problem, therefore, was to guess the exact invasion beaches. Two were chosen, one at Kagoshima and the other near Ariake. Behind these sandy avenues to the interior, intensive construction was begun. The Japanese pinned their defense of Kyushu on a calculated gamble that the Americans would attempt to walk across these white strips of ground.

They guessed correctly. On May 28, 1945, a document had begun to circulate among the senior officers of the United States Army in the Pacific.

On the cover was a simple title: *Downfall, Strategic Plan*. It was the blueprint for the invasion of the Japanese Home Islands. *Downfall's* aims were boldly stated:

1. To force the unconditional surrender of Japan by lowering the Japanese ability and will to resist by establishing sea and air blockades, conducting intensive air bombardments, and destroying Japanese naval and air strength.

2. To invade and seize objectives in the industrial heart of Japan.

Operations on the Japanese mainland would be divided into two phases. First Kyushu must be taken; then Honshu, particularly the Tokyo plain, must be overrun. The date for the invasion of Kyushu, code-named Olympic, was November 1, 1945. The main beaches chosen for assault were around Kagoshima and Ariake.

General Walter Krueger's Sixth Army, spearheaded by the Second, Third and Fifth Marine Divisions plus the First Cavalry Division, would land in the midst of concentrated fire from well-entrenched Japanese defenses. The bloodshed might be enormous.

There was one great omission from both the Japanese and American plans.

In the Imperial General Staff's estimate of the whereabouts of American units, a notation was appended to the list of B-29 squadrons still assumed to be in the United States. Dated May 8, the notation read: "One other unit is available but its identity has not been ascertained as yet." The missing squadron was the 393rd, then leaving the United States under the strictest security for its new home on Tinian. The 393rd's mission was specific. As part of the 509th Composite Group, it was to drop atomic bombs on the cities of Japan.

FOUR

The Project

The bomb had been evolving for over six years. It began with a discovery made in the laboratories of the Kaiser Wilhelm Institute in Berlin. In the fall of 1938, just before Europe went into the convulsions of another war, two scientists, Otto Hahn and Fritz Strassmann, repeated an experiment first tried in 1934 by an Italian, Enrico Fermi. The results of bombarding a piece of uranium metal with neutrons led them to conclude that the nucleus of the metal had split into two lighter elements and that a portion of the enormous energy required to hold it together had been released.

They reported their findings to a colleague, Lise Meitner, who had been involved with their preliminary experiments but had recently been forced to leave Germany because she was a Jew. She communicated the startling theory to her friend Niels Bohr, a Danish pioneer in physics, who urged further experiments to validate the conclusions.

It was Bohr who brought the news to the United States. Shortly after he came to New York from Copenhagen in January 1939, he received a telegram from Lise Meitner's nephew reporting that the theory she had described to him had been confirmed by further tests. The atom had indeed been split. Bohr then went to the Institute for Advanced Study at Princeton and shared the information with scientific colleagues there; he later published a report on it in the magazine *Physical Review.*

As Adolf Hitler plunged the world into war, knowledgeable men realized the ramifications of the discovery. Because of the fantastic energy potential involved, it was now theoretically possible to produce a weapon which could alter the course of history. It was unthinkable that such a power should fall into the hands of a dictator.

On October 11, 1939, Franklin Roosevelt entertained an old friend, Alexander Sachs, a director of the Lehman Corporation, an influential economist and a friend to scientists. Sachs came to the White House with a terribly important message contained in a letter he began to read:

Sir:

Some recent work by E. Fermi and L. Szilard, which has been communicated to me in manuscript, leads me to expect that the element uranium may be turned into a new and important source of energy in the near future. Certain aspects of the situation which has arisen seem to call for watchfulness and if necessary, quick action on the part of the Administration. . . . It may become possible to set up a nuclear chain reaction in a large mass of uranium, by which vast amounts of power and large quantities of new radium-like elements would be generated. . . . It is conceivable—though much less certain—that extremely powerful bombs of a new type may thus be constructed. . . .

The letter was signed by Albert Einstein.

Though impressed, Roosevelt seemed preoccupied with other things, He broke off the discussion, but asked Sachs to come back again the next day for breakfast.

The economist returned on Columbus Day to renew the assault. Well aware of the President's personality, he had decided on a different tactic in presenting the "atomic" plea.

Sachs told Roosevelt a story. He brought the President back to the year 1805 when Napoleon hungered to invade England but lacked the means to navigate the English Channel. An American inventor, Robert Fulton, came to the dictator and proposed building a fleet of steamboats which could easily make the crossing. Napoleon considered the idea for just a few moments, then threw Fulton out as an idiot.

Alexander Sachs paused in his story, then asked Franklin Roosevelt the crucial question: How might the history of the world have been altered if Napoleon had listened to this inventor?

Roosevelt got the point immediately. He looked up at his friend. "Alex," he said, "what you are after is to see that the Nazis don't blow us up." To his secretary, "Pa" Watson, Roosevelt added, "This requires action."

Accordingly, Roosevelt formed a committee to explore the potential of the uranium atom. He installed Lyman Briggs, a Government scientist, as its head, and Commander Gilbert Hoover and Colonel Keith Adamson as members. The greatest scientific brains in America became involved in the race to build the bomb before Germany could achieve it—among them, James B. Conant, Harvard's lean, sober president; Ernest Lawrence, brilliant, aggressive leader of the University of California Science Laboratories; Enrico Fermi, whose earlier work was the basis for so much that followed; Leo Szilard, a Hungarian physicist; Kenneth Bainbridge, a Harvard professor recently returned from observing similar efforts in Britain; Arthur and Karl Compton, genius brothers, Karl the President of M.I.T. and Arthur chairman of the Physics Department at the University of Chicago. The work of these men was coordinated into the Office of Scientific Research and Development under the direction of Dr. Vannevar Bush. This office was also to take under its wing Roosevelt's original Uranium Committee. From then on, the project had direct access to the President for guidance and money.

Almost two years to the day after Alexander Sachs first approached the Chief Executive with Einstein's letter, Dr. Bush

met with Roosevelt and Vice-President Wallace and outlined
the latest findings. He told them that British physicists were
confident that they had determined the approximate amount of
uranium needed to make a bomb. He gave the President the tentative cost for a production plant needed to concentrate the metal
and an estimate of the time needed actually to achieve a weapon.
Together, Roosevelt, Wallace and Bush conferred on the urgency
of moving the program past the theoretical stage. They discussed
military policy, the probable state of German research, and even
the problems associated with postwar control of the new power.
Franklin Roosevelt agreed that work on the bomb must be expe-
dited and told Bush that money could be made available from
secret funds within the governmental budget. Vannevar Bush left
the White House knowing that he and his colleagues must proceed with all possible haste toward making certain that an atomic
bomb could in fact be produced.

Two months later, following the Japanese attack on Pearl Harbor and the United States' entry into the war, Roosevelt released
emergency monies into the bomb program. Thousands of men
were recruited for a unit officially known as the Manhattan Engineering District, later called the Manhattan Project. The Project
included a vast building program necessary to the manufacture
of bomb ingredients. General Leslie Groves, a forty-six-year-old
West Point engineer who had recently played a key role in the
construction of the massive Pentagon, was chosen as coordina-
tor of this building program. Blunt and unreasonable in his demands, Groves had acquired a reputation for being difficult. At
his first meeting with Dr. Bush, he got off to a bad start. Unfortunately, Bush had not been informed about Groves' new status
and quickly resented the general's probing questions. Groves was
dumbfounded by the scientist's lack of cooperation and left the
office wondering exactly what had gone wrong. Bush in turn telephoned and tried to find out just what Groves' position was in
the hierarchy. When he was told that the general would oversee

the operation of plant facilities, he expressed strong doubts about Groves' ability to work with people. He said, "I'm afraid we're all in the soup."

Despite this memorable first confrontation between the two men, they managed to work out an excellent relationship based on mutual respect for each other's abilities. A committee of four, including Bush, Conant, General William Styer and Admiral William Purnell, sat in judgment of Groves during the next three years as he guided the Manhattan Project toward its elusive goal. The four found General Leslie Groves a remarkable man, as they watched him proceed with the formidable task of creating a new industrial complex across the American landscape.

Research and production were centered at three remote places: Los Alamos, New Mexico; Oak Ridge, Tennessee; and Hanford, Washington. In Los Alamos the workable weapon was to be designed under the supervision of Julius Robert Oppenheimer, a shy, frail scholar, a theoretical physicist. Oppenheimer was a man versed in Oriental literature, an aesthete who abhorred the violence of war. In his earlier life, he had associated with various Communist organizations, contributed to left-wing groups, and been intimate with many "fellow travelers"—in his time, completely predictable in an academic community espousing the utopia being preached by Moscow. When he first became involved in the security-ridden life of the Manhattan Project, his past produced violent opposition to his appointment. At this point, General Groves personally insisted that Oppenheimer be cleared immediately as "essential to the project." Oppenheimer went on to prove beyond doubt Groves' wisdom in selecting and championing him.

At Oak Ridge, a sprawling complex in the isolated mountains of Tennessee, the task was to pry the highly fissionable U-235 from U-238, the predominant isotope in natural uranium. Two separation methods, gaseous diffusion and electromagnetic, were employed to extract the vital material. Mammoth buildings were erected in two valleys for the purpose of collecting this rare metal that could be measured in thimblefuls. Thousands of men and women labored at their assigned duties in a contest against time. Most of them were as ignorant of the final purpose as mystified local onlookers. No product emerged from an assembly line. No trucks carried off goods. The only tangible evidence of achievement was the two huge cities of brick created for the scientists.

At Hanford, in the scrubland of eastern Washington, another sprawling factory complex was constructed. There, the most amazing part of the atomic quest was enacted. Inside windowless buildings, a man-made element was separated from uranium by chemical means. Plutonium was produced.

In the spring of 1940, Drs. Edwin M. McMillan and Philip H. Abelson had identified a new element in their laboratory at Berkeley. Neptunium, element 93, was born through the emission of an electron by U-239, which in turn had been produced by the capture of a neutron by U-238, an isotope in natural uranium. The scientific report of the discovery stressed that another element, 94, was undoubtedly present, since neptunium "had been observed to emit an electron." The new force was too minute to detect.

When the work of Abelson and McMillan was interrupted by other duties, Dr. Glenn Seaborg, another researcher at Berkeley, had asked to continue the job of finding the elusive element. On March 1, 1941, he, Dr. Joseph Kennedy, Arthur Wahl and Dr. Emilio Segré bombarded one kilogram of uranium with neutrons. The experiment lasted six days. Suddenly the uranium was turned into neptunium and then metamorphosed into the exciting discovery, element 94, plutonium.

Twenty-two days later, the same scientists bombarded one-half microgram of plutonium with slow neutrons. They were jubilant on finding that it split its atoms just like uranium U-235. Man had manufactured his first element in nature's periodic table. Instead of depending on the rare uranium U-235, he could now produce practically limitless quantities of fissionable material. When the Manhattan Project got under way, scientists realized that, in plutonium, the United States had the ingredient to manufacture a bomb in time to alter the balance of power. The major problem was to build the facilities to create it.

On December 2, 1942, scientist Enrico Fermi supervised the first self-sustaining, chain-reacting atomic pile. It had been built on a squash court at the University of Chicago. Later that day, Arthur H. Compton telephoned his friend James Conant at Harvard and said, "Jim, you'll be interested to know that the Italian navigator has just landed in the New World." Conant asked whether the natives were friendly. Compton assured him that they were.

At Hanford, several plants rose up on the south bank of the Columbia River. Inside them, there was no sound, only an eerie silence that belied the incredible drama going on behind thick, lead-shielded walls. No human eye witnessed the strange alchemy. Through a complicated system of control panels, metal moved through various stages to the final process. Huge atomic piles, the first atomic power plants on earth, generated cosmic fires as microscopic amounts of plutonium were created. Here at Hanford, man reached a summit of intellectual and utilitarian attainment as the material for the bomb was prepared.

Satisfied with the progress of his industrial facilities, General Groves put into motion the next phase of the Manhattan Project: Operation Silver Plate, leading ultimately to the bomb drop itself. From bases scattered around the world men were summoned to a secret installation in the Utah desert—fifteen hundred of them by the end of September 1944. Wendover Field, code-named Kingman or W-47, was a desolate oasis, only 125 miles west of Salt Lake City but a light year away from civilization. It was a sinkhole, a dusty, hot scar in a bleak, forbidding landscape.

    Commander Fred Ashworth, a weapons specialist who would help to field-test the new bomb and who was to supervise ballistics design improvements at Wendover, first saw the base on a Sunday afternoon and was appalled. Since he would be commuting between Los Alamos and Wendover, he requested that his family be allowed to live in New Mexico rather than endure the hardships at the new airfield.

Personnel at Wendover included military specialists of all kinds. They formed the newly created 509th Composite Group. As group commander, Colonel Paul Tibbets, twenty-nine years old, was responsible for perfecting the ability of the 509th to carry out the mission flawlessly.

Tibbets' credentials were impressive. He was one of the first pilots to fly a B-17 over Europe when the Luftwaffe still dominated the air. Decorated several times, he eventually returned to the United States to lead modification work on a new bomber, the B-29, just then beginning to come off the assembly line. In the summer of 1944, an urgent telephone call ordered him to report to General Uzal Ent in Colorado Springs. There Tibbets met Captain William Parsons, chief of weapons development under Oppenheimer at Los Alamos, and Dr. Norman Ramsey, a Harvard professor and a specialist in bomb development. The three men briefed him on the job the Government wanted him to do—a job that required him to train the newly formed 509th Composite Group to drop the product of billions of dollars of research monies on an unnamed target at an unannounced date.

In the summer of 1944, Tibbets reported at Wendover, and quickly arranged for some of his old flying companions to join him and become key members of the 393rd Bombardment Squadron. This was the section of the 509th to be entrusted with the actual delivery of the weapon. Among Tibbet's friends were Major Tom Ferebee, a mustachioed bombardier who had been with him during the trying days in England, and Dutch Van Kirk who had navigated for him over Europe. Others were called upon because of their work with Tibbets on the B-29 modification program in the United States: Bob Lewis, an excellent pilot, and Major Chuck Sweeney, who had probably flown the B-29 more than anyone else. Earlier in the summer Sweeney had been stationed at Grand Island, Nebraska, to train pilots in handling the new bomber—among them, General Curtis Lemay, who later commanded the initial super-bomber effort in the Pacific. Sweeney was a cherubic-faced, heavyset Irishman from Boston, a man of great ability and personal charm who quickly attracted the affection and respect of those who worked under him. Under the direction of Colonel Tibbets, Major Sweeney was to train one of the crews: Number 15.

Crew 15 was formed in the fall of 1944. The navigator was Jim Van Pelt, a handsome, sensitive West Virginian who had washed out as a pilot but was graduated from Navigation School in September of 1942. He had become friends with Tom Ferebee at a dice table at Ardmore, Oklahoma, and it was through Ferebee that he came to Wendover. At his suggestion, Kermit Beahan also came from Ardmore with him. Beahan was a bombardier, a tremendously efficient technician known to his fellow airmen as "The Great Artiste." He was a Texas boy, an authentic hero from the skies of Europe where he had been shot down several times and on one occasion had saved a tail gunner's Me by administering oxygen during a raid.

Captain Don Albury was another B-29 pilot whose superb flying skills were obvious to Tibbets and Sweeney. This native of Miami, Florida, was called by some of his contemporaries the "most competent twenty-five-year-old" they had ever known. The father of one child, Albury was especially popular with the enlisted men, who continually brought their problems to him.

Lieutenant Fred Olivi served as copilot or third pilot on the crew. A bulky Italian boy of twenty-three from Chicago, he neither smoked nor drank and was therefore the object of much good-natured ribbing from his fellow officers.

There were five enlisted men in the crew. Master Sergeant John Kuharek was the only Regular Army man on board, a veteran of fourteen years' service and an extremely competent engineer. The radio operator was Sergeant Abe Spitzer, born in the Bronx and an old-timer of thirty-five. The gunner and assistant engineer was Sergeant Ray Gallagher, the youngest of the group at twenty-three. Sergeant Pappy Dehart, the tail gunner, was a sad-eyed Texan who passionately hated the army and loved farming but performed his duties competently and without complaint. Sergeant Ed Buckley operated the radar along with Van Pelt. He also doubled as mechanic, radio operator and general handyman.

The 509th Group held the highest priority rating in the matter of securing the necessary tools for the task ahead. Fourteen new B-29's disappeared from the rolls of various Air Force installations. Generals who raised loud voices in complaint at the transfers from their squadrons were silenced by phone. The top Air Force man in Washington, General Hap Arnold, had given the word that there was good reason for the action.

Under Tibbets' direction a number of plane crews initiated curious flights out over the western part of the United States. Each aircraft took one large, bulbous bomb aloft, always to an altitude of more than thirty thousand feet. Bombardiers released them over painted white circles on the desert floor. Immediately the planes turned sharply at a 60-degree angle, then came around in an arc of 156½ degrees.

Toward the end of the training period, dummy weapons were filled with high explosives. At all times the bomb drops were photographed from bomb bays and other planes in order to record the efficiency of each bomb's external configuration. (Wendover's personnel included twenty-seven scientists working on the ballistics phase of the superweapon.) Although Crew 15 constantly speculated on the purpose of the unvarying method of attack and maneuver, no one ever guessed at the purpose of the special training.

Security regulations at Wendover were stringent to an extreme. Special agents followed men on leave into neighboring cities and eavesdropped on their conversations. One high-ranking officer who revealed too much information in a casual meeting at another Air Force base returned to Wendover to find his bags packed and his orders for transfer processed. He spent the rest of the war near the Arctic Circle. A few men of the 509th were gradually made aware of the nature of the project. Chuck Sweeney was driven into the desert one day and told of it. But the vast majority remained uninformed.

By January 1945, most of the 509th Group had moved to Cuba for two months as part of a plan to train the unit as a completely self-sustaining entity capable of moving by itself over a long distance. There, crews were also able to practice radar bombing over water areas as preparation for the eventual move to the Pacific.

The base they would occupy in the Mariana Islands had already been chosen by Commander Fred Ashworth of the Navy, who, in February, had gone to Guam to see Admiral Chester Nimitz. In a money belt the commander carried a letter signed by Admiral Ernest King, Chief of Naval Operations, which revealed the story of the atomic bomb and gave Ashworth the highest priority. Nimitz had been curious about the new unit detailed to come into his area, but Ashworth's arrival ended his confusion.

The commander then chose the northwest corner of Tinian as headquarters for the 509th Group. Several factors weighed heavily in making his decision: the Seabees were transforming the coral table into an unshakable aircraft carrier; Tinian was one hundred miles closer to Japan than Guam, and the great weight of the bomb might make that shorter distance crucial to the success of the flights; Tinian also had better harbor facilities.

Back in the United States, the Manhattan Engineering District was moving at an accelerated pace during the spring of 1945. The plants at Oak Ridge and Hanford were operating. U-235 and plutonium were being produced in small quantities. As two designs for the bomb became finalized each was given a nickname. The narrow uranium bomb was called "Thin Man" for Roosevelt, as opposed to the bulbous plutonium bomb which was named "Fat Man" after Churchill. Choice of these nicknames was more than casual. It was believed that if messages concerning Thin Man and Fat Man were monitored, the eavesdropper would assume that the names actually referred to Roosevelt and Churchill. In its final stage, the gun barrel of the Thin Man was shortened, and it was thereafter known as "Little Boy."

Theoretical tests left little doubt that the uranium bomb would work. Little Boy would not need to be tested before the actual detonation over Japan. The problem at the moment was to provide enough U-235 to explode the weapon.

The plutonium bomb, however, still had to be test fired. No one was completely sure that Fat Man would detonate. In the desert of New Mexico, scientists planned to set up a tower to hold a device containing a tiny amount of the metal for testing.

In March 1945, the 509th returned from Cuba to practice again over the western part of the United States. Cameras recorded each free fall of the tear-shaped bombs to make sure of the design. Chuck Sweeney and Don Albury wheeled their B-29 over in fast turns as before. They flew the ship for great distances while Jim Van Pelt obtained extensive experience navigating the plane alone.

In the spring, the 509th began to leave its desolate home. Eight hundred men sailed out of Seattle in May and the advance air echelon left shortly afterward.

Though the war in Europe ended on May 8, fighting in the Pacific was becoming increasingly brutal. The 509th Group now embarking for Tinian from the West Coast hopefully would bring that conflict to an abrupt end. But Harry Truman would face a grave decision because of what the 509th was training to accomplish.

On June 18, at a meeting in Washington, D.C., President Truman had talked with his military and civilian advisers:

TRUMAN: As I understand it, the Joint Chiefs of Staff, after weighing all the possibilities of the situation and considering all possible alternative plans, are still of the unanimous opinion that the Kyushu operation [invasion of Japan] is the best solution under the circumstances.

ANSWER: That is correct.

TRUMAN: Mr. Stimson, what is your opinion?

STIMSON: I agree that there is no other choice. . . . I do think that there is a large submerged class in Japan who do not favor the present war and whose full opinion and influence have not yet been felt. . . . I feel something should be done to arouse them and to develop any possible influence they might have before it becomes necessary to come to grips with them.

Truman asked Admiral William Leahy for his views:

LEAHY: I do not agree with those who say that unless we obtain the unconditional surrender of the Japanese that we will have lost the war. I fear no menace from Japan in the foreseeable future, even if we are unsuccessful in forcing unconditional surrender. What I do fear is that our insistence on unconditional surrender will only result in making the Japanese more desperate and thereby increase our casualty lists. I don't think this is at all necessary.

TRUMAN: . . . don't feel that I can take any action at this time to change public opinion on the matter. . . . I am quite sure that the Joint Chiefs should proceed with the Kyushu operation.

As the meeting was adjourned, Truman asked John McCloy, Assistant Secretary of War, to add his comments before leaving. McCloy said that all the talk of invading Japan struck him as rather "fantastic." The secretary asked, "Why not use the atomic bomb?"

The meeting was once more called to order and McCloy's remark was discussed. Truman listened intently as the men at the table argued the merits of first warning the Japanese to surrender and then using the new weapon if the enemy ignored the ultimatum. The dialogue broke down because of one basic truth. No one in the room knew whether the device being readied in New Mexico would actually work. Without that knowledge, strategy was pointless. Truman again affirmed his approval of the invasion of Kyushu.

Crew 15 lingered at Wendover until late in June. Sweeney, now commanding officer of the 393rd Squadron, was issued a new plane, serial number AC 44-27353, a highly modified B-29 incorporating the latest improvements. Besides fuel injection engines, the plane had reversible pitch propellers, which acted as brakes on landing. These would save the lives of the entire crew one day.

On June 21, Chuck Sweeney took his men out of Utah for the last time. He flew them to Hawaii for a few hours in the sun and surf. On the next morning he had the B-29 blessed by a Catholic priest before taking off to the southwest. On June 27, Sweeney brought the huge silver plane down on the runway of North Field at Tinian.

There, the Seabees had performed a miracle. The island had changed markedly since Fred Ashworth first visited it in February. Hundreds of B-29's sat at hardstands in row after gleaming row. Wide asphalt roads were laid out to correspond with the street plan of New York City. There was a Broadway, a Forty-second Street and an Eighth Avenue. The 509th made its home in upper Manhattan.

Tinian was a white coral rock. It was also a lush tropical island on which the Japanese had cultivated a thriving sugar cane business. Natives from Korea and Okinawa had been brought to the island to labor in the fields and mills. Now some of them hid in the hills too frightened to surrender. With Japanese soldiers, they sometimes raided the garbage cans at North Field in order to stay alive. The men of the 509th tried to ignore the possibility of being killed by one of these scavengers as they entered their final training.

Security had dictated that this group be isolated from the other fighting units based on Tinian. Surrounded by barbed wire and armed guards, the men of the secret outfit endured mounting criticism from airmen flying to Japan every week and losing their friends to Japanese fire.

Occasionally one plane from the 509th went out over the ocean on a long distance familiarization mission against an enemy-held island. It carried a single orange high-explosive bomb, dubbed "Pumpkin," which was dropped and detonated in the air above the target. Some of the men in the planes wondered openly whether the Pumpkin was the only reason for all the specialized training in the past year. They hoped not.

In the meantime, the airmen on Tinian acquainted themselves with their new home. They swam, kibitzed at card games, drank beer, read, did the things that men do with time on their hands. Kermit Beahan managed to persuade Fred Olivi to take his first drink. The results were disastrous and Olivi spent several days in bed. Tom Ferebee constructed a "professional" dice table and gamblers stayed at it for eight hours at a time. The men had movies nightly; the officers could buy a fifth of liquor a week at $1.30 a bottle.

Mostly they wondered among themselves when the big mission would come. Few were aware of the tension building around them.

On July 16, as Crew 15 dawdled in front of their Quonset huts or swam in the ocean, the experimental plutonium bomb had exploded in the New Mexican desert. In an appalling burst of heat, man had liberated that very energy which, through eons of time, lights the stars.

Three men had lain face down as the white light engulfed them. Leslie Groves, Vannevar Bush and James B. Conant had looked at each other and silently clasped hands as they beheld their creation born of urgent dreams and grown to terrifying reality in seconds.

◆   ◆   ◆

In Potsdam, Germany, Secretary of War Henry Stimson received the following dispatch from his assistant in Washington:

SECRETARY OF WAR FROM HARRISON
    DOCTOR HAS JUST RETURNED MOST ENTHU-
SIASTIC AND CONFIDENT THAT THE LITTLE BOY
IS AS HUSKY AS HIS BIG BROTHER. THE LIGHT IN
HIS EYES DISCERNIBLE FROM HERE TO HIGHHOLD
AND I COULD HAVE HEARD HIS SCREAMS FROM
HERE TO MY FARM.

Highhold was Stimson's summer place on Long Island, 250 miles from Washington; Harrison's farm was fifty miles away in Virginia.

Stimson was elated. Though he had continually wrestled with the moral implications of the weapon, he never wavered from his determination to end the war with it, if necessary. In writing to his wife after the New Mexico test explosion, he said he had just had "good news from my baby at home." On the morning of July 17 he told the good news to President Truman in the "Little White House" at Babelsburg outside Potsdam, and urged that the Japanese be duly warned of the utter destruction that awaited them if they continued the war.

Success of the plutonium bomb test and the power potential it established produced a marked change in American attitudes. Prime Minister Churchill later noted that from July 17 on, Truman, the novice in Big Three meetings, seemed to lose any feelings of inferiority he might have possessed in the company of Stalin and himself. As their meetings continued, when the Russian leader balked at certain proposals, Truman would cut him short and show an aggressiveness which Churchill found "stimulating."

One of the major items on the agenda at Potsdam had been the inclusion of Russia as a belligerent in the Pacific war at the earliest possible moment. By agreement at Yalta, Stalin was committed to entering the war within three months after the end of hostilities in Europe. With the deadline only a few weeks away, General George Marshall, Army Chief of Staff, wanted Russian troops to invade Manchuria so that Japanese soldiers would be drawn off from the Home Islands. As of July 16, the need for Soviet help in Asia completely evaporated. The war could be won without it.

President Truman knew this. Already disenchanted with Stalin, he wanted no part of a Red claim that their armies had broken the back of Japanese resistance. Nor did he relish the prospect of coping with Stalin's intrigues in newly liberated lands on the Asia mainland. Nevertheless, he realized there was no way to keep the Soviets out of the war if they wanted to honor the letter of the agreement at Yalta and attack Japan in August. He merely stopped pressing for their pledge and awaited developments in the coming weeks. The cynical round of talks at Potsdam continued.

On July 20, OSS chief Allen Dulles arrived at Potsdam with an important message. He told Secretary Stimson that a Swedish banker, Per Jacobbson, had approached him as a go-between for Japanese officials working at the International Trade Bank in Switzerland. The Japanese wanted to work out peace terms with Dulles and then act on them back in Tokyo. Like Commander Fujimura, they hoped to convince their own Government to agree to end the war immediately. Dulles was particularly interested in this overture because he respected Jacobbson's reputation and trusted in his motives.

Dulles found Stimson a harried man, immersed in the myriad details of the conference. He showed only slight interest in Dulles' story.

Both men were well aware of the deteriorating situation in Japan. Dulles had been able to gain access to Japanese cablegrams sent to Germany before the Nazi regime fell. Through an agent working at the German Foreign Office, he had read many dispatches sent from Tokyo to Japanese attachés in Berlin. The messages outlined the grave state of affairs in the Far East.

Stimson had read intercepted telegrams from Foreign Minister Togo to Ambassador Sato in Moscow. He and Truman had discussed the fact that the Japanese seemed to be looking for a way out, though on the basis of several conditions. The American leaders wondered whether the Japanese had other motives behind these apparent peace feelers. For in the United States, the Combined Intelligence Committee, a group which reported to Truman on enemy capabilities, had issued a study on the situation:

. . . In general, Japan will use all political means for avoiding complete defeat or unconditional surrender.

a. [It will] continue and even increase its attempts to secure complete political unity within the Empire . . .

b. Attempt to foster a belief among Japan's enemies that the war will prove costly and long drawn out . . .

c. Make desperate efforts to persuade the USSR to continue her neutrality . . . while at the same time making every effort to sow discord between the Americans and British on one side and the Russians on the other. As the situation deteriorates still further, Japan may even make a serious attempt to use the USSR as a mediator in ending the war.

d. Put out intermittent peace feelers, in an effort to bring the war to an acceptable end, to weaken the determination of the United Nations to fight to the bitter end, or to create inter-Allied dissension. . . .

Japanese leaders are now playing for time in the hope that Allied war weariness, Allied disunity, or some "miracle" will present an opportunity to arrange a compromise peace. . . .

The Japanese believe . . . that unconditional surrender would be the equivalent of national extinction. There are as yet no indications that the Japanese are ready to accept such terms. . . .

Suspicious of Japanese intentions, buoyed up by the success of the Bomb, American statesmen could not get excited over such peripheral approaches to peace as were emanating from Switzerland. Per Jacobbson had come to Allen Dulles far too late in the game of high level diplomacy.

On Tinian, Crew 15, which had already emblazoned bombardier Kermit Beahan's nickname, *The Great Artiste*, on the nose of their plane, flew two missions. One, on the twenty-first, was aborted due to engine trouble. The second trip was more successful. With a Pumpkin in the bomb bay, Chuck Sweeney piloted the B-29 to Japan and saw the bomb released over the Kobe marshaling yards. Sweeney performed the same evasive action practiced so often over the deserts of Utah and the Caribbean, then wheeled back toward the Marianas.

On the same day, Henry Stimson told his diary that the United States "didn't need Russia anymore."

On the twenty-fourth of July, Harry Truman had that thought in mind as he went up to Joseph Stalin and mentioned that America had developed a new weapon "of unusual destructive force." Stalin seemed only mildly interested and did not ask for further details.

A day later, Henry Stimson went to the Cecilienhof Palace, a huge brownstone building set in gardens near the ruins of Berlin. There, he sat with Stalin amid the splendor of another age and discussed the roles of the two great powers. Stimson said that he welcomed Soviet participation in the struggle against Japan, and Stalin answered by saying that since both countries had worked so well together in the European conflict, he too was happy to share in the hardships of a joint effort against Japan. Both men knew that S-1, the atomic bomb, would be used shortly, Stimson through his official function and Stalin through his espionage channels. Yet both adhered to the formalities of diplomatic exchanges and parted in a cordial atmosphere, which ignored the basic fact that the monstrous weapon would alter the partnership irrevocably.

On both the twenty-fourth and the twenty-sixth, American military groups met with their Russian counterparts to plot details of Russian participation in the Far Eastern war. The meetings were friendly, free from friction, but perfunctory. The need for cooperation had dwindled to the point of absurdity.

In Tokyo, attention was irrevocably centered on Moscow. There, however, Ambassador Sato sensed the cold wind blowing from Potsdam. On July 20, he had wired Togo: "I recommend acceptance of virtually any terms. . . ."

Togo was extremely annoyed at his man in Moscow. He was also desperate for a channel leading to peace negotiations.

> July 25, 1945 1900 hours
> To: Sato
> From: Togo
> No. 944 (urgent, ambassador's code.)
>   . . . Navy Captain Zacharias said on the 21st that Japan had two choices: she could either accept a dictated peace after her ruin, or surrender unconditionally and enjoy the benefits of the Atlantic Charter. We would be wrong to consider such statements trick propaganda. We must admit that they are partly intended to invite us to come to their cause. . . . We, for our part, are desirous to inform the United States through some feasible method that, although we are unable to accept unconditional surrender under any circumstances, we have no objection to the restoration of peace on the basis of the Atlantic Charter.

As Sato read this telegram in Moscow, an American cruiser, the *Indianapolis*, stood in Tinian Harbor unloading components of the uranium bomb. Before Sato replied to the cable, the Allies issued the Potsdam Declaration, a last warning to the Japanese Empire.

The month-long meeting in Potsdam closed with the issuance of an ultimatum that promised the Japanese complete destruction unless they surrendered. The communiqué was dated July 26, just before Clement Attlee had been elected British Prime Minister and had arrived back in Potsdam to replace Churchill.

When the declaration was being drafted, Secretary Stimson took great pains to insist to Truman that the Japanese people be reassured of the continuation of the dynasty under Emperor Hirohito. As a student of Japanese affairs and a former resident of the Far East, Stimson fully understood the importance of the Emperor in Japanese life and feared that they would balk at any surrender terms which reflected adversely on the Ruler's position. He knew that certain elements in the American Government were vociferous in their stand that the Emperor must go. In particular, Harry Hopkins, Roosevelt's chief adviser, and Dean Acheson, Undersecretary of State, held apparently strong feelings against the retention of the Imperial Household.

President Truman maintained a flexible attitude toward the Emperor. Both he and Byrnes feared public opinion in the United States would reject any "appeasement" at this stage. Therefore, they felt that the question of Hirohito's future role should be held in abeyance as a bargaining feature of any forthcoming negotiations with the Japanese. Neither was stubborn with Stimson about the issue, but they ordered the provision struck out of the Declaration of July 26.

On July 27, in Tokyo, the Japanese cabinet sat down to study the document transmitted from across the world.

Attention focused on topics related to surrender terms:

Point Six: There must be eliminated for all time the authority and influence of those who have deceived and misled the people of Japan into embarking on world conquest. . . .

Point Seven: . . . points in Japanese territory to be desig-
                  nated by the Allies shall be occupied to secure
                  the achievement of the basic objectives we are
                  here setting forth.

Point Eight: The terms of the Cairo Declaration shall be
                  carried out and Japanese sovereignty shall be
                  limited to the islands of Honshu, Hokkaido,
                  Kyushu, Shikoku and such minor islands as
                  we determine.

Point Nine: The Japanese military forces, after being com-
                  pletely disarmed, shall be permitted to return
                  to their homes with the opportunity to lead
                  peaceful and productive lives.

Point Ten: . . . stern justice shall be meted out to all war
                  criminals, including those who have visited
                  cruelties upon our prisoners. . . .

Point Twelve: The occupying forces of the Allies shall be
                  withdrawn from Japan as soon as these objec-
                  tives have been accomplished and there has
                  been established in accordance with the freely
                  expressed will of the Japanese people a peace-
                  fully inclined and responsible government.

Point Thirteen: We call upon the Government of Japan to
                  proclaim now the unconditional surrender
                  of all Japanese armed forces, and to provide
                  proper and adequate assurance of their good
                  faith in such action. The alternative for Japan
                  is prompt and utter destruction.

"Prompt and utter destruction" had little meaning at this
point to the men in Tokyo whose nation was being destroyed
daily by fire raids and who could not possibly have construed
the threat to mean imminent use of an atomic bomb. The points
included in the Declaration contained nothing surprising to the
Japanese cabinet; the terms were what they could expect. What

the Potsdam paper did not cover was what the men in Tokyo most wanted clarified: the future status of their Emperor.

Rather than make a decision on the Declaration, Japan preferred to wait for some progress in Moscow. When reporters asked Premier Suzuki for a reaction to the Allied message, he meant to tell them that the Government would "withhold comment" on it for the time being. Unfortunately, he used the word *mokusatsu* to describe his attitude. In Japanese, *mokusatsu* means "take no notice of, treat with silent contempt, ignore." The news agencies broadcast it just that way. After the damage was done, Suzuki reinforced the meaning by repeating it two days later at a press conference. This time he had little choice because the military had demanded that the cabinet stand firm against Potsdam. The Allies were told that the ultimatum was not worthy of comment.

The blunder in Tokyo went uncorrected by any official. Foreign Minister Togo concentrated on Moscow, where his ambassador, Sato, realized that Tokyo was out of touch with reality. Sato hastened to warn Togo that "there is absolutely no necessity for him [Stalin] to go out of his way and conclude an agreement with Japan now."

Sato was a prophet, crying vainly across the mainland of Asia to his superiors at home.

In Potsdam, Harry Truman reacted predictably to Suzuki's "mokusatsu." He allowed the atomic bomb mission to proceed according to schedule.

Secretary of War Stimson agreed. Noting regretfully that "we could only proceed to demonstrate that the ultimatum meant exactly what it said," Stimson concluded that for such a purpose "the atomic bomb was an eminently suitable weapon."

By the end of July, enough fissionable material had been transported to Tinian by plane and by ship to kill every living thing on the island. It was stored in heavily guarded Quonset huts, and scientists and weapons specialists such as Doctor Ramsey and Captain Parsons were frequently seen going in and out of the restricted buildings.

On July 31, a message was sent from Tinian to Washington: "Lemay needs eleven hours more which would be August 1, 1000 hours E.W.T." After that the bomb would be ready to drop over Japan. Truman had insisted on giving Japan several days to reply to the surrender demand. That time was about gone.

FIVE

The Little Boy

On August 4, seventy men of the 509th filed into a briefing hut on Tinian and sat down to watch a movie. Seven crews saw a colossal fireball rise up from the floor of the New Mexican desert and turn darkness into day. Awed by the pyrotechnics and power, they realized instantly the reasons for their peculiar training routine. One bomb, steep turns; their questions were answered by the film shot only nineteen days earlier.

Captain Parsons gave a speech in which he outlined the significance of the new weapon. He avoided using the word "atomic" as he told the men the bomb would be detonated in the air, that its full destructive effect was not known, that airplanes near the explosion would have to be extremely careful not to fly near the cloud rising from the burst. When Parsons mentioned the term "radioactivity," some of the listeners blanched as they connected it with another term, "sterility."

Tibbets then discussed the procedures for the first flight. He went over the air-sea rescue plans, the schedule for takeoff, routes and other aspects of the mission. Then the seven crews filed out of the hut into the bright sunlight of Tinian knowing that the next few days would see remarkable moments in the history of the world. Though the words atomic bomb had not been mentioned, the privileged group that had witnessed the movie knew that something horrendous was about to happen to the Japanese.

On Sunday, the fifth of August, scientists began the job of packing the Little Boy for shipment to Hiroshima. Two pieces of the deadly metal U-235 were delicately positioned at opposite ends of the cylindrical casing. A charge of cordite was placed behind one of them. On command it would blast this piece of uranium toward the other section with the velocity of a .45-caliber bullet. When the two collided, the temperature over Hiroshima would become that of a sun. All these calculations had been worked out at Los Alamos by minds normally devoted to peaceful pursuits.

On the sixth of August, Colonel Tibbets led the way to Japan with the Little Boy tucked inside the bomb bay of the *Enola Gay*. Chuck Sweeney and Crew 15 flew *The Great Artiste* nearby as an instrument ship. In its rear section, three scientists occupied a section set up as a darkroom. George Marquardt commanded the third plane, Number 91, equipped with cameras.

At 7:30 A.M., in brilliant sunlight, they sighted the Japanese coast. Claude Eatherley, flying as weather scout over the primary target, radioed back that conditions were perfect.

Tibbets called Sweeney: "Chuck, it's Hiroshima."

The planes turned toward the Initial Point for the run to the city. Underneath, the mass of Shikoku Island was a dark green. There were only a few clouds in the sun-drenched sky.

The placid Inland Sea appeared below and then the coastline of Honshu. Tibbets turned west at a point sixty miles from the target and shortly thereafter Hiroshima lay exposed and beautiful under the B-29's. Sweeney and Albury could even see in the center of the city the old castle that served as Japanese Army Headquarters in the area. The men in *The Great Artiste* kept reminding Beahan to yell when the Little Boy fell from the other B-29 because Sweeney needed every second of time to bank away safely.

At precisely 8:15 and 17 seconds Beahan shouted "Bombs away!" Sweeney pulled the plane over in a 60-degree bank and

Beahan dropped a cluster of instruments on parachutes to gauge the intensity of the explosion.

The Little Boy, a black and orange shape weighing nearly five tons, fell down on the 255,000 people of Hiroshima. At an altitude of 1,870 feet, the nine and one half pounds of cordite drove the uranium chunks into each other and the equivalent of 13,500 tons of TNT exploded in the sky.

A brilliant purplish-white flash lit the interiors of the three B-29's. Tibbets was momentarily blinded. Captain Parsons, who had daringly armed the Little Boy in flight to avoid any danger of explosion on takeoff, was staggered by the flash and the unfolding destruction.

In *The Great Artiste*, the film in the scientists' darkroom showed jagged lines as the instruments, still suspended on parachutes, attested to the death of a city.

At the Japanese Naval Academy on the island of Eta Jima, nearly sixty miles southeast of Hiroshima, students in classrooms heard a dull thunder and felt an unusually warm breeze touch them through open windows.

The three B-29's flew away from the devastation. Kermit Beahan had been so awed by the Little Boy that he forgot to turn on a tape recorder to preserve Crew 15's comments for posterity. George Marquardt's camera plane had photographed the boiling cloud, but only dust and smoke were visible beneath it. On the ground, more than sixty-four thousand people were dead or about to die.

Major Tom Ferebee had dropped his special bomb within feet of the prescribed aiming point. The Little Boy was released only seventeen seconds later than planned. The first atomic bomb mission was almost perfectly executed. Nothing had gone wrong.

Half a world away, Harry Truman heard the news while he ate lunch with men of the cruiser *Augusta* carrying the President home from Potsdam. An aide handed Truman a dispatch:

"Big bomb dropped on Hiroshima August 5 at 7:15 P.M. Washington time. First reports indicate complete success which was even more conspicuous than earlier test."

Truman was greatly moved. The *Augusta* sped onward across the Atlantic while the President shared the tremendous story with James Byrnes and ordinary seamen on the cruiser.

Tokyo also had a reaction:

> 6 August 1945   1700 hours From: Togo
> To: Sato
> No. 991 (urgent, ambassador's code.)
>   It is reported that Stalin and Molotov returned to Moscow today. As we have various arrangements to make, please see Molotov immediately, and demand his earliest possible reply.

The first word was in from Hiroshima, where a strange weapon had caused tremendous damage.

Before he heard from Sato, Togo was propelled into sending another frantic cable. An eyewitness to the atom bomb had come back to the capital with a chilling description: "The whole city of Hiroshima was destroyed instantly by a single bomb."

> 7 August 1945   1540 hours From: Togo
> To: Sato No. 993
>   Regarding your No. 1519. The situation is becoming so acute that we must have a clarification of the Soviet attitude as soon as possible. Please make further efforts to obtain a reply immediately.

Sato answered within hours:

> 7 August 1945   1950 hours Moscow
> 8 August 1945   1200 hours, Ministry of Foreign
>   Office, Tokyo From: Sato
> To: Togo
>   No. 1530 (urgent, ambassador's code.)

Regarding my No. 1519. As soon as Molotov returned to Moscow, I requested a meeting. I also asked Lozovsky to help arrange it. On the seventh, Molotov notified me that he would see me at 1700 hours tomorrow, the eighth.

Molotov kept his promise. At 5:00 P.M. on the eighth of August he met with Ambassador Sato and promptly declared war on the Japanese Empire.

Late that same night, in a room at Secret Police Headquarters in Osaka, Japan, two men stood over the figure of an American flyer, Lieutenant Marcus McDilda. Shot down that day on a strafing mission, McDilda had been picked up from the water and brought to shore. As soldiers marched him blindfolded through the streets, civilians closed about him and smashed him repeatedly with their fists. Bruised and bleeding, he was taken to a building where Japanese officers began to interrogate him. The pilot was asked questions about his home base at Iwo Jima. He lied consistently about the number of aircraft on the island, about other details of the P-51 fighter plane he flew.

For several hours he endured constant harassment. At intervals, officers stepped up and beat him. Then the same questions were asked again. When he said that 300 planes were based on Iwo, his captors displayed photographs showing that approximately 150 fighters actually operated from there. Trapped in this lie, he was rewarded with another beating.

The questioning became more intense. One officer demanded that he tell what he knew of the atomic bomb, dropped two days before on Hiroshima. McDilda assured him that he knew absolutely nothing about the weapon. The Japanese kept returning to the theme of the atomic bomb. McDilda repeatedly denied any knowledge of it.

Before midnight, a door opened and a general stepped in. He, too, insisted that McDilda tell about the bomb. When the lieutenant did not, the general drew out his sword and held it up before the captive's face. Then he jabbed forward, cutting through an open sore on McDilda's lip. Blood streamed down onto the American's chin and flying suit. The general screamed, "If you don't tell me about the bomb, I'll personally cut off your head." Then he stalked from the room.

McDilda was badly shaken. He hurt terribly from the many beatings. His face was cut, his torn lip throbbed from the sword slash. As the interrogators picked up the familiar questioning about the bomb, the pilot wondered just what he could tell them about it in order to stay alive. He could recall having heard someone on Iwo talking about the splitting of atoms, of negative and positive charges. Marcus McDilda began to tell the Japanese secret police about the atomic bomb.

Hoping his heavy southern drawl would confuse the interpreter, the pilot from Florida began: "As you know, when atoms are split, there are a lot of plusses and minuses released. Well, we've taken these and put them in a huge container and separated them from each other with a lead shield. When the box is dropped out of a plane, we melt the lead shield and the plusses and minuses come together. When that happens, it causes a tremendous bolt of lightning and all the atmosphere over a city is pushed back! Then when the atmosphere rolls back, it brings about a tremendous thunderclap, which knocks down everything beneath it!"

The interrogators prodded him to go on. McDilda continued: "The bomb is about 36 feet long and 24 feet wide."

The Japanese asked, "Do you know the next target for this weapon?" McDilda thought a minute, then chose the two cities whose destruction might be most demoralizing. He said, "I believe Kyoto and Tokyo. Tokyo is supposed to be bombed in the next few days."

The excited secret policemen pressed him for further details but McDilda was running out of ideas. He kept going back to his original lies. One of the interrogators left the room and went to a phone. He put through a call to Tokyo to the main headquarters of the secret police in Japan.

Back in the small room, Marcus McDilda continued to tell his preposterous story to fascinated officers, who were appalled at the news that Tokyo might become a victim of the terrible new bomb.

SIX

The Genie

On the afternoon of the eighth of August, Chuck Sweeney had flown *The Great Artiste* over the Pacific and released another dummy bomb into the sea. This one contained all component parts of the Fat Man except the deadly core of plutonium. All fuses, switches and detonators worked perfectly. Up until that moment, all the varied components needed to trigger the bomb in flight had not been assembled together inside the casing. When the first plutonium device was exploded in New Mexico in July, it was on a stationary tower and lacked some of the sophisticated gadgetry vital to a drop from the bomb bay of a B-29. Commander Fred Ashworth, aboard with Sweeney, was elated by the performance of the weapon. He knew that the Fat Man would be dropped on Japan within twenty-four hours.

When *The Great Artiste* got back to Tinian, Crew 15 was told that it would fly again the next morning. Since weather reports from Japan indicated unsettled conditions would prevail for five days after the ninth of August, the Fat Man would leave within hours.

Admiral Purnell and General Groves had often discussed the importance of putting a second bomb on target as quickly as possible after the first in order to impress the Japanese with the fact that the United States was actually in production of the weapon, that the future held only the prospect of more and more atomic warfare. It was Purnell who had initially proposed that it would take two bombs to end the war. Groves concurred in that belief. Harry Truman evidently did, too. He ordered atomic bombs dropped on "the two cities named on the way back from Potsdam." Unless expressly countermanded by radio from Washington, field commanders on Tinian could proceed accordingly. Orders for the second atomic mission were cut.

While Sweeney talked to his men about the mission, scientists completed the assembly of the Fat Man. Just before they inserted the plutonium itself, General Tom Farrell, Groves' deputy on Tinian, held in his hands the dark-grayish metal. It felt warm to his touch and he found it almost impossible to believe that this amount of matter, cupped in his palms, could actually destroy a city.

The officers of Crew 15 moved into a guarded Quonset, where they pored over maps of targets as they had done for a week. After leaving for a brief supper, they returned to the tedious chore in the hut. At nine o'clock, intelligence specialists seemed satisfied and the tired and tense men walked out to their barracks and a brief rest.

In the enlisted men's area, tension also gripped the five sergeants from *The Great Artiste*. Normal horseplay was missing. Abe Spitzer brooded. Ray Gallagher thought of what he'd seen over Hiroshima and felt queasy. He tried to write a letter to his family but was not able to concentrate. Ed Buckley and Pappy Dehart were almost silent, not even bothering to kid with Gallagher or John Kuharek.

Shortly after 11:00 P.M. the five men dropped their wallets on the beds of friends not flying that night and strolled across the field to the bustling briefing room for their last instructions.

The map on the wall clearly indicated the primary target, Kokura, in the northern part of Kyushu. The alternate target would be Nagasaki, on the western side of the same island.

Colonel Tibbets rose and made a short speech, in which he told the men that the Fat Man was radically different from the Hiroshima model and would make the first bomb obsolete. He mentioned that Washington was watching this mission closely, cautioned the crews to do a good job, and wished them luck.

Intelligence officers followed with the details of the mission.

Three planes would fly together to the target. Chuck Sweeney would carry the bomb, Fred Bock the instruments, and Major Jim Hopkins the movie cameras plus scientific personnel from England as observers. Since *The Great Artiste* had been outfitted for the Hiroshima flight as an instrument laboratory, it had been decided to leave it that way for the second mission. Fred Bock would fly *The Great Artiste* while Chuck Sweeney used Bock's own plane, *Bock's Car*, to carry the Fat Man.

Three officers had been added to the ten members of Crew 15. Navy commander Fred Ashworth would be in charge of the weapon. Lieutenant Philip Barnes would be his assistant. Lieutenant Jake Beser, an electronics specialist, would handle the radar countermeasures unit, monitoring Japanese frequencies and those on which the fuses for the Fat Man operated. It was his job to see that the enemy did not jam the bomb's fuse frequencies and prematurely detonate the Fat Man.

Weather experts told the assembled crews that a typhoon was wandering about off Iwo Jima. Therefore, rendezvous had been arranged at Yakoshima, a tiny island off the southern coast of Kyushu. The three planes must join there within fifteen minutes of the appointed moment.

Two weather planes would have reported conditions over the designated cities by that time. Sweeney and Ashworth would then proceed to their target based on the data given them by the reconnaissance craft.

Ashworth and Beahan were cautioned again that under no circumstances was the bomb to be dropped other than by visual, naked-eye observation of the aiming point in each city. Officials in Washington had insisted on this requirement in order to minimize any chances of a wasted drop, a negligible result.

The location of air-sea rescue units was outlined. Four B-29's were deployed to guide stricken aircraft to submarines which would pick up ditched personnel. The B-29's themselves carried survival equipment to be dropped to crash-landed crews.

Cruising and bombing altitudes were set. Sweeney was to come over the target at thirty-one thousand feet. One by one, the minutiae of the special flight were discussed.

On one point, the intelligence people were disquietingly vague. They seemed unable to forecast the strength of Japanese fighter opposition in the Kyushu area. Since the bombing of Hiroshima, no one could venture a prediction as to how the enemy would react to a small number of planes trying to penetrate the mainland. It was entirely possible that the Japanese were lying in wait for Crew 15.

After Chaplain Downey said a short prayer, the crews filed out to the mess hall. Most ate sparingly as pre-flight tension knotted their stomachs. When they reached the runway, several hundred men were milling around the three planes.

Number 77, *Bock's Car*, stood in the glare of over thirty klieg lights set up around it. In its bomb bay, the Fat Man waited. Shiny black and bulbous, it measured 10 feet 8 inches long by 5 feet in diameter. Inside its casing, meticulously machined pieces of plutonium were carefully arranged. When they came together under violent pressure, people in a Japanese city would burn to death.

Cameramen were on hand to record the takeoff. Generals hovered around the plane. Armed guards stood by to prevent any close inspection of the weapon. Fire-fighting equipment lined the strip in case the ship failed to negotiate the takeoff. Bob Lewis, the *Enola Gay's* copilot, teased Jim Van Pelt about this possibility. Van Pelt was not amused. Should the plane crash, aviation gas might ignite the high explosive in the bomb and trigger a release of nuclear energy. A senior officer on Tinian, terrified that the Fat Man might explode prematurely, had insisted on a written assurance that such a thing would not happen. Parsons and Ramsey had freely given it to him. If they were wrong, no one would be left to call them to account.

On *The Great Artiste*, three cylinders containing instruments for measuring the blast had been loaded into the bomb bay. Fastened to the outside of each one was an envelope, containing a white piece of paper on which Dr. Luis Alvarez had written a plaintive appeal in longhand.

Earlier, he and two other scientists on Tinian, Phil Morrison and Robert Serber, had recalled that Professor Ryukochi Sagane, a Japanese physicist, had studied with them at the University of California in 1938. Reasoning that Sagane, a nuclear expert, would be able to explain to his own government the chilling truth of Hiroshima, Alvarez penned an eloquent message to his colleague in Japan and taped it to the instruments that would record the death of another Japanese city.

Headquarters
Atomic Bomb Command
August 9, 1945

To: Prof. R. Sagane
From: Three of your former scientific colleagues during your stay in the United States.

We are sending this as a personal message to urge that you use your influence as a reputable nuclear physicist, to convince the Japanese General Staff of the terrible consequences which will be suffered by your people if you continue in this war.

You have known for several years that an atomic bomb could be built if a nation were willing to pay the enormous cost of preparing the necessary material. Now that you have seen that we have constructed the production plants, there can be no doubt in your mind that all the output of these factories, working 24 hours a day, will be exploded on your homeland.

Within the space of three weeks, we have proof-fired one bomb in the American desert, exploded one in Hiroshima, and fired the third one this morning.

We implore you to confirm these facts to your leaders, and to do your utmost to stop the destruction and waste of life which can only result in the total annihilation of all your cities if continued. As scientists, we deplore the use to which a beautiful discovery has been put, but we can assure you that unless Japan surrenders at once, this rain of atomic bombs will increase manyfold in fury.

The letter was unsigned.

Colonel Tibbets came to the side of *Bock's Car* and spoke quietly to the men. As he discussed the mission, Sergeant Kuharek, the engineer, came down from the ship and spoke to him and Major Sweeney. His words chilled the listening crew for he had found a serious problem inside the plane. The lower rear bomb bay auxiliary transfer fuel pump was not operating and six hundred gallons of gas were trapped. This would mean going on the lengthy trip without the reassurance of the reserve fuel supply.

Sweeney and Tibbets discussed the situation for a few minutes. To abort the flight would be calamitous. It was important to drop the Fat Man in quick succession following the Little Boy to convince the Japanese that there was an unending supply of the new weapons. To delay now would give the enemy time to reflect, to rationalize, to gain his balance.

Sweeney turned to his men. "To hell with it," he said. "We're going anyway." The plane could land at Iwo Jima on the way back and refuel.

On Tinian that night, jagged streaks of lightning laced the sky. Crew 15 sweated in the oppressive heat as the giant silver plane rolled from its hardstand toward Able Runway. Afraid that the Japanese might be eavesdropping on the wavelengths, Chuck Sweeney kept radio silence. He neither spoke nor was spoken to by the control tower.

Number 77's motors roared as the engines were checked for power. Sweeney strained to see down the runway, then released his brakes. *Bock's Car* rumbled down the strip toward the west. To Jim Van Pelt in the navigator's seat, the direction of takeoff itself seemed a bad omen. Always before Crew 15 had taken off from North Field into an east wind.

The air speed indicator reached toward 100, then 120 as the heavily laden plane raced over concrete. Spectators watching the hazardous takeoff tried mentally to lift it into the air but *Bock's Car* was being held right to the end of the field by the weight of the Fat Man in its belly.

As the Pacific rushed at him, Chuck Sweeney pulled up on the controls and the bomber rose slowly over the water. Normally a bright spotlight marked the ocean's edge but on this night it was unaccountably turned off. The B-29 held at fifty feet in level flight and turned ponderously to the north, climbing as it went.

It was 1:56 A.M. Japanese time. On the ground, scientists and generals breathed a collective sigh, and Dr. Ramsey went straight to his quarters and wrote a letter to Robert Oppenheimer, outlining the need for better safety precautions on the next takeoff with a Fat Man.

Shortly thereafter, the other two planes took off. An hour later, Dr. Robert Serber, who had last been seen taxiing off in the camera plane, suddenly turned up at the headquarters building. Because Serber had forgotten his parachute, Major Hopkins had dismissed him from the aircraft and he had walked the long way back through the darkness to report to General Farrell. Farrell was infuriated because Serber was vital to the mission. He was the only man of the crew who was trained to operate the high-speed camera needed to photograph the bomb's detonation. The general immediately ordered radio silence broken and contacted the airborne camera plane. For the next half hour Tinian instructed Hopkins on the proper use of the vital photographic equipment. The disconsolate Serber then joined the rest of the people on Tinian in their long wait for word from Japan.

At 2:32 A.M. *Bock's Car* reached seven thousand feet and was on top of the clouds. Some turbulence buffeted the ship as it headed into the edge of the typhoon that had been reported earlier. Chuck Sweeney went back to the tunnel to get some sleep. Don Albury handled the controls in Sweeney's absence. Jake Beser napped near his special equipment. In the nose, Kermit Beahan completed his first assignment. Asked to record the mission for posterity, he had all the crew members say a few words for a tape recording. One by one he solicited their home towns, their vital statistics. When he finished, Beahan put his gear down and went to sleep on his favorite pillow. John Kuharek fussed over his fuel gauges. The thought of the trapped gas weighed heavily on him. Abe Spitzer read a *Reader's Digest* condensation of *Our Hearts Were Young and Gay*, while Pappy Dehart, alone in the tail, gazed out at the receding cloud formations. Jim Van Pelt worked over his charts quietly. He could not afford a navigational error. Intermittently, he and Ed Buckley tested the radar to make sure that it was operating properly. Huddled in his seat, Fred Olivi slept soundly.

Commander Ashworth and Lieutenant Barnes worked over a little black box. Ashworth was the man most responsible for the Fat Man that day, the officer personally chosen by General Groves as accountable for "the care and operation of the bomb until its release on the target and for decisions concerning its tactical use." In effect, Ashworth and Sweeney would hold a joint command. They would consult on any difficulties in identifying the target, on any question of ditching the bomb or of choosing a secondary target—on any emergencies that might arise. In case of disagreement between them, Ashworth, as project officer, would have the final decision.

Ashworth watched while Barnes monitored the insides of the black box, connected to the Fat Man by an inch-thick umbilical cable. Just after takeoff, Ashworth and Barnes had checked out the systems in the weapon. Nearly halfway to Japan, they were shocked to see that the red light on the black box was on, signifying that all firing circuits were closed. The enormity of this discovery was terrifying. Barnes calmly opened up the console and methodically checked every wiring sequence. After a tense half hour, he smiled and sighed, "I've found it." A switch had failed and caused the arming light to glow. Barnes promptly corrected the problem.

Number 77 went west of Iwo Jima at 5:04 A.M. On Iwo, a substitute B-29 waited to take the Fat Man to Japan in case *Bock's Car* had run into mechanical difficulties. But the solitary bomber kept on going, climbing steadily to its assigned altitude of thirty-one thousand feet. In the Plexiglas nose, Kermit Beahan could see an almost solid blanket of clouds which obscured the ocean from view.

At 7:45, the cloud cover broke and someone pointed out an island dead ahead. It was Yakoshima, the rendezvous point. Near it part of the air-sea rescue team was on duty. A Dumbo Catalina patrolled idly. A Super Dumbo B-29 droned in a wide circle. Two submarines cut through the sea.

Several minutes later Crew 15 silently monitored a coded message. The weather plane at the alternate target, Nagasaki, reported: "Hazy, clearing rapidly, two-tenths cloud coverage, wind 250 degrees at 50 knots." Sweeney smiled in satisfaction. Earlier he had received similar good news from the primary area around Kokura. The weather over Japan seemed almost perfect. Sweeney moved the B-29 toward the southwest tip of Yakoshima.

Sergeant Ray Gallagher sat looking out his scanner window. He had been preoccupied and apprehensive during the long journey. He imagined each cloud to be a fighter waiting to strike. He thought of his family in Chicago and tried to connect them with what he was doing on this day. It was impossible. Just a few feet away from him lay a monstrous black weapon which would soon snuff out thousands of lives. Ray Gallagher's reverie ended as he saw another B-29 coming out of the clouds behind him. At 8:09

A.M. Japanese time, *Bock's Car* and *The Great Artiste* made their rendezvous.

In the second plane, pilot Fred Bock sat talking to a small, gray-haired man occupying the copilot's position. William Laurence was a *New York Times* reporter who was riding on his first combat mission. Laurence's job was unique. He was aboard to record the greatest story any journalist had ever been permitted to witness. His copy would be read around the world. Less than a month before, Laurence, again uniquely privileged, had stood on the New Mexico desert and watched as the atomic age began. Now he sat in the front end of a B-29 on its way to the heartland of the enemy. As the instrument plane came up to Yakoshima, he and Fred Bock were discussing the writings of Saint Thomas Aquinas and Plato. In front of them, the shape of Number 77, carrying the Fat Man, emerged from the clouds. Laurence left the ordered world of logic to put on a flak suit and survival belt.

Ralph Curry, the radio operator, and Len Godfrey, the navigator, helped him as he struggled into the cumbersome equipment. Dressed in the paraphernalia of war, Bill Laurence returned to his seat to gaze at the strike ship looming directly ahead of him.

The two planes began to circle the southwest corner of Yakoshima, while waiting for Major Hopkins' camera plane to appear. Minutes went by as the B-29's dallied over the tiny spot of land. Tempers began to flare in *Bock's Car* as the crew thought of the gas problem growing more acute with each lost moment.

Hopkins was actually in the area but at a higher altitude and over another point. Instead of lingering over the southwest portion of Yakoshima, he made a huge circle which encompassed islands to the northeast of the rendezvous area. John Cantlon, copilot in the camera plane, thought visual sighting of the other ships was made once but he could not be sure. At that great height, it was virtually impossible for any of the three planes to see each other unless they made a precise rendezvous.

In the lead ship, Chuck Sweeney grew increasingly concerned. On board the missing craft were two British scientists, Dr. William

Penney and Group Captain Cheshire, acting as observers for His Majesty's Government. Also, Hopkins had the cameras needed to record the explosion of the Fat Man. Sweeney was in a quandary.

The Major circled and circled and, after forty minutes, gave up the vigil. He waggled his wings at Fred Bock, who closed in to the right and followed *Bock's Car* toward Kyushu where Kokura, the primary target, basked in the summer sun. Nagasaki, the alternate, was enjoying the same pleasant morning.

The radar scope in *Bock's Car* locked onto Kokura before the crew could actually see it. Kermit Beahan, gazing into the rubber eyepiece of the bombsight, waited for the city to appear. The bomb bay doors opened and a sustained humming signal, signifying that the bomb was ready for release, sounded through the ship. Most members of the crew put on their arc welder's glasses with special Polaroid lenses designed to protect their eyes from the bomb's glare.

Beahan's aiming point was the enormous arsenal which was supplying arms to the Japanese Army. He picked up the city in his sight now and waited for the factory to pass under him. He saw the river that flowed by it, he saw the streets and buildings of Kokura, but the arsenal never came into view. A mixture of industrial haze and smoke from a nearby fire hid the one thing in Kokura that mattered at that moment. Beahan shouted, "No drop." Sweeney spoke to the crew: "Relax. We're going around again."

The plane wheeled about to approach Kokura from another angle. Abe Spitzer felt increasingly nervous as he thought of the Japanese antiaircraft batteries stationed below, in what he knew was the most heavily defended sector of the Empire. Just to the west were the steel mills of Yawata, a prime target in previous raids. Heavy guns formed a belt around its industrial complex.

Bock's Car thundered in again, the bomb bay doors open, the Fat Man poised in the open bay. The humming signal sounded. Fred Ashworth watched the black box which showed that the bomb mechanisms were in order. Again Kermit Beahan's face was fast to the rubber eyepiece.

The city flowed beneath. The river next to the arsenal emerged clearly in the sight, but the arsenal remained hidden. No drop. Beahan was following orders to the letter. Since he could not see the one specific building that served as the aiming point, he took no chances.

As the plane turned once more to come in from still another angle, Ray Gallagher looked down to watch orange mines bobbing in the sea. Jim Van Pelt saw a stadium close to the arsenal and hastened to point it out to Beahan. The stadium was not the aiming point, Beahan said, and therefore he could not sight on it.

John Kuharek agonized over the fuel supply. The delay at Yakoshima, and now at Kokura, had compounded a dangerous situation. Kuharek knew that *Bock's Car* had no chance of getting back to Iwo Jima.

On the final approach, Spitzer was wishing that they would get the hell out of there and go to Nagasaki. When Ed Buckley spoke to him, Spitzer told him to shut up. He was thinking of the guns around Yawata.

By now those guns were following *Bock's Car* closely, gauging its height and speed. The B-29's had lingered too long. In Kokura itself more and more people paused momentarily in the streets to watch the planes whose actions were unusual for reconnaissance aircraft. Civilians began to crowd into shelters as the specks in the sky hovered over them.

As Sweeney brought his B-29 across the target for the third time, Beahan again bent to his task. The humming of the tone signal sounded in his ears as he looked carefully for the arsenal. Jake Beser, watching his frequency band closely, noticed signs of activity on the Japanese fighter-director circuits. Someone was coming up to meet them. Gallagher was thinking to himself, "God, let's get in and get out of here."

Beahan saw the streets and the river glide under his gaze. He never saw the arsenal. It was still shrouded in a smoky haze.

Pappy Dehart called Sweeney on the intercom. "Major, we're getting flak. It's short but the altitude is perfect." "Roger, Pappy," Sweeney said. "Major, the flak is coming in closer." Sweeney answered, "Roger." Pappy Dehart then said, "Major, this damned flak is right on the tail and coming closer all the time." Sweeney answered, "Forget it, Pappy. We're on a bomb run."

As Beahan shouted "No drop" once again, Pappy Dehart spoke into the intercom: "Fighters below. Coming up." John Kuharek told Sweeney, "Fuel getting very low."

In the second plane, the *Times* reporter noticed black puffs mingling with the fleecy cumulus clouds. A novice at war, Laurence did not immediately recognize the signs of flak. At least fifteen shells burst near the two planes before he understood their significance. His eyes fastened on the small black book in which he was writing notes about the mission. Then, suddenly, he went to Sergeant Ralph Curry, the radio operator, and said: "Here, son, take this book. If anything should happen to me, give it to the first American officer you see when you get back." Over Curry's reassurances, he added: "If we have to bail out, you'll probably survive a landing in the ocean better than I can. Be sure and tell the officer that this is the last story Bill Laurence ever wrote." Curry took the book. Laurence looked out at the puff balls in the sky and cursed loudly at the possibility of missing the greatest news-beat in history.

In *Bock's Car*, Chuck Sweeney made up his mind. After talking with Beahan and Ashworth, he knew that it was foolish to stay over Kokura any longer. Several fighter planes were trying to climb to the great height of the B-29's while antiaircraft fire came closer by the minute.

He waggled his wings to Fred Bock and turned away from the city. Abe Spitzer, who had been muttering "How about Nagasaki?" found his prayers answered. *Bock's Car* droned away with the Fat Man still secured in its belly, leaving the people on the ground below alive—and annoyed at the two planes that had come to spy on them.

When the two bombers had left the target area, Bock's plane momentarily drifted out of Sweeney's line of vision. Sweeney spoke into his intercom: "Where's Bock?" Inadvertently, he had thrown the radio command switch open, and his voice carried over a wide area, breaking radio silence. Suddenly the men in both planes were startled to hear Hopkins from the missing camera plane: "Chuck, where the hell are you?" Sweeney chose not to protract the radio violation. Without answering, he closed the command switch. The third plane stayed lost.

Sweeney had enough problems of his own. Sergeant Kuharek gave a reading on the gasoline supply which caused Sweeney to moan "Jesus!" He announced that he must turn directly over the fighter fields of Kyushu to make a run on Nagasaki. He could not afford the extra fuel it would take to skirt the east coast before crossing west over the mainland.

Ashworth, in complete agreement with this move, sat before his black box trying to figure ahead to the situation at Nagasaki. What if *Bock's Car* ran into trouble there? He had to have ready an alternate plan. The thought of bombing Tokyo flashed quickly through his mind. There had been frequent discussion at Tinian about dropping an atomic bomb on Tokyo, thereby completing the destruction of that city and destroying the Government and the Emperor. He tried to dismiss the thought. Aside from the gas problem, the idea of making such a drastic move without express orders was staggering. The Fat Man rode on toward its secondary target.

At that moment, one city was reprieved, and another substituted. But to the population of Nagasaki, danger seemed remote. The morning was mild. The city pulsed with a steady hum while 200,000 people worked as usual. Bicycles and military vehicles clogged downtown streets. Children chased dragonflies in the park. There had been an air-raid warning earlier, but at 8:30 A.M., the single American weather plane had passed over, and the city had reverted to a standby status. Despite this, two thousand people still remained in the caves which served as shelters, unaware that others had already gone back to work. Overhead, banks of puffy clouds moved in to momentarily obscure the sun and etch fleeting shadows on the sidewalk.

Ninety percent of the labor force in the city worked in the Urakami Valley on the northwest side of town. Here, surrounded on both sides by low-lying ridges, the Mitsubishi complex of war plants manufactured torpedoes and small arms for the armed forces of the Empire. On this day, they were operating at full capacity, though scarcity of materials promised to cut production schedules in the coming weeks. The workers in the plants knew the war was going badly, but they kept hoping for the miracle that would save the country from defeat. Plans were already being made to counter the expected American invasion of their island. Civilians were being told that they must fight in the streets and in the hills to defend the homeland. There seemed no other choice.

One man in Nagasaki that morning was preoccupied with a sobering problem. Just the day before, Prefectural Governor Nagano had met with municipal officials to discuss the startling news from Hiroshima. His guest of honor had been Takejiro Nishioka, publisher of the *Minyu*, a local paper. Nishioka had come from that doomed city, where he had suffered burns and radiation exposure. He wanted to warn everyone of the awesome effects of the atomic explosion and to suggest countermeasures for the inhabitants of Nagasaki. The city officials had listened attentively as the publisher described the brilliant light and the following blast and heat. Nishioka's recommendations included placing the people in mass shelters at the approach of any single plane. Failing that, he had stressed that everyone should fall to the ground or behind any kind of cover if the white light burst over them.

Governor Nagano, troubled deeply by the publisher's recital of the facts of Hiroshima, planned a major indoctrination program for his constituents in the next week. This morning he initiated the necessary paper work for the project.

Over on the right-hand side of the Urakami Valley, hundreds of people had massed in the huge church on the bluff. Nagasaki was the center of Catholicism in Japan. Our Lady of the Immaculate Conception was the largest Roman Catholic cathedral in the Far East. It had been built by parishioners as a memorial to the centuries-old quest for religious freedom by converts to the teachings of Saint Francis Xavier, who visited the area in 1549. Persecuted for three centuries by the rulers of Japan, the Catholics had been left in peace after the American, Matthew Perry, forced the reigning Shogun to recognize their right to freedom of worship in 1853. On this Thursday morning they had come to make confessions in preparation for the Feast Day of the Assumption.

At the Nagasaki Medical College, Dr. Shirabe, a surgeon, finished a lecture to his students. In a second-floor room, Dr. Tsuneo tried to forget the horror of the destruction at Hiroshima, which he had witnessed at first hand. Tsuneo had miraculously escaped serious injury in the holocaust and had hurried back to his school to recuperate.

At the Urakami railroad station, the baggage master prepared to go out to the platform to unload an incoming train. His assistant, Aiko Tagawa, a girl of twenty, worked inside the cavernous room, sorting various articles. The clock on the wall registered 10:55 A.M.

North of the station, a man stood at the base of a water tower at the Mitsubishi factory and gazed through a pair of binoculars toward the east. As the sound of loud motors broke into the lazy morning, air-raid sirens began to shrill. The man with the binoculars picked up a plane heading toward Nagasaki.

Bock's Car was in serious trouble. The B-29 was facing a deteriorating fuel situation and might not be able to reach even Okinawa after dropping over Nagasaki. There was barely enough gas for one pass over the city before heading for safety. Any further delay would mean crash landing in Japan or dumping the atomic bomb into the ocean.

Sweeney told Spitzer to radio the air-sea rescue team off southern Kyushu to alert it to the possibility of ditching. Spitzer called out several times, but was unable to get an answer. Crew 15 was very tense by now. The strain of flying over the Japanese islands for so long was wearing down their nerves. So was the awesome weapon that continued to lie in the belly of the plane. The mission was a nightmare, a terrible joke being played on them. First the reserve gas problem, then the missed rendezvous, then the haze at Kokura. Nothing had gone right.

The nightmare intensified as the plane came near Nagasaki. The two-tenths cloud cover reported by the weather plane at 7:48 A.M. had changed by now to an apparent nine-tenths. In the past three hours a front had moved in across the East China Sea and nearly blanketed the city.

Sweeney called for Ashworth and came right to the point: "We have enough gas for one pass over Nagasaki. Just one pass. Otherwise we won't make it to Okinawa. How about dropping it by radar?"

It was a question Ashworth had been dreading. He was under explicit orders from Washington not to unleash the bomb unless the bombardier could actually see the target through the cross hairs. Because of that directive, Kermit Beahan had three times refrained from dropping the Fat Man over Kokura. Now Chuck Sweeney was mentioning the unmentionable.

Ashworth hesitated, then said firmly, "No."

Sweeney kept talking. "I'll guarantee we come within a thousand feet of the target, and that's better than dropping it in the ocean. I'm sure the radar will work right."

Hearing this, navigator Van Pelt shuddered. It would be his responsibility to bring the bomb over the aiming point by radar, and he did not share Sweeney's confidence.

Ashworth knew that his would be the final decision. If he vetoed Sweeney's suggestion, the Fat Man would probably have to be jettisoned in the ocean. Tokyo was officially out of bounds, there was no other worthwhile target within range, and he had no right to drop it on any other center of population. One city, Niigata, had originally been on the approved list of target cities, but had since been removed because it was too far from Tinian. And it was now too far from *Bock's Car* to be used as a dubious alternate.

Ashworth said, "Chuck, let me think about it for a moment." He walked back to his position and made a last analysis of the dilemma. To dump the bomb into the ocean would be a waste of the entire Manhattan Project effort. To attempt to bring the bomb all the way to Okinawa could result in disaster, since its weight increased fuel consumption. Yet it would be so simple for him to obey his orders to the letter and not take the chance of bombing by radar.

Ashworth balanced the scales. Knowing he was disobeying orders from above, he returned to Sweeney and said, "Go ahead and drop it by radar, if you can't do it visually." In that instant, Nagasaki began to die.

On Tinian, officials were thoroughly alarmed. No word had come from Sweeney after Kokura. General Tom Farrell went to lunch deeply troubled. When he emerged, a message was handed to him from Hopkins' wandering camera plane. It read: "Has Number 77 aborted?" General Farrell threw up on the floor.

Van Pelt and Buckley went to work on the radar. Nagasaki already showed on the scope as a light blue center surrounded by a darker background, with the water and the mountains around the city showing still darker. It was a difficult area to track and pinpoint. They asked Ashworth to verify their reading. He checked the scope and confirmed that it was, in fact, the outline of Nagasaki.

The city has a distinctive shape. Formed like the letter X, the upper arms are populated valleys split by a range of hills which reach to a height of thirteen hundred feet. The lower arms are heavily congested commercial and residential sections spreading out on either side of a magnificent harbor. According to the strategic plans, Ground Zero would be just to the southeast of the middle of the *X*, in the heart of downtown Nagasaki. Fat Man was supposed to drop below the hill range and spread its devastation through the relatively flat land around the bay. As in Hiroshima, the fireball could then run out unchecked and achieve maximum devastation.

As the plane neared the outskirts of the city, the cloud cover seemed to break somewhat. Van Pelt's eyes were glued to the scope as he directed *Bock's Car* toward the dropping point.

At thirty seconds to bomb release nothing had changed. Sweating faces reflected the intense concentration on the most difficult job of maneuvering the big ship over a precise target.

Five seconds later, a firm voice called, "I'll take it." Kermit Beahan had found a huge hole in the cloud layer and absolved Ashworth and Sweeney of the burden of deciding to bomb by radar. At the radar scope Van Pelt and Buckley felt reprieved from the responsibility of pinpointing the drop.

The humming signal droned through the plane. The ship shuddered as the open bomb bay doors caught the air. Beahan spotted the oval outline of a stadium a mile and a half up the Urakami Valley northwest of the intended Ground Zero. He sighted on it. He asked for a correction to the right, received it, and was able to put his cross hairs on the stadium. Then he was silent.

Seconds later the humming signal stopped abruptly. *Bock's Car* lurched upward as the Fat Man fell toward the ground. Over the intercom, Beahan said, "Bombs away," then quickly corrected himself: "Bomb away." Sweeney turned the plane to the left at a steep angle while the fuselage groaned.

In the other ship someone shouted, "There she goes!" Fred Bock executed a similar turn as the cluster of instruments and the letter to Professor Sagane fell down on parachutes several miles to the rear of the Fat Man.

When the atomic bomb left the B-29, arming wires were extracted, enabling the weapon to run on its own internal power.

Safe-separation timing clocks held switches open so that the bomb could not detonate near the aircraft. As it fell farther toward earth, additional switches were closed by barometric pressure. Then radar fuses were actuated to sense the exact height above ground. As the shiny black weapon neared an altitude of 1,540 feet, arming and firing switches closed, and the high voltages already built up in massive condensers were released to a series of detonators attached to a layer of high explosive. The detonators triggered an implosion, a bursting inward. The resultant shock wave quickly pressed the separate sections of plutonium together. In turn, the now dense plutonium sphere compressed a tiny "initiator," composed of particles of beryllium and polonium. Alpha rays emitted by the polonium acted on the beryllium, which sent a shower of neutrons out into the surrounding dark gray metal. In a millisecond, Nagasaki became a graveyard.

The Fat Man was detonated over the northwest leg of the X, just northeast of the stadium in the Urakami Valley. At the moment of ignition, there was an intense bluish-white flash as though a large amount of magnesium had exploded. The entire area grew hazy with smoke. Simultaneously there was a tremendous roar, a crushing blast wave and searing heat.

Twenty-four hundred feet to the northeast, the roof and masonry of the Catholic cathedral fell on the kneeling worshipers. All of them died.

At the Nagasaki Branch Prison, just north of the explosion, 118 guards and convicts saw the brilliant light but nothing more. There were no survivors.

The baggage master at the railroad station never rose to meet the incoming train. The roof of the building dropped onto his head. His assistant, torn by flying glass, ran into the street where people were beginning to jump headlong into the river to find relief from burns.

The approaching train had stopped for a moment to discharge passengers near the entrance to the Urakami Valley. Most of the people never left their seats as the white light flooded over them.

The windows blew in and ripped flesh into flayed meat. Severed heads rolled down the aisles as uninjured Japanese stumbled over the dead and ran from the train, too stunned to offer any help to others.

Out in the harbor, two and a half miles from the center of the blast, a seaman watched the explosion from his boat. As he stood transfixed, a small craft near him burst into flames and burned to the waterline. Beside him on his own deck, crew members screamed from burns on exposed portions of flesh.

Four and a half miles to the south of the blast, a wooden barracks at Kamigo simply fell down.

When the bomb exploded, Fusa Kawauchi was working inside a cave pumping out water. She did not see the intense flash but heard a noise like the sound of machinery running. She looked at a girl across from her and noticed that her face was streaked with dirt and soot. The two girls got up and went to the mouth of the cave. What they saw was unbelievable.

The fireball of the bomb had broadened in seconds to fill the valley. It lapped at the ridges on either side. The blast wave leaped the crests and raced through the seaport. People by the hundreds lay on the streets, in the fields, in wreckage, and screamed for water. Creatures that barely resembled human beings walked dazedly, skin hanging down in huge flaps, torsos blackened.

A mile and a half north of the center of the fireball, Ensign Jolly of the Netherlands Navy lay under a table in a prisoner-of-war camp. He had seen the parachutes drop, and he had seen the flash. Instinctively he plunged under the furniture as the building crashed around him. He lived, but several of his fellow prisoners died in the first seconds.

Another prisoner of war was an American, Motorman's Machinist Mate Second-class Jack Madison, captured three years before at Corregidor. He was standing before a coal-washing pit nearly two miles away. Guarding him and six other prisoners was a solitary Japanese policeman, who glanced idly into the sky as *Bock's Car* passed by. None of the captives paid much attention to that one plane as it headed over the Urakami Valley. Madison continued working and neither felt the blast nor saw the light as Fat Man burst below the layer of clouds. He was thrown to the bottom of the pit, unconscious.

At the Nagasaki Medical College, southeast of the epicenter, Dr. Shirabe heard the plane and started for the door of his offices. The room collapsed behind him and left him in total darkness. When the light returned, Shirabe stumbled to the corridor and walked outside to join survivors struggling to reach the high ground behind the building. At their backs were the terror-filled cries of patients trapped in their beds by crackling fire.

Over the wreckage of the Urakami Valley towered a monstrous expanding pillar of smoke shooting upward from the middle of the explosion at incredible speed. Like a genie released after countless ages of captivity, the column writhed and twisted toward the stratosphere. At its feet lay incredible devastation, as though the living thing had wreaked a special vengeance on its jailers. The deadly apparition seethed up toward the circling planes. It changed faces, it changed colors from purple to salmon to gold to soft white. It escaped into the boundless sky where it sprouted a new head and hovered menacingly over the dying valley.

The men in *Bock's Car* and *The Great Artiste* were overwhelmed by the sight. The brief, blinding, purplish white flash lit up the sky. Below they could see only a pall of smoke in the Urakami Valley. The center of the city seemed undamaged. Around the periphery of the blast they saw countless fires on the slopes of the hills.

Pappy Dehart sat in the tail of *Bock's Car*, photographing the explosion with a movie camera given him by Dr. Alvarez. His excitement at what he was witnessing made him almost incoherent. As he focused on the scene, two aftereffects of the blast threatened the lives of the fliers.

The first was a violent series of shock waves. As Sweeney turned to come back over the city to verify the bomb's point of detonation, he and Albury saw the waves coming through the air like ripples on a pond. When they hit, Commander Ashworth felt as though he were inside a garbage can with someone striking a baseball bat against the cover. By the third blow, he wondered whether the plane was being attacked by antiaircraft fire. Jim Van Pelt distinctly counted five blows against the fuselage—not two or three, as he had expected.

In *The Great Artiste*, Laurence scribbled furiously in his notebook. He too experienced five distinct shock waves which bounced the ship about like a matchstick. The navigator, Len Godfrey, was "startled and amazed" at the size of the explosion. As his mind raced to comprehend the enormity of Nagasaki's disaster, observers in the rear of the aircraft shouted the fact that the mushroom cloud was racing toward them.

In the lead plane, Ray Gallagher was as quickly aware of the second threat, the approaching radioactive cloud. From his position in the left scanner's window he saw the spiraling monster apparently heading directly up under the B-29. He shouted into the intercom at Sweeney, "Major, let's get the hell out of here."

Van Pelt and Albury also had seen it coming. Albury said to Beahan, "Well, Bea, there's 100,000 Japs you just killed." Beahan did not answer. He was watching the advancing pillar of fire—which was much too close.

Sweeney pulled away in a turn, and the mushroom soon loomed above them nearly ten miles away. It was black and gray at the base, white and reddish above. Commander Ashworth thought it "vicious-looking." *Bock's Car* and *The Great Artiste* headed away from Nagasaki.

Five minutes after leaving the scene, Spitzer transmitted a message to Tinian:

Bombed Nagasaki 090158Z visually with no fighter opposition and no flak. Results "technically successful" but other factors involved make conference necessary before taking further steps. Visible effects about equal to Hiroshima. Trouble in airplane following delivery requires us to proceed to Okinawa. Fuel only to get to Okinawa.

As *Bock's Car* flew south from Nagasaki, it carried a relaxed crew. With the Fat Man finally delivered on target, the strain built up over the past hours quickly dissipated. Even the seriousness of the fuel shortage could not dampen the men's spirits, and shouts of congratulations continued to sound over the intercom as they climbed out of thin flak suits and survival equipment. Eventual ditching in the ocean was something they were willing to risk if necessary. Beser said as much. So did Buckley, who also commented to Gallagher, "I never said many prayers in my life, but today I really prayed."

On the scant remaining three hundred gallons of gas, Sweeney took the B-29 down the chain of islands between Kyushu and Okinawa. He told Spitzer to call the air-sea rescue people again and alert them to the possibility of a ditching in the area. Repeated messages got no answer. The rescuers had gone home. Having been told nothing of the mission's delays at the Yakoshima rendezvous and over Kokura, they assumed that the bomb had been dropped at Kokura and that the strike planes had successfully returned to Tinian.

An hour out of Yontan Field on Okinawa, *Bock's Car* tried to contact the tower. There was no response. As the B-29 bored in, increasingly desperate messages were sent to the ground. No one answered. After nearly twelve hours at the controls, Sweeney and Albury were close to exhaustion; but as they came within sight of safety, they saw yet another hazard ahead. The tower at the field still failed to recognize the approach of the plane, and squadrons of P-38's and B-25's were taking off and landing below. Because of *Bock's Car's* fuel problem, there was no time left to circle. The plane had to make a direct descent.

At the pilot's order, Van Pelt and Spitzer shot off flares. On the ground no one paid attention to the signals.

Just behind Sweeney, Commander Ashworth sat on the floor and braced himself against the wall in anticipation of a rough landing. The pilot called into his voice radio, "Mayday, Mayday," as he steered the ship toward the long runway.

The ground ignored him.

Sweeney roared, "I want any goddamn tower on Okinawa." Then he shouted to Van Pelt and Spitzer: "Shoot every flare you've got." Twenty-four of them, all colors, arched into the sunlit sky. The interior of the ship smelled like a battlefield from the acrid smoke. Outside, the multicolored lights—signifying "dead and wounded on board"—hung over the airport.

The fireworks display finally attracted attention below. Formations began peeling off as *Bock's Car* flew along the runway high above the ground; the plane had to have the concrete under it in case a dead-stick landing was necessary.

Bock's Car descended rapidly and hit the strip halfway down at 120 miles per hour. It bounced into the air once and settled. The two outboard engines suddenly quit cold and the plane veered to the left, narrowly missing a line of B-24's parked to the side. Fighting to slow it, Sweeney threw the propellers into reverse pitch. The new Curtis props caused enough drag to tame the wild ride of the B-29 before it plunged off the concrete. Even then, the men in the rear were tossed about like chaff as Sweeney, still at high speed, turned into the taxiway.

A jeep appeared, prepared to lead Number 77 to a hard-stand. Fire engines and ambulances waited for the plane to come to a full stop. When Sweeney cut the functioning motors, silence enveloped the interior of the plane. A man came to the door as it opened and asked where the dead and wounded were. None were aboard *Bock's Car*. The dead and wounded, thousands of them, were several hundred miles to the northeast.

In Nagasaki, the mushroom cloud became less vertical, more diffused, as the wind gradually altered its appearance. The scene beneath it had become even more horrifying.

Within twenty minutes, American POW Jack Madison had regained consciousness at the bottom of the coal-washing pit. His head was bleeding and two ribs were broken. Near him a British prisoner, bloodied, held his hands over his face.

Madison looked up and saw a silver B-29 circling slowly around the mushroom cloud. He was watching the missing camera plane, which was finally attracted to the area by the flash of the Fat Man. Nearly a hundred miles east and heading south at the time, pilot Hopkins brought his crew across the stricken valley at thirty-eight thousand feet. Bombardier Myron Faryna noticed that the northwest portion of Nagasaki was covered by a blanket of dust and smoke; in the other parts of the city he could clearly see buildings, apparently undamaged. Above the camera plane, the cloud extended for another twenty thousand feet. Hopkins took the B-29 south toward Okinawa.

On the ground, Jack Madison rose from the coal pit. No one with him had been killed because an intervening hill range had deflected the blast and flame. While he wondered whether an ammunition dump or oil storage depot had been exploded by a bomb, a group of Japanese guards appeared and ordered the POW's to go with them. Madison walked away from the disaster, but he kept looking over his shoulder at the fires spreading out from the Urakami Valley.

Much of the city was in flames. Lines of refugees streamed out of the inferno. Many were walking dead, soon to collapse to the ground and expire. Not only had the heat charred and destroyed their skin, but the invisible gamma radiation from the split atoms had invaded their bloodstreams and marked them for sure death. They croaked continually for water.

Almost one half of the medical personnel in Nagasaki had died in the first minutes, and, as a result, casualties received little or no relief from their wounds. The burned continued to scream, the torn bled to death, and those dosed with radiation never received the transfusions which might have saved them. Over everyone hung a wall of crackling fire which rained down sparks and consumed the slow of foot.

One of the doctors who died was Dr. Tsuneo, the man who had just returned from Hiroshima. The second atomic bomb caught him in his room at the Medical College. Though carried to a nearby hill by friends, he was beyond help.

Some of the doctors and nurses were so shocked by the enormity of the catastrophe that they turned their backs on helpless survivors and scurried away to the safety of the high ground. By the time their consciences functioned, it was too late.

A light rain began to fall on the Urakami area shortly after noon. It was black, a result of the condensation of the mushroom cloud, filled with dirt and debris. It acted as a brake on the spreading fires which ate at the wooden wreckage and the bodies sprawled about on all sides. The dirty rain streaked the faces of those still walking and running out of the flames. It put out some fires, but others grew from sparks of smoldering debris.

Trees had been snapped off, not merely blown down. Seven miles from Ground Zero, in the village of Mogi, one of every ten windows was blown out. Within an area of a thousand acres around the point where the bomb detonated, there was total destruction of all buildings except those of heavily reinforced concrete, and these were completely gutted on the inside. Every structure in the valley and at the northeastern end of the harbor was either destroyed or badly damaged.

Eighteen schools were smashed to rubble. The street railway system lost almost all of its cars. The Mitsubishi steel complex was rendered inoperable. The huge torpedo factory was stripped like the skeleton of a prehistoric beast and lay naked under the blood-red sun, its steel ribs exposed, its guts scorched by blast and flames.

Governor Nagano survived the holocaust, thanks to the warning given him and others by publisher Nishioka. When the light shone above him, he dove to the ground and lived to fight for his city. All fire-fighting equipment had been burned up. Telephone lines were nearly all down. Water mains had sprung leaks in hundreds of places. Nagano called outside Nagasaki for help. Though the main Omura highway was badly damaged over a distance of five miles, relief teams went to work in the early afternoon to bring aid.

By one o'clock lines of refugees began to straggle eastward over the hills into Nishiyama and down into the less damaged portion of the city around the harbor. Most of them were naked. Most had no hair, or what there was of it was frizzled and singed. They cried mournfully. Their burns were black and swollen. Many had no faces, just indentations where eyes and nose had once been. They vomited continually or suffered from diarrhea as they stumbled along.

Rescue workers going past them toward the valley sobbed as they watched the hellish procession move along under the specter of the mushroom still lingering above. When American reconnaissance planes flew over to try to ascertain the damage, they were scarcely noticed.

Later in the afternoon, Tatsuya Koga sat on the hillside behind the Medical School. Around him the remnants of the hospital staff tended to the dying. Below, the west wing of the college was still burning and patients trapped by the fire had ceased to scream. Across the valley, antlike columns of Japanese men and women still struggled up the slopes of the hill leading to Nishiyama. Children rode the backs of the less seriously injured.

Koga felt a wave of nausea and vomited into the grass three times. He continued to retch bile as the effects of radiation gripped his body. He put his head down and fell into a fitful sleep.

By four o'clock rescue workers had cleared a stretch of the railroad leading to the shattered Urakami station. The first trainload of wounded was shepherded out of the area and on to the Omura naval hospital twenty-eight miles north of the city.

Governor Nagano acted quickly to head off another calamity. Aware that the summer heat would accelerate decomposition of the thousands of cadavers lining the streets, he ordered mass cremations begun as soon as possible.

Twilight came early that afternoon to the Urakami Valley. Smoke hung over the land. A sea of fire had spread across the entire valley. The living clung to the slopes and watched their homes burn to the ground. From the edges of the fire people ran haltingly, blindly toward the highlands. Some had skin hanging in huge folds from their arms and legs, and cried when they brushed against anything in their path. As darkness fell, volunteers began to collect the corpses by the light of the burning trees and buildings. Row after row of blackened and blistered bodies were formed into mounds. Torches were applied to wood underneath the piles. Human forms lay stiff and naked in a welter of meat soon to be reduced to ashes and remnants of bone.

Many families buried or burned their own dead rather than have them collected and thrown on the mountain of flesh. Many others did not need to.

Kikuo Fukahori arrived back from his job several miles away to find his home completely destroyed. He went to a nearby cave to look for his family. In the dusk he could see nothing inside and went away. His family was beyond help. His five children had been pinned under the roof of their home and died in an inferno of fire. His wife was inside the cave, her tongue protruding from a swollen and blistered face.

In the darkness, small fires dotted the landscape as other survivors returned to the ruins and put their relatives to rest. There was little else they could do that awful night in the sorrowing land around the Urakami River.

The crew of *Bock's Car* spent less than two hours at Okinawa. Within a few minutes after its nearly disastrous landing, it was joined by Fred Bock's *The Great Artiste*. Nearly an hour later the missing camera plane finally made its rendezvous with its companions. Its crew received some sarcasm from disgusted fliers in the other ships. Meanwhile, Sweeney and Ashworth had reported their mission to General Jimmy Doolittle, commander of the Eighth Air Force based on the island. When they departed for

Tinian, only he, of all the men on Okinawa, knew what *Bock's Car* had accomplished that day.

En route to the Marianas nearly all the men aboard the plane slept. At 10:25 P.M. they touched down on Tinian—nearly twenty hours after the mission had begun.

There was a briefing attended by Purnell, Farrell, Ramsey, Tibbets and others. Then the crews of the three planes were dismissed. *Time* reporter Bill Laurence sat down to write the story of the raid. It would win him the Pulitzer Prize. Bombardier Kermit Beahan went to bed, exhausted. It was his twenty-seventh birthday. Some of the others were too tense to rest. Two officers of the 509th stood at the bar of the officers' club and drank until 5:00 A.M. Then they stole a general's jeep and tried to drive it through the hut where Kermit Beahan and Don Albury were sleeping. Some of the men on Tinian had trouble settling down that night.

In the communications center, General Tom Farrell sent a coded message to his superior in Washington:

TO GROVES PERSONAL FROM FARREIX APCOM 5479 TOPSECRET

Strike and accompanying planes have returned to Tinian. Ashworth's message from Okinawa nr 44 is confirmed by all observers. Cloud cover was bad at strike and it will be necessary to await photographs to give exact point of strike and damage. . . .

After listening to accounts, one gets the impression of a supremely tough job carried out with determination, sound judgment and great skill. It is fortunate for the success of the mission that its leaders, Ashworth and the pilot Sweeney, were men of stamina and stout heart. Weaker men could not have done this job. . . .

Fifteen hundred miles to the north, the enemy could not sleep either. While the interrogations droned on at North Field, nervous men sat around an air-raid shelter in Tokyo and waited for the Emperor of Japan to appear. The past day had been calamitous. Russia had invaded Manchuria, and a second atomic bomb had killed thousands. The men in the shelter had come to discuss the dread word *surrender* and the Emperor was on his way to listen to their arguments. He wanted a decision that night.

Thirteen hours after *Bock's Car* dropped the Fat Man over Nagasaki, the officials sat tensely, waiting for their Ruler to enter the room and listen to them debate ending the war. As Captain Ellis Zacharias' Plan I-45 predicted months before, they were divided by doubt, debate, difference of opinion, and the fear of being held responsible for such an awful decision.

SEVEN

The Air-Raid Shelter

Eleven men sat in extraordinary session around the long, cloth-covered table. The room they had gathered in was small, only 18 by 30 feet. Its ceiling was steel-beamed, its walls paneled in a dark wood. Its most striking characteristic that particular evening, however, was a complete lack of ventilation. In the August humidity, the assembled conferees, all dressed formally in morning attire or high-collared uniforms, perspired heavily as they talked.

Four of the men were aides or secretaries. One man was a guest. The others were the Big Six, Japan's "inner cabinet," formally named the Supreme Council for the Direction of the War. To these six men—four cabinet ministers and two military chiefs of staff—was entrusted the formulation of policies, subject to full cabinet approval, which influenced the destinies of eighty million citizens of the Japanese Empire.

The "inner cabinet" operated very cautiously because, in the summer of 1945, real power in Japan was vested in the Army and Navy General Staffs. The Diet, similar in makeup to the United States Congress, was now a rubber-stamp assembly. The Privy Council, once a powerful group advising the Throne, was now consulted after the fact. The jushin, ex-Premiers, held no official authority, but managed to exert some pressures on events as they had in forcing General Tojo's downfall in 1944. The cabinet, modeled like those in America and England, nevertheless had little mind or authority of its own; the military dictated its actions.

Above all these governmental branches sat the Emperor of Japan, who could express his opinions, show his feelings, but who by tradition did not order his own subjects to do his bidding. He had no veto power. On this night, for instance, he could only suggest courses of action to the men in the shelter.

The titular leader of the Big Six was Premier Kantaro Suzuki, a venerated hero of the long-ago Russo-Japanese War. Then, as a young officer, he had led a suicidal charge against the Czarist fleet off Tsushima. By that exploit, he had earned lifelong prominence in Japan. Now in his eighty-first year, the aged admiral held the highest office his nation could offer a commoner. Revered by most, he puzzled some by his contradictory statements on the conduct of the war. One day, he would tell everyone he would prosecute it to the bitter end. The next day, he would reassure the peace party that he was in favor of immediate moves to terminate hostilities.

The Japanese people delight in oblique tactics, but Suzuki's actions confused even his closest confidants. Some whispered that his apparent indecisiveness could be traced to his advanced age. Deaf in one ear, Suzuki dozed frequently at conferences, missed points in debates, and generally let others hold the spotlight while he sat in the twilight of his career. Though he had been an inveterate cigar smoker in the past, he puffed only two a day by 1945. He loved to sit and play solitaire or read books on Taoism, while sipping part of his quota of five cups of sake a day. His wrinkled, moustached face, framed by enormous ears, smiled often as he went about among his peers. Even those violently opposed to his policies liked and admired him. Premier Suzuki was one of the few men in government without personal enemies.

Yet the Premier was beset by fear of assassination. He knew first-hand the force of military fanaticism. Nine years earlier, on

February 26, 1936, hundreds of Army officers and men had gone wild in an orgy of killing. Shot three times, Suzuki had narrowly escaped death. His mind as well as his body still retained those scars of violence. In the summer of 1945, as he surveyed the ruins of his beloved Empire and tried to carry out the Emperor's mandate to end the war, the Premier could not perform effectively. During the intensive series of high-level discussions, he vacillated, contradicted himself, trod carefully through the camp of the enemy, the military. He wanted to surrender, but he knew, as did others in Tokyo, that a premature declaration of intent would probably mean his death. His realization of the futility of continued war did not need to be confirmed by the bombing of Nagasaki. When the first Soviet troops broke across the Manchurian border that morning, Suzuki had cried, "The game is up." Now, hours later, as he sat with his colleagues, he was at last prepared to show his hand and take his country out of the "game."

Beside Suzuki in the Emperor's shelter sat Foreign Minister Shigenori Togo, sixty-three years old and a strong supporter of surrender. Though later the Allies would brand him as a war criminal for his actions as Foreign Minister at the time of Pearl Harbor, Togo had assumed a dominant role in the summer's efforts to take his nation out of the war. A brilliant intellectual, he had little use for sensitivities in his daily contacts. He was a dogmatic man, scornful of opinions contrary to his own, and given to venomous eloquence in frequent temper outbursts. A mild-looking, bespectacled face masked an aloof, acerbic personality which caused his friends much embarrassment and his enemies much pain.

From 1942, when he had been deposed owing to a dispute with the military, until 1945, when Suzuki became Premier, Togo had lived in retirement. At the urging of the jushin he then again took charge of the Foreign Office. He agreed to do so only after he was assured that Suzuki intended to end the war as soon as possible. Like Suzuki, however, Togo was forced to proceed carefully to forestall a coup by military fanatics. He too feared for his life in the long summer of 1945.

The third member of the peace faction was a military man, Navy Minister Admiral Mitsumasa Yonai, whose weather-beaten face had been a familiar sight among top circles in the Government for nearly twenty years. At sixty-five, the Navy Minister sat once more with old friends and rivals and championed the cause of peace. His features betrayed an enthusiasm for good whiskey. Once handsome, his facial muscles now sagged, huge pouches hung under his eyes, deep lines creased his cheeks, and veins stood out on his nose. Yet a warm smile constantly wiped away these signs of debilitation and attracted people to his side.

Yonai had many enemies among the military, who resented his "pacifist" attitude. When he had been Premier in 1940, he ran afoul of the generals because he opposed any alliance with Germany and Italy. For that the Army forced his resignation.

He was an ardent critic of war with the United States and was subjected to much harassment when the Japanese marched south in 1941. Called pro-American, he was sent into retirement. For nearly three years, Yonai languished in relative obscurity while the United States armed forces battered their way to the Marianas. When Tojo fell in July of 1944, he was catapulted back into service as Navy Minister under Koiso. Actually he was more than that. Because the jushin had forced the Army's hand, Yonai was in effect assistant Premier, standing in Koiso's shadow, subtly trying to influence the course of events. When Suzuki took over, Yonai continued as Navy Minister.

As noted in the Fujimura affair, he walked carefully to avoid extremists. He had the same fears, the same memories as did Suzuki and Togo. Death lurked in the barracks, in the officers' clubs, in the hearts of young men unable to comprehend defeat. Yonai had to wait for the right opportunity, the moment when the scales would be heavily weighted in his favor. Tonight he sat near his inseparable companion, Kantaro Suzuki, and prepared to strike. The events of the past few days—Hiroshima, Nagasaki, the Russian invasion of Manchuria—had unbalanced the scales.

Ranged against Togo, Yonai and Suzuki were the other members of the Big Six. Their leader was General Korechika Anami, War Minister, spokesman for the Army and the most powerful man in Japan.

Only four months before, Anami had arrived at the summit of his military career. The fifty-seven-year-old general had been given the War Ministry post when Suzuki formed his new cabinet. His new power, however, offered him little satisfaction. Beneath him lay the ruins of an empire. His Army numbered in the millions, but it was doomed to defeat. Supplies for the war machine had begun to dwindle and disappear. Though tactically the Imperial Japanese Army could still inflict cruel punishment on the enemy, strategically it had lost the war.

But Anami had one hope left. His forces might bleed the Americans so badly on the beaches of Kyushu and Honshu that Japan could extract better peace terms from the conquerors.

The general was a stubborn man, whose career reflected a tenacious determination to succeed. As a youth, he took and failed the entrance exams for the Military Academy four times before passing. After graduating from school, he served a typical apprenticeship in the Japanese Army in the period during and after World War I. In 1926, he was placed in the much sought-after position of aide to Hirohito. As such, Anami became friendly with Marquis Kido, also an Imperial aide, who later became Hirohito's most influential counselor.

Anami was not one of the original fanatics who usurped power in Manchuria. Not a firebrand, he chose a middle path between the disputing factions of the Imperial Army, thus avoiding the bitter factional warfare that erupted in the turbulent thirties. After Pearl Harbor, the rapidly rising officer commanded Japanese armies in the Dutch East Indies. From there his path led back to the intrigues of Tokyo. When Koiso fell, he was acceptable to both peace and war advocates as War Minister.

Anami possessed a relatively colorless personality. Compared to predecessors like Tojo, he seemed almost a shadow figure in the military hierarchy. Grandfatherly in appearance, Anami's only affectation was a neatly trimmed moustache. His face was full, his figure ample but not portly. The general kept in excellent condition through his favorite pastimes, archery and *kendo* (Japanese fencing). Every morning he tried to spend a few minutes shooting a bow and arrow because he felt that it helped discipline his mind.

To the young officers under him, Anami was always calm and almost paternal. To the men who argued for peace in the cabinet meetings, he was infuriatingly obstinate. Frequently, the general would agree to a main point of discussion, then spar over side issues interminably. Such a man now grasped the leadership of the most dominant force in Japan, the Army. He must either disarm it forever or see it overwhelmed on the beaches. Thus far no one had been able to convince him not to fight. He had insisted on one last battle.

His Chief of Staff sat next to him. General Yoshijiro Umezu, who looked like an oriental version of Benito Mussolini, also managed to typify the American image of a Japanese warlord. His head was shaven, his eyes were narrowed slits, hooded and menacing. His thick lips were constantly pursed, lending a perpetual scowl to his face.

Umezu was a rigid, gruff martinet, a product of the fanatical Kwantung Army. Like Tojo, he had been in the center of the drive into Manchuria and China from 1931 to 1940. As one of the small nucleus that guided Japan's destinies overseas, he was partially responsible for the disaster that engulfed his nation. But Umezu was not blind to the truth of impending defeat. He merely wanted better terms than those offered so far by the Potsdam Declaration. From the tip of his visored cap to the spurs on his shiny boots, the Army Chief of Staff epitomized the dilemma facing Japan. The Army must have peace with honor or it would fight on without quarter to the enemy.

The sixth member of the council was Admiral Soemu Toyoda, a beefy man with a pockmarked face, who was Navy Chief of Staff. As such, he was the most recent addition to the select group and had been appointed by Navy Minister Yonai both for his competence and for a less apparent reason. Toyoda came from the same clan and region as General Umezu. Assuming that Toyoda leaned toward immediate peace, Yonai felt that the admiral would be a positive influence on Umezu in the final weeks of discussion. He guessed wrong.

In these discussions, Toyoda vigorously defended the Army's position. With his Navy lying on the floor of the Pacific, the Admiral lent full moral support to his fellow officers. Probably the most astute of the three, he dissected arguments brilliantly and found flaws in every position held by the opposition. His speeches were eloquent and reasoned. The sixty-year-old Toyoda was known as extremely nationalistic, and his hatred of foreigners was intense. Instead of being a subversive force against the generals, he had proven a worthy compatriot to the military clique in the last days.

The guest, Baron Kiichiro Hiranuma, had no legal right to be there. As President of the Privy Council, an advisory body to the Emperor, he approved decisions already laid down by the full cabinet. Hiranuma had been invited merely to observe and report back to his own group on this meeting, thereby speeding up the decision-making process within the Government. However, the bespectacled, long-faced old politician intended to do more than just listen to the dialogue. Hiranuma had decided to become a devil's advocate, soliciting facts, seeking out loopholes in arguments, generally pressing the participants closely in order to help them break through to a conclusion.

As a veteran of high-level negotiations in Japan, Hiranuma was admirably suited for the job. At eighty, he had miraculously survived many decades of the in-fighting that typified his nation's politics. An artful, wily tactician, the baron had lost little of the zealot's fire he showed in his earlier career. Then he had been an ultranationalist, a strict constitutionalist, lending his support to various patriotic societies whose avowed purpose was to strengthen the Imperial institution. As a leader of the

THE FALL OF JAPAN 121

Kukohonsha, a rightist organization, he wielded tremendous influence on formation of cabinets in the turbulent years that followed World War I. By 1927 he managed to cause the overthrow of the reform-minded Wakatsuki cabinet and the establishment of Giichi Tanaka, an Army general, as Premier. From that point on, Japan's policies were increasingly determined by the militantly ambitious groups within the Army, and Hiranuma learned to repent his action.

In 1939, Hiranuma was made Premier. As often happens, the office helped tone down the man's reactionary tendencies. He tried to slow the Army's drive to expand into China and elsewhere but failed. Though he worked most of his life for continuation of the Emperor system he in no way wanted the dictatorial monster that emerged from Manchuria in the guise of the Kwantung Army, which slowly spread its tentacles throughout the Government. Compared to this army, Baron Hiranuma was a flaming symbol of reform. Disillusioned, he continued to combat the military even after the Army forced him out of power. Terrorists tried to kill him in 1941. In the same year, he opposed war with America. When Tojo came to power as Premier, Hiranuma went into eclipse.

As the long war came to a close, he once more began to play a pivotal role as he struggled to shore up the Imperial institution and protect it from extinction. Hiranuma saw the necessity of convincing the warring factions within the government to agree on some form of answer to the Allied Powers.

The Big Six, their aides and Hiranuma waited twenty-five minutes in the underground shelter before the door to the Emperor's quarters opened and the Divine Ruler walked in, accompanied by an assistant. Hirohito moved quickly to a straight-backed chair at the head of the table and sat down. His subjects bowed to him and sank back into their seats.

All of them were dismayed to see that their Sovereign's hair was unkempt, hanging down in disarray on his forehead. His harried look was hardly that of a godlike leader.

Hirohito cleared his throat and waited for the meeting to begin.

The Emperor was not an impressive figure. Short-statured, bespectacled, he was shy to an extreme. His right cheek was marred by a nervous tic. His chin receded. His shoulders twitched. His voice was high-pitched. Yet to millions of his subjects he was a divine being, beyond worldly criticism, safe from any comparison to a mere mortal. The introverted, ineffectual-appearing Hirohito was nothing less than a direct descendant of the Sun Goddess, Amaterasu.

Born in 1901, Hirohito had been brought up in a traditional pattern. His world was ruled by advisers, who saw to it that the young prince was indoctrinated in the mystical origins of his ancestors. Even he had trouble digesting the myth. In his teens, he clashed with Professor Shiratori, a history instructor, over the legend of his succession. Declaring that it was biologically impossible, the youthful Prince refused to accept the teacher's thesis. Shiratori was thoroughly alarmed and reported Hirohito's blasphemy to court advisers, who brought in Prince Saionji to reason with him. This aged relative was a poor choice; he did not believe the ancestral lore either. Saionji worked out a compromise. As long as Hirohito kept his suspicions to himself and did not upset the popular image of the Imperial family, no harm would be done. The masses could still worship the Emperor and find in him a strength of purpose. Hirohito agreed not to rock the ship of state. He spent less time with his history professor and more in the study of marine biology, at which, in later years, he became a world-renowned expert.

As Crown Prince, he shocked the conservatives at the court by insisting on taking a trip to Europe. Never before had a Japanese heir apparent ventured out of the country. Over strenuous objections, he traveled to London, Paris and Rome where he was thrilled by his glimpse of Western life and enjoyed the companionship of such men as Edward, Prince of Wales, who also would inherit an Empire.

Within two years after he returned to his cloistered world in the Imperial Palace, he married Nagako, a princess to whom he had been engaged for five years. In that period, he had seen her only nine times. Their betrothal had sparked warfare at the court as opposing factions jostled for the honor of supplying the bride for the next Emperor. Though Nagako was vilified by hostile elements, she persevered through the engagement period and married the nervous Prince on January 26, 1924. Slightly less than two years later, on Christmas Day, 1926, Hirohito became the 124th Emperor of Japan. His father Taisho, who had been insane during most of his reign, died, to the regret of practically no one at court. A man who spent his days in a world of unreality, who once sat gazing at legislators through a rolled-up newspaper "telescope," Taisho had been a ruler in name only.

Now his eldest son carried on the royal tradition. Like previous leaders, he chose a new name for his reign. Hirohito called it Showa, which means *Peace*.

The new Emperor settled down to ceremonial routine, which marked the main function of his office. He and Nagako raised a family and he continued with his other love, the study of the sea. A retiring man, he watched passively as Japan fell under the sway of the militarists, whose acts in his name had terrible consequences. Hirohito could possibly have spoken out, but the Emperor of the Japanese people was not supposed to get involved in worldly intrigues. While he sat behind the gray walls of his compound, his subjects set the Pacific on fire.

Three years and eight months after Pearl Harbor was attacked, the Emperor of Japan saw visible evidence around him that his Showa reign was a mockery. Sickened and depressed by the appalling casualty figures, he began to insinuate himself into discussions of peace. Already he had insisted that Prince Konoye approach Russia with a bid for peace. Now, in the twilight of his Empire, he was ready to lend his authority to his faltering statesmen. Legend and history had bestowed power on him. Hirohito intended to use it.

Premier Suzuki stood up at the Emperor's left and addressed the assemblage:

"I would like the Cabinet Secretary to read the Potsdam Declaration once more."

The Secretary, bushy-browed Hisatsune Sakomizu, quickly recited the terms laid down by the Allies, terms that every man in the room knew. Suzuki then outlined the difficulties in reaching agreement. In two previous meetings of the Big Six, opinion on the note was divided 3–3. In a cabinet session of fourteen ministers that afternoon, no harmony had been achieved. Six ministers were for peace providing only that the Emperor's status was left unchanged. Anami, Umezu and Toyoda wanted this provision plus three others: Japan must be allowed to try its own war criminals; Japan must be permitted to disarm its own men in the field; and America must not occupy the Home Islands. They insisted on the last two to insure against friction between conqueror and vanquished. The five other ministers advocated peace with varying omissions of the conditions set forth by Anami, Umezu and Toyoda.

As Suzuki continued to describe the deadlocked discussions of that day, presumably for the Emperor's benefit, General Anami sat glowering. Since he had come into the room, Anami had been building into a rage because of the presence of the guest, Hiranuma. Leaning over to Umezu, he whispered: "Hiranuma has no business being here. They're trying to trick us, so let's stand fast." Umezu stared across the table at the elderly intruder and grunted agreement.

After his prefatory remarks, Suzuki asked Togo for his opinions. The Foreign Minister rose, bowed to the Emperor, and began to speak. He admitted, "It is disgraceful to have to accept the Potsdam Declaration. Yet we must." Glancing from time to time at notes, he pointed out the folly of sitting still while Japan burned to the ground. His round spectacles glinted in the light as he fervently concluded, "We must accept the Potsdam

Declaration with the sole condition that the Emperor's status remain as it is." He sat down.

Suzuki quickly stepped into the vacuum and asked Admiral Yonai for his opinion. The sleepy-eyed Navy Minister did not bother to stand. Staring straight ahead, he said quietly, "I agree with the Foreign Minister."

Anami leaped to the attack. Pointing his finger at Yonai, he shouted: "Absolutely not! There is enough determination left in the armed forces to wage a decisive battle in the homeland. Unless all four conditions are met, there is no other choice for us. We will fight on."

General Umezu swiftly echoed that determination, and added, "I have no objection to a decision in favor of accepting the Potsdam Declaration but the four conditions must be included."

Premier Suzuki switched tactics. Ignoring Admiral Toyoda, he asked Baron Hiranuma to give his opinion. Toyoda was left with his mouth open.

Hiranuma rose to assume a role he relished. Immediately he baited Shigenori Togo: "Why did Russia declare war?"

Togo hotly retaliated, "Russia had no intention of being a mediator. It wanted to get into the war."

The devil's advocate continued to press for details. "Russia said that on July 28 the Japanese Government refused the Potsdam proposal. Is it true?"

Togo patiently replied, "No, we didn't refuse."

"Then why do they say so?"

Togo shrugged and answered, "It's all in their imagination." For himself, the Foreign Minister was speaking the truth. He had not rejected the Potsdam Declaration. Suzuki's "mokusatsu" speech had caused the damage.

After several more questions to Togo on the various conditions put forth by the two generals and Admiral Toyoda, Hiranuma addressed the war faction directly: "You said you had the means to continue the war but air raids come now every night and day. Do you have the means to defend against the atom bomb? I wonder."

General Anami did not answer. He was still annoyed by Hiranuma's presence at the meeting, and he was also plagued by a sobering thought which had been with him since morning. Osaka intelligence officials had informed him of their interrogation of the captured American fighter pilot, Lieutenant Marcus McDilda. The pilot's marvelously embroidered lie about the size and design of the atomic bomb, its inner workings and other details did not impress Anami as much as the information that Tokyo itself might be the bomb's next target. McDilda had been discussed seriously at the morning's meeting of the Big Six, for no one could deny that this obscure American pilot might be telling the truth. It was an appalling possibility.

Umezu instead responded to Hiranuma's question:

"We have a new plan and hope for good results. Regarding the atomic bomb, it might be checked if proper antiaircraft measures are taken against the planes."

Hiranuma asked Toyoda if the Navy, too, had a plan. The admiral agreed that it did, adding: "We wanted to use our planes against the American fleet but in preparing for homeland defense we couldn't. From now on, we'll attack."

Hiranuma called on Umezu to account for the Army's contingency plans against invasion. Haltingly, Umezu replied: "Our biggest problem is weapons production. That is the major deterrent to completion of beach defenses."

"What about the Tokyo area? Is the Kujikuri Beach ready?"

"No."

"What about the division that is supposed to be guarding it?"

"The equipment for that unit will not be available until September 15."

An undercurrent of dismay ran around the table. Anami and Umezu shifted uncomfortably.

Hiranuma pursued the military men on several more points, then suddenly asked in disgust, "How on earth can you believe it is still possible to continue the war under the existing conditions?"

Anami, Umezu and Toyoda sat dumb.

The baron finished his fact-finding mission with a warning to the group about the danger of a leftist revolution by the masses. He said, "I'm worried about keeping the public peace—"

Suzuki interrupted: "I am too. The people are uneasy."

Hiranuma continued: "Therefore, I think that some form of answer should be sent to the Allies. Perhaps negotiations on the conditions imposed by the Army and Navy might even be appropriate—"

Suzuki interrupted him to let Toyoda speak. The admiral recovered from the onslaught by Hiranuma and launched into an explanation of the military position, which he felt could salvage some sort of honorable terms from the Americans. His chief fear was that the Army would revolt if not catered to in the last emergency, and he wanted to do as much as possible to help General Anami keep a firm grip on his staff. The four conditions were a necessary prerequisite to that stability.

The opinions had been given. Now the moderator, Kantaro Suzuki, prepared for his own master stroke. Since early in the morning of the ninth, just after the news of the Russian entry into the war, he and the Emperor had shared a secret with Togo and Marquis Kido. At 7:30 A.M., he had gone to the palace and agreed with Hirohito that the Potsdam Declaration must be accepted that day. Suzuki had told the Emperor that he would be needed that night for the last thrust. Then he had outlined a course of action. "I will make sure that there is no final vote taken in any meeting in the morning or the afternoon sessions." Though a consensus would be ascertained, no formal ballot would be taken until the Emperor could be ushered in to break the stalemate. Hirohito was only too willing to be an active participant and the stage was set for a dramatic move.

At 2:00 A.M., over two hours after the discussion began, deep under the streets of Tokyo, Suzuki did the unprecedented. He stood up in the humid room and said: "I believe that everyone has fully expressed his opinion but I regret that we did not come to an agreement. As it is a matter of great importance, there is no way left but to rely on the decision of His Imperial Majesty." He addressed the Emperor: "Your Imperial Decision is requested as to which proposal should be adopted, the Foreign Minister's or the one with the four conditions." Suzuki had trumped the opposition, which had never expected the Emperor to speak. He had asked the 124th Emperor of the Japanese people to take the matter out of his subjects' hands and decide the best course for them.

The only visible reaction in the room was an immediate stiffening in posture and sharp attention to the man at the head of the long table.

Hirohito rose. He began to speak slowly, as though feeling for the proper words.

"I agree with the Foreign Minister's plan. I have given serious thought to the situation prevailing at home and abroad and have concluded that continuing the war can only mean destruction for the nation and a prolongation of bloodshed and cruelty in the world. Those who argue for continuing the war once assured me that new battalions and supplies would be ready at Kujikurihama by June. I realize now that this cannot be fulfilled even by September. As for those who wish for one last battle here on our own soil, let me remind them of the disparity between their previous plans and what has actually taken place. I cannot bear to see my innocent people struggle any longer. Ending the war is the only way to restore world peace and to relieve the nation from the terrible distress with which it is burdened."

Hirohito was spelling the end for the die-hards; and in personally assuming the onus of breaking the deadlock, he was giving them a face-saving way out.

His face lined with grief, the Emperor continued: "I cannot help feeling sad when I think of the people who have served me so faithfully, the soldiers and sailors who have been killed or wounded in far-off battles, the families who have lost all their worldly goods, and often their lives as well, in the air raids at home. It goes without saying that it is unbearable for me to see the brave and loyal fighting men of Japan disarmed. It is equally unbearable that others who have rendered me devoted service should now be punished as instigators of war. Nevertheless, the time has come when we must bear the unbearable."

There was absolute stillness in the tiny room. No feet moved, no sound escaped the lips of the other twelve in audience.

The Emperor paused, then concluded, "When I think of the feelings of my Imperial Grandfather, Emperor Meiji, at the time of the Triple Intervention, I cannot but swallow my tears and sanction the proposal to accept the Allied Proclamation on the basis outlined by the Foreign Minister."

Hirohito did not wait for a reaction, but rose from his chair and went to the door opened by his aide. He walked through it and was gone.

Eleven men remained with their own private thoughts, absorbing the import of his speech. The Emperor had spoken. He had supported the peace faction, recommending surrender on the condition alone that the Imperial status be preserved. No one raised his voice in either protest or agreement. There was no sound.

Finally Suzuki rose to his feet, his masterful plan accomplished. He quietly stated, "His Majesty's decision should be made the decision of this conference as well." No one disagreed. Then the Premier adjourned the group to a full cabinet meeting at three o'clock in the morning at his official residence. The meeting broke up and the participants made their way up the long flight of stairs into the night air of Tokyo.

At the top of the steps, a scuffle broke out. Silent through the whole meeting, General Yoshizumi, an aide to Umezu, lost his temper and rushed at Premier Suzuki. Trying to get his hands on the aged man, he screamed over and over, "Are you happy? Are you satisfied now?" As the bewildered Suzuki dodged his assailant, General Anami stepped between the men and wrapped his arms protectively about the old statesman. Yoshizumi was pulled away by other witnesses while Anami escorted Suzuki into the beautiful gardens in the center of Tokyo. Overhead, a brilliant moonlight brought even pine cones lying on the grounds into sharp relief. It was a perfect summer's night.

From the cloistered garden of the Imperial Palace the eleven men went to join other cabinet members assembled at Suzuki's house, to consider an appropriate answer to the American offer of peace. They began another argument immediately. This time it was over the phrasing of the sentence dealing with the preservation of the Emperor's status. Not one of the men disputed the necessity of that stipulation. The only problem now was in correctly stating it to the Allies.

Hiranuma, the defender of the royal function for most of his life, was adamant that his sentence be the one chosen. It was put in by Toshikazu Kase, a Foreign Office secretary, who admitted later that he had severe doubts about the phrase "with the understanding that the said declaration does not comprise any demand which prejudices the prerogatives of His Majesty as a Sovereign Ruler." But he included the phrase, and the full cabinet approved it to go out over the airwaves just that way.

The message ended with the remark, "The Japanese Government hopes sincerely that this understanding is warranted, and desires keenly that an explicit indication to that effect will be speedily forthcoming."

At four o'clock, the cabinet members walked out to their cars and were driven through the pre-dawn quiet of the city streets while civilians slept on in their beds.

Chief Secretary Sakomizu went to bed in an armchair downstairs in Suzuki's home. The old admiral went upstairs satisfied with the day's work, but utterly exhausted by his efforts. General Anami returned home heartsick. Though he knew that the Emperor was right, nevertheless he felt that the Army had been disgraced and he worried that the Emperor's position was in great danger.

Marquis Kido, the Emperor's closest adviser, was in bed by four o'clock, after talking with his Ruler about the meeting in the shelter. When Hirohito had told him what happened there, Kido listened, "filled with emotions and trepidation." His fears were justified shortly.

At 7:33 A.M., wireless operators in the Foreign Ministry Building in downtown Tokyo began clicking off the momentous news in code to Switzerland and Sweden, for transmittal to the appropriate parties in Allied capitals. Reaction to the news would come swiftly and it would indicate trouble ahead, both at home and abroad.

EIGHT

Reaction in Washington

Later in the day Tokyo broadcast the news of the pending acceptance directly to the United States. Since Eastern War Time was thirteen hours behind Far Eastern Time, it was during the early hours of August 10 when the Japanese radio report was received. Consequently, the first intimation of a break came to officials as they lay in bed. James Forrestal, Secretary of the Navy, was awakened by an aide who informed him of the dramatic development. He dressed hurriedly and rushed to his office on Constitution Avenue. There his secretary told him that President Truman wanted him at the White House at 9:00 A.M. for discussions. The Navy Secretary hurried to the meeting.

Harry Truman greeted Forrestal warmly and showed him to a seat. A group of officials and aides joined him around the table as the President prepared to open the discussion. Three of them, together with Forrestal, formed an inner circle of advisors, a "war" council most directly concerned with operations on the diplomatic and military levels. All but one were holdovers from the preceding administration.

Forrestal himself had come to Washington in 1940 as Undersecretary of the Navy. He had left the presidency of a New York brokerage firm, Dillon, Reed, to become part of Roosevelt's new look in the military sphere. When Navy Secretary Frank Knox died in 1944, Forrestal had accepted the top job in the department.

Forrestal's rugged face was his trademark. His nose was spread and battered from catching too many punches in college boxing matches at Princeton. An intense man, he drove himself and others around him unmercifully. He worked well with Truman, though the President's decision-making processes annoyed him. Recently he had crossed swords with Truman over a minor point. Slighted at not being invited to the Potsdam Conference, Forrestal had simply turned up unannounced at the Big Three sessions, thereby resolving the issue to his own satisfaction and Truman's annoyance.

The pressures of his office always weighed heavily on him, so much so that in later years, as the first Secretary of Defense, Forrestal broke down under constant criticism by the press and lobbyists, and, in 1949, jumped to his death from a hospital window. But on August 10, 1945, he was ready to savor the victory and share in the planning for peace.

Admiral William D. Leahy, a veteran of fifty-two years of naval service, functioned as the President's personal chief of staff. In his late seventies, the crusty old salt, nicknamed "Sandpaper," tended toward blunt assertions and a cynical outlook. He was one of the few who had categorized the atomic project as "a silly brainstorm" that would never work. He also deplored its use as a weapon of war.

Leahy's career mirrored the emergence of the United States Navy to a preeminent position in the world. At one time he served on the frigate *Constellation*. Later he served during the Boxer Rebellion and fought in World War I. In 1945, he helped guide the vast armada that ruled the oceans of the earth. A widower, the admiral was left with only two loves, tobacco and hard work. He smoked sixty cigarettes a day while exerting every ounce of energy toward helping the Chief Executive over the rough spots of the Presidency.

Henry Stimson, Secretary of War, was the last of the old guard. He had served the Government for many years. As Secretary of State under Herbert Hoover in 1931, he watched the growing challenge to world peace in Manchuria. His warnings to the League of Nations went virtually unheeded as European nations grappled with their own problems at home.

Stimson bridged the years between the old America of the nineteenth century and the awesome international giant of the mid-twentieth century. A patrician by birth, he grew up surrounded by the trappings of inherited wealth, then amassed another fortune as a Wall Street lawyer. He lived well. Fox hunting and deck tennis were his hobbies. He was a highly moral gentleman, an aristocrat dedicated to serving his nation. Though aloof and unbending, he tried nobly to project warmth to his aides and others. This mild, courtly man found himself responsible for a gigantic war machine which destroyed nations. It was he who decided that since "war is death," the atomic bomb was a legitimate weapon to use on human beings.

The only Truman appointee in the room was the Secretary of State, James F. Byrnes, from South Carolina. But for an ironic twist of fate, he might have been sitting in Truman's chair that day. Positive that he would be Roosevelt's running mate in 1944, Byrnes was stunned when Harry Truman was nominated at the convention. When Roosevelt died, Truman called Byrnes out of retirement to head the State Department. The nattily dressed Secretary worked well with the new President and had, in fact, just returned with him from Potsdam where they had faced the intransigent Russians for the first time.

United in their suspicions as to Soviet intentions, the two statesmen had returned to Washington on the seventh of August to face the swift onset of peace in the Far East. Three days later, in the cabinet room, they were confronted with a new dilemma. It was found in the wording of the Japanese message, specifically in the phrase injected by Baron Kiichiro Hiranuma:

The Japanese Government is ready to accept the terms enumerated in the joint declaration which was issued at Potsdam on July 26, 1945, by the heads of the Governments of the United States, Great Britain and China, and later subscribed to by the Soviet Government with an understanding that the said declaration does not comprise any demand which prejudices the prerogatives of His Majesty as a sovereign ruler.

The Japanese had brought into the open the problem of the Emperor's future. Truman asked Stimson what he would do about the "conditional acceptance" aspect of the message. The Secretary reiterated his plea for retention of the Emperor. "Even if the question hadn't been raised by the Japanese," he said, "we would have to continue the Emperor ourselves under our command and supervision in order to get into surrender the many scattered armies of the Japanese. . . . Something like this use of the Emperor must be made in order to save us from a score of bloody Iwo Jimas and Okinawas all over China and the New Netherlands." Admiral Leahy supported this view. Forrestal also concurred. At this time he was more concerned about Russia's designs in the Far East. If keeping the Emperor would end the war quickly, he was in favor of it.

The council adjourned swiftly to await official notice from Japan. Byrnes and Stimson went to an anteroom to discuss the wording of a reply. There the Secretary of War mentioned an urgent request from General Marshall, who wanted Allied prisoners released as soon as possible and moved to some accessible area of Japan from which they could be flown out for medical treatment.

Stimson left the White House before 10:00 A.M. to go back to the War Department. Outside the building, large crowds had formed on Pennsylvania Avenue as rumors of peace swept through the streets. Washington—the entire United States—was ready to explode at the first official declaration of an end to the war.

James Byrnes returned to the White House shortly after noon with the official message from the Swiss Embassy. President Truman promptly called a full cabinet meeting for two o'clock. Here he outlined the text of the answer formulated by Byrnes and others and discussed methods of notifying the Allies of its contents in order to obtain their approval prior to dispatch of the reply by telegram to Japan.

Only the Russians were expected to cause trouble. Truman did not want them interfering in the government of the fallen nation. Wary after the joint rule instituted in Berlin and Vienna, the President wanted no part of Soviet "cooperation" in Japan. He specifically wanted MacArthur as the sole commander responsible to Allied controls.

By four o'clock in the afternoon notes had been sent to London, Chungking and Moscow. Work on the final draft of the answer to Japan continued into the night.

Britain and China agreed promptly to the terms. Predictably, Russia balked. When Ambassador Averell Harriman presented Truman's message to Molotov in Moscow, the Russian stalled, then later recalled Harriman and told him that the Soviets would agree to the settlement with the condition that they participate in the Allied High Command. Harriman had been briefed by Truman at Potsdam on just such an eventuality, and despite Molotov's insistence, he refused to transmit such a proposal to Washington. Minutes after he got back to his office at the American Embassy, he received a call from the Kremlin and was told there had been a misunderstanding: the Russians merely wished to be consulted on the choice of a Supreme Commander; they had not meant to imply that agreement on the choice was required. The USSR's bluff had been called.

By the end of the hectic day of August 10, the last draft of the Byrnes statement replying to the Japanese was being readied for transmission.

In China, worried American officers worked over a secret plan. In July, General George Marshall had sent a cablegram from

Washington expressing concern about Allied prisoners behind Japanese lines. To General Albert Wedemeyer and his aides in Chungking, Marshall entrusted the job of saving the prisoners in case of a sudden surrender.

This assignment was staggering. The prison camps were thousands of miles to the north and northeast. Chinese divisions could not possibly reach them. Tanks could not batter their way through the lines to effect lightning rescues. Some other way had to be found.

At dinner one night, Wedemeyer solicited opinions from staff members. Several ideas were broached, then rejected. Colonel Arthur Dobson, from Lincoln, Nebraska, finally suggested the possibility of sending in teams of parachutists who would confront the Japanese and demand access to the captives. He reasoned that the element of surprise might stun the enemy into inaction and prevent bloodshed.

Dobson's idea was well received. At Kunming, the OSS had a base for clandestine activities. From it, some form of task force could be scraped together. Wedemeyer's assistant, General George Olmstead, was given command of the special project. As the atomic bombs fell on Japan, he and his staff rushed to implement the "mercy missions."

The China theater was an extraordinarily difficult arena of war. It had been that way since before Pearl Harbor, when the Flying Tigers under General Claire Chennault helped the Nationalist armies defy the Japanese invader. It had continued that way during the dark days of 1942 and 1943 when the Burma Road, lifeline to China from India, had been sealed off.

Conditions had improved after the Japanese were driven out of North Burma in 1944, and road traffic into China was resumed. Increased air transport over the Himalayas helped even more. Still, the Chinese command posed a continual problem to high officials in Washington.

The country was beset by factional strife. Though united against a common foe, the Japanese, both the Nationalists, under

Chiang Kai-shek, and the Communists, led by Mao Tse-Tung, fought each other repeatedly. The Chiang government held the reins of power but the Reds lurked in the background. From their headquarters in the caves of Yenan in northwest China, Mao's lieutenants broadcast about the excesses of the Nationalists and promised a "people's government" after the Japanese had been thrown off the mainland. The charges hurt Chiang because they were based on fact.

In a nation that had not had a strong central government for centuries, the ruling class was riddled with corruption and greed. A bribe could win an official's favor. A bribe could wean a general away from his loyalty to Chiang. The Japanese themselves employed such tactics to disrupt, confuse and subvert their foes. The Communists did the same.

When General Vinegar Joe Stilwell went to Chungking in 1944 to help Chiang organize the Chinese armies, he was disgusted with the situation. Contemptuous of the Chinese leader, whom he referred to as "The Peanut," Stilwell told Washington that Chiang intended "to go on milking the United States for money and munitions." Because he thought that the Communists would eventually win the allegiance of the peasants, he felt that America was supporting the wrong side. Stilwell did not last very long in China. He was recalled from what he termed "as merry a nest of gangsters" as one could find.

General Albert Wedemeyer came from Washington to heal the rupture. He managed to soothe Chiang and induce him to cooperate more fully in training a total of thirty-nine Chinese divisions for combat against the Japanese. By the summer of 1945, Wedemeyer had reversed a prevailing defeatist sentiment among Chinese generals and had embarked on the first phase of Operation Carbonado, a drive to the sea near Canton.

The Japanese now ruled a shrinking continental empire. Though capable of offering stern resistance to their enemies, they could not control the land mass of China. One and a half million troops in the field failed to stop constant harassment by guerrillas,

Nationalist and Communist, who blew up bridges, seized towns, and terrorized individual units on patrol. The Japanese had won the big cities but not the countryside. Battle lines were fluid and porous, stretching over thousands of miles.

In this incredibly complex situation, American advisers, numbering nearly seventy thousand, strove to wage effective warfare. The latest message from the War Department concerning prisoners of war was therefore particularly unsettling. It seemed to ask the impossible.

Elsewhere, it was necessary to continue the business of war. General Leslie Groves called on General Marshall to discuss the next shipment of nuclear material to the battle zone. Finding him involved in conferences, Groves returned to his office and arbitrarily ordered a hold on delivery of plutonium and other vital bomb parts until further notice. Later in the day Marshall agreed with Groves' action. A third bomb could be prepared for drop at any time if the Japanese did not surrender.

In Washington, a special alert had gone out from the Navy Department to all clerical personnel in the area. Full reports of a naval disaster in the western Pacific had just reached headquarters. On the moonlit night of July 30, tragedy had overtaken the cruiser *Indianapolis*. As it steamed toward Leyte after delivering part of the core of the Hiroshima bomb to scientists at Tinian, it moved past the periscope of the I-58, a large Japanese submarine homebound for the Inland Sea. Its captain, Hashimoto, quickly fired torpedoes into the side of the cruiser, which sank in moments. Hundreds of Americans spilled into the darkness and began floating on the tranquil ocean. The I-58 moved out of the area and proceeded toward Japan. On the surface of the Pacific, survivors waited for dawn and rescue.

Rescue did not come. Owing to an incredible lapse, authorities at Leyte did not take action when the *Indianapolis* failed to make an appearance. For days the sun beat mercilessly on the helpless sailors bobbing on the sea. They weakened gradually and lost hope as the countless hours went by without a friendly ship coming over the horizon. Men gave up. Some swam away toward imagined oases. Others simply fell asleep and sank from sight.

On the fourth day, a plane wandered over the pitiful remnants of the *Indianapolis* crew. By the time ships lifted survivors out of the water, over eight hundred officers and men had died. At least half could have been saved if prompt action had been taken.

On the tenth of August, mounting casualty lists from the *Indianapolis* poured into Washington. Telegrams were composed and dispatched across the nation as the Navy fought to notify the next of kin before peace was declared.

But plenty of time remained. On the other side of the international dateline, Tokyo seethed with unrest. The forces of opposition to surrender had rallied swiftly. Sakomizu, the Cabinet Secretary, was the first to feel the wrath of the angered military. Asleep in an armchair at Premier Suzuki's residence, he was rudely awakened at seven o'clock by four young officers from the War Ministry, who had just heard about the message sent to Switzerland. They cornered the Secretary and demanded to know why the council had done such a thing. Sakomizu was outraged but knew that he must proceed cautiously. He decided that his best defense was a good offense, and shouted at them to get out. They refused. Then he walked into an adjoining room and sat down. The officers followed, but before they could continue the verbal abuse, Sakomizu ordered them to take off their ceremonial swords and leave them outside the house. At this point, the soldiers became flustered and walked out.

War Minister Anami slept for several hours after the meeting with the Emperor. He was exhausted by the strain of the past few days. At fifty-seven, Anami was in excellent health but his eyes were baggy from lack of rest and his body was leaden with fatigue. Yet at nine o'clock, he was in his office in the Ichigaya Heights War Ministry building, where the senior officers were assembled for a meeting.

Anami knew the temper of his men and spoke prudently: "I do not know what excuse to make to you, but since it is the Emperor's decision, it cannot be helped." There was no sound from the assembled officers. Anami continued: "The important thing is that the Army shall act in an organized manner. Individual feelings must be disregarded. Those among you who are dissatisfied and wish to stave it off will have to do it over Anami's body." Some officers broke out into protest at the remark. Anami waved them quiet. "This decision, however, was made on the condition that the upholding of our national polity [way of life] be guaranteed. Consequently, it does not mean that the war has ended. The Army must be prepared for either war or peace." Grumbling erupted from the close-packed body of men. Anami dismissed them, and they turned back to their own sections to argue the situation.

Rebellion became a common topic in the corridors of the War Ministry. Anami had his hand on the pulse of the officer corps and realized that he was dealing with volatile men, who, if provoked, could overthrow the best-laid plans of the Government. The atomic bomb did not matter to these zealots, who still believed surrender a worse fate than death.

One of the plotters in the War Ministry was Colonel Masao Inaba. Sincerely convinced that it was important to maintain the spirits of the soldiers until such time as a surrender was actually consummated, Inaba composed a speech for broadcast to the troops overseas. His message urged continued vigilance and sustained opposition to the enemy.

Though he got approval for it from various senior officers, he could not reach General Anami, then engaged in discussions with cabinet officials. While Inaba waited for Anami to initial the document, two other officers came to his office and demanded that it be released in time for the evening radio news program. They found a copy of the speech in a wastebasket and began to rework it into still harsher terms. Inaba finally gave in to their urging and permitted them to take the strong declaration without Anami's approval.

The War Minister was immediately placed in a most embarrassing position, for at this time he himself was helping to draft a statement of a different kind, intended for the civilian population. Hiroshi Shimomura, Chief of the Cabinet Information Board, had wanted to advise the masses that something was in the wind. Without actually telling them that surrender was being discussed, he wished to warn them of crucial developments to be announced soon. Anami was in agreement with this plan and helped to write the declaration.

Later, when Shimomura learned of the existence of the dangerous Army proclamation, he called Anami to ask just what he was trying to accomplish by attempting to broadcast an inflammatory message to the armed forces. When the War Minister was at a loss to explain, Shimomura immediately sensed that the general had been duped by his own men. Realizing that Anami might be killed if his subordinates were thwarted, he allowed the broadcast to be carried to the outermost areas of the Empire.

Throughout the Pacific, soldiers of the Japanese Imperial Army heard their leader exhort them to "crush the enemy." In Japan itself, civilians were exposed both to that and to Shimomura's message about ominous developments in the near future. The contradictory statements only served to confuse the issue for the populace.

The civilian population of Japan was dying in ever-increasing numbers. Curtis Lemay had sent hundreds of B-29's up the long path from far to the south to lend authenticity to the Allied message. High above darkened cities bomb bay doors opened and thousands of incendiaries cascaded down onto wooden homes and steel factories. Hundreds died in bed, in makeshift shelters all over Japan.

Though unaware of events unfolding in the Imperial Palace, the Japanese civilians had already had more than enough. In five short months the Twenty-first Bomber Command had changed day-to-day living in Japan to a bitter struggle for survival. In the same five months, the B-29's had effectively paralyzed sixty-six metropolitan centers in the Home Islands. Tokyo, Osaka, Kobe—the names included the vital centers of Japanese war industry.

Air strikes had repeatedly concentrated on workers' houses, where much of the decentralized war production system was based. Eight million people were homeless. Many workers had simply left their jobs and taken their families into the country to escape the bombers. Others crowded in with relatives or friends. Five or six families frequently shared three rooms. Hunger was a constant torture. The rice ration had been cut to almost a quarter of its prewar subsistence level, and fish, a staple, had become a luxury because boats could not venture far enough or often enough into the enemy-dominated waters. Clothing materials were almost unavailable and the average citizen patched and repatched what remained of his wardrobe.

Social deterioration kept pace with economic decay. The foundations of the traditionally strong family unit were eroded as parents abandoned children to the public care. Because use of the cherished public baths was sharply curtailed, owing to air raids and fuel rationing, for the first time in their lives the normally fastidious Japanese stank.

Even the rites for burial were affected. Almost no lumber was available for coffins used to transport the dead to crematoriums.

Overriding all these concerns was fear. The B-29's and the planes from the carriers dominated the people's every movement. The civilian in Japan was on the edge of desperation.

Lieutenant Marcus McDilda had become a Very Important Person to the Japanese Secret Police. After nearly twenty-four hours of questioning, he had been taken to a plane and flown with another American prisoner to Tokyo. On the morning of August 10, McDilda was ushered into a room at Kempei Tai headquarters. Seated at a desk was a Japanese civilian, wearing a pin-stripe shirt and sipping tea. He was very cordial to the American pilot and served some tea to him. "I am a graduate of CCNY College," he told McDilda, "and most interested in your story about the atomic bomb." McDilda repeated his lie.

After several minutes, the Japanese official knew that Marcus McDilda had committed a hoax, that he knew nothing at all about nuclear fission. When McDilda said that he had been trying to tell that to his interrogators in Osaka, the Japanese laughed. After more friendly conversation, McDilda was taken to a cell and given some food. The beatings ceased.

NINE

August 11—
The Conspiracy Begins

While statesmen in Tokyo waited impatiently for the Allied answer, a small group of Army officers on Ichigaya Hill, the nerve center of the Army, were plotting a revolution. For more than two weeks, ever since the Potsdam declaration had been issued, these men had been preparing for the day when they might have to act against the Government. Loose plans were formulated. Tactics were analyzed. Slowly, the officers evolved a design for action.

The inflammatory Army proclamation of August 10 had been only one of their many maneuvers. Now, on August 11, fifteen officers met in an air-raid shelter under the War Ministry Building to discuss implementing their strategy.

Colonel Masahiko Takeshita presided. As a brother-in-law of General Anami, he was in a singularly favorable position. He had learned the decisions of the Big Six and knew approximately how much time was left to alter the course of events.

The emotional, intense colonel found willing accomplices in men serving in staff positions at the Ministry. Some were sober, intelligent professional officers such as Colonel Masao Inaba and Colonel Masataka Ida; others were volatile, impressionable young men like Majors Jiro Shiizaki and Kenji Hatanaka. The pale, soft-featured Hatanaka, a "pet" of General Anami, was a man who could not imagine Japan in defeat. He was growing increasingly reckless as the men at Ichigaya went over the situation carefully.

While cigarette smoke filled the air, the conspirators sketched out a rough strategy. Their ultimate aim was to reject the peace terms. To attain that goal, they would have to seize the palace and dispose of the appeasers, Suzuki, Togo and Kido. As an afterthought, they added Baron Hiranuma to the list of victims.

They realized they needed support from four generals. Anami was the key man. Takeshita was sure of his brother-in-law: "I can guarantee that the general will join with us."

General Umezu would naturally follow along if Anami agreed. Like dominoes, General Seiichi Tanaka, commander of the Eastern District Army, and General Takeshi Mori, of the Imperial Guards at the palace, would fall into line when they realized the revolt had the blessing of the highest officers in Tokyo.

Takeshita brought up the question of timing. Aware that the Allied answer was expected within hours, the rebels agreed that they must move no later than midnight on the thirteenth.

Major Kenji Hatanaka was detailed to contact General Mori and his regimental commanders to ascertain their feelings. If, despite their hopes, Mori proved recalcitrant, the men under the general were to be weaned away from their loyalty to him.

The approach to Anami would be a joint effort. Led by Takeshita, the group would confront him within twenty-four hours and solicit a quick answer.

As the last cigarette was stubbed out, optimism ran high in the conference room. Hatanaka was visibly excited. The others, though more restrained, spoke enthusiastically of the coming adventure. They separated outside the room and disappeared into the maze of corridors.

Once again in a time of crisis, the young officers of the Japanese Army had decided to take matters into their own hands. When they did so, blood always flowed in the streets and peaceful men died brutally.

The last great orgy of killing had taken place little more than nine years before, on February 26, 1936. It had been brought about by increased unrest in the Army over the direction of Japan's future and was triggered by an order posting the Tokyo-based First Guards Division to Manchuria. The officers of the unit felt that opposing factions within the Army had taken this means to eliminate the division from any influence on events in Japan itself. A *coup d'état* was immediately decided upon.

Over fifteen hundred men went out into the streets of the capital that night to hunt down statesmen and generals known to be in opposition to Army plans. Finance Minister Takahashi was shot to death. General Jotaro Watanabe's throat was cut as he lay in bed. Count Makino was assaulted, but survived. Baron Suzuki was shot in his bedroom and only saved by his wife's presence of mind. As an army officer bent over his crumpled body to slash his throat, she rushed forward and said, "Please let me do it if it must be done." The unnerved officer left without delivering the *coup de grâce*. Viscount Makoto Saito was also assaulted in his bedroom, but his wife's efforts could not save him. He was found cradled in her arms on the floor, with a total of forty-seven bullets in his dead body.

Several of the victims of the coup had dined that evening at the American Embassy as guests of Ambassador Joseph Grew. Suzuki had been among them, as had Saito. The occasion had been pleasant and relaxed. It had included the showing of a Hollywood movie, *Naughty Marietta*, and a generous amount of wine and whiskey.

Another of Grew's guests, the then Premier of Japan, Keisuke Okada, was also marked for death by the Army rebels. Like the others, he had been driven home through the beginnings of a snowfall late that night and had gone to bed. Because he had drunk too much, Okada slept like a drugged man. When the soldiers came for him in the predawn, he was still drowsy and unable to comprehend the danger. The officers had surrounded the house, broken in, and were flooding into the various rooms.

Okada's brother-in-law, Matsuo, and two bodyguards managed to get the Premier up from his bed and lead him toward an emergency exit at the back of the house. Seeing men milling about in the rear yard, one of the bodyguards pushed Okada and Matsuo into the bathroom, where they cowered behind a screen. In the corridor outside, several guns were fired simultaneously and one of the guards died instantly. The other guard grappled with the advancing soldiers but fell to the floor mortally wounded by sword cuts.

As Okada and Matsuo waited for their own deaths, the bathroom door opened. A soldier stepped in and gazed quickly around. Then the trapped men heard the door close and footsteps retreat down the corridor.

Matsuo wasted no more time. Warning Okada to be quiet, he calmly walked out of the refuge to his own doom.

As Okada paced the floor, he heard the weak voice of the surviving bodyguard lying in the hall outside: "Please stay where you are." The man repeated it twice more, then died.

Matsuo had left Okada for only one reason. He bore a superficial resemblance to his brother-in-law, and he hoped that the soldiers would mistake him for the Prime Minister and deal with him alone. He would gamble on trading his life for Okada's freedom. Within minutes the soldiers caught Matsuo as he scampered through the rooms of the house. An officer ordered his men to fire, but at first they did not. When he repeated the instructions, twenty bullets ripped into Matsuo's body.

The rebels carried his lifeless form into a bedroom and compared his face with a picture hanging on the wall. One officer said, "Yes, that's Okada, all right." Within a few minutes, the band of insurrectionists departed, leaving behind three dead men and one live Prime Minister, who now scurried into a maid's room and squatted down in a closet. For the next forty-eight hours, while the Army rebellion rocked Tokyo, Okada hid in the darkness. He escaped from his refuge by mingling with mourners following Matsuo's corpse as it was taken from the residence. With them, he calmly walked past rebel soldiers still patrolling the streets. He survived to attend his own funeral, which was staged in the belief that Matsuo's body was truly that of the Prime Minister.

Though the rebellion of February 1936 ultimately failed to bring down the Government, it was symptomatic of increasing Army interference in national affairs. Year by year the military assumed more control of policy-making apparatus. Month by month the civilian government danced to the Army's tune. Ahead lay the road to Pearl Harbor.

But even in the face of certain defeat in the summer of 1945, Army confidence remained high. Defeat was not real to the men still alive and healthy at the War Ministry in Tokyo. Takeshita, Hatanaka, Shiizaki, the names were different but the breed was the same as in the thirties. In both decades Army schemes were hatched in the name of the Emperor. In each case the victims were chosen from the same class: statesmen who blocked the Army plans. By 1945 nothing had changed the Army mentality despite the fact that it had led Japan to destruction. The night of the assassin was about to be repeated.

In the midst of the confused drift to violence, a man named Makoto Tsukamoto appeared at the War Ministry in Tokyo. He was a colonel in the Kempei Tai, the Japanese secret police, and had recently been transferred from Formosa. He had spent years before that as an undercover agent in China where he had witnessed the depredations carried out on both sides of the fighting lines during the Sino-Japanese conflict. Though he had lived on the edge of death, he was an intellectual, a sophisticated soldier who abhorred the brutality many of his fellow officers practiced. In the frenzy of total war, he maintained his own code of conduct and upheld his reputation as an honorable man.

On the twenty-seventh of July, Tsukamoto had received orders in Formosa to leave for Tokyo at once. He was mystified. There was no apparent reason for his transfer.

He left that same day by way of Shanghai. Because of faulty airplane maintenance and the increased bombings, his arrival in Tokyo was delayed until the sixth of August. Tsukamoto was stunned at the wreckage in the capital. When he had last been there in January, before General Lemay had sent the fire bombs down from five thousand feet, Tokyo had hardly been touched by the B-29's. Now a wasteland lay before him. He hurried from the plane to the headquarters of the secret police and his new assignment.

At headquarters his arrival was a total surprise. No one had ordered his return, no one expected him, no assignment awaited him. Both Tsukamoto and his commanding officer were baffled, and neither could discover any clue to the origin of the mysterious summons to Tokyo.

Later the Kempei colonel went to the office of General Okido, commandant of the secret police, and reported the strange circumstances. Okido too was confused by the peculiar situation, but offered him a temporary assignment. He had been talking with General Anami, who was concerned about the unrest in the officer corps. Okido explained: "I have been instructed by the general to look into the talk of a coup. He wants me to watch over these people and report on their plans." Tsukamoto accepted the job of surveillance and decided to go to the War Ministry where he had many friends among the staff.

On August 11, Colonel Tsukamoto drove up the winding road to the massive cement building at the top of Ichigaya. As he entered the office area, Colonel Masataka Ida saw him and rushed up. "Tsukamoto, where have you been? We've been waiting for you."

The pieces fell quickly into place. It was Colonel Ida who had sent for him. The two had been friends for years, and since 1944 Tsukamoto had felt he owed the officer his life. At that time, when he was assigned to the jungles of Burma, a special order from Ida had brought him out before the Allies overran the Japanese defenses. Now his old friend needed him. As a participant in the officers' conspiracy at Ichigaya, he wanted Tsukamoto to help in the coup. Because of his prominence in the secret police, the colonel would be an invaluable ally when trouble began.

Tsukamoto asked the obvious question: "What is this talk of a coup?"

Ida explained the situation at the Ministry in detail. The men were unhappy with the talk of surrender and might do something about it. "Suzuki is a Badoglio (traitor). He and others have surrounded the Emperor and have talked him into surrendering. We intend to take him away from them. Will you join us?"

Unaware of the intimate details of the cabinet negotiations with America, Tsukamoto cautiously answered: "I'll cooperate on two conditions. First, if the Emperor's decision goes against us, then it's all over. Second, the entire Army must rebel, not just a group here and there."

Ida was incredulous. "You mean you won't come with us in any case?" He had thought that Tsukamoto would wholeheartedly endorse the plan.

Tsukamoto laughed. "I'll talk to you later." He walked away from his good friend, who was both annoyed and puzzled at the tenor of the conversation.

Having thus quickly uncovered the focal point of the pending coup, the Kempei colonel went directly to Okido's headquarters and reported. Tsukamoto was ordered to keep closer watch on the situation at the War Ministry and to pay special attention to Colonel Ida's movements in the days ahead.

On August 11, in Fukuoka, one hundred miles north of the burning remains of Nagasaki, some Japanese army officers sat in their headquarters and discussed murder. Just recently, news of the atomic bombings had inflamed opinion against the Americans. In Fukuoka, it occasioned a day of violence. There, the Japanese had under their control a group of captured American B-29 crewmen who had been shot down on raids mounted from the Marianas during the past three months. The jailers had already executed eight fliers in formal rites carried out on the twentieth of June. Now they were preparing to kill again.

At 8:30 A.M., a truck pulled up to the rear of Western Army District Headquarters. Thirty-two men got into the back and sat down. Eight of them were Americans. The rest were Japanese soldiers. The truck went out through the rear gate and down the road to a place called Aburayama, several miles south of Fukuoka City. In a field surrounded by dense undergrowth, the prisoners were led down from the back of the vehicle and arranged in a loose line. They were stripped to shorts or pants and forced to watch as Japanese soldiers began to dig several large holes in the ground. The Americans said nothing to each other.

Shortly after 10:00 A.M., a first lieutenant from a Japanese unit training for guerrilla warfare stepped forward and brandished a gleaming silver sword. As one of the Americans was prodded forward and forced to a kneeling position, the Japanese officer wet his finger and ran it across the sharp edge of his weapon. Then he looked down at the bowed head of the prisoner and gauged the distance. Suddenly his sword flashed in the sun and crashed against the bared neck. It cut nearly all the way through to the Adam's apple.

The line of captives silently watched their comrade die. Some turned away. Others saw the body roll sideways onto the grass.

A second flier was pushed forward to be killed. A third, a fourth was decapitated. The fifth one was butchered by an executioner who required two strokes to sever the head.

The Japanese officers introduced a new torture on the sixth prisoner. He was brought in front of a group of spectators and held with his arms behind his back. A Japanese ran toward the American and smashed him in the stomach with the side of his hand. The flier slumped forward but was pulled upright again to receive another karate blow. Three, four times, the powerful chops to the body were repeated. When the victim did not die, his head was cut off.

The seventh prisoner suffered the same cruelty from men practicing the art of killing with their bare hands. When he too survived the vicious karate, one of the officers, angered by his own failure, rushed up and kicked him in the testicles. The prisoner fell to the ground, his face contorted by nausea and pain. He pleaded, "Wait, wait," but his tormentors had no pity. He was pulled into a kneeling position while the captors debated another manner of execution. They settled on *kesajiri*. Another sword glinted in the sun over the bowed form and cut down through his left shoulder and into the lungs. The American died in a froth of blood.

The last prisoner had seen seven men hacked to death before his eyes. His last moments were a blurred image of blood, steel slashing through skin and bone, cries of pain from his friends and shouts of glee from his enemies. Now he knew it was his turn. He was pushed into the center of the maddened group of soldiers, who made him sit down on the ground. His hands were tied behind him. Ten feet away, another officer from a guerrilla unit raised a bow and placed an arrow on it. The American watched as the Japanese pulled it back, sighted on him, and let go. The arrow came at his head and missed. Three times the officer shot at the American, and the third arrow hit him just over the left eye. Blood spurted out and down his face.

Tired of the sport, his captors prodded him into the familiar kneeling position and chopped his head from his body. On the field of Aburayama, eight torsos stained the meadow grass.

In China on August 11, control of the prisoner rescue operation was handed over from General Olmstead in Chungking to Colonel Richard Heppner in Kunming. Heppner would handle the next phase. As director of all undercover activities in China for the OSS, the colonel controlled networks of spies and saboteurs working throughout the mainland. From these he could draw personnel to mount the ambitious scheme.

As he labored over the details of the mission, a telegram came in from the advance base at Hsian, far to the north, at the edge of the vast Gobi Desert. Major Gus Krause, commanding officer of that vital espionage center, was advising Heppner that he was ready for any change in the war situation:

WE HAVE AVAILABLE HERE FULLY TRAINED AND EQUIPPED OBOE SUGAR SUGAR [OSS] PERSONNEL . . . TO DROP OR PLACE IN STRATEGIC AREAS. PLEASE ADVISE YOUR DISPOSITION REGARDING THIS PERSONNEL.

A later telegram from Krause expanded on the readiness of the Hsian garrison:

KELLIS AND TEAM ARE TO BE DROPPED ONE ZERO ZERO MILES SOUTHEAST OF PEIPING. BY THE ABOVE MEANS WE SHALL HAVE OBOE SUGAR SUGAR PERSONNEL SO LOCATED AS TO MOVE INTO EITHER PEIPING OR TIENTSIN UPON YOUR DIRECTION.

Gus Krause, aware of the imminence of capitulation by the Japanese, was moving to take advantage of the few hours or days left. In Kunming, Colonel Heppner began to organize his own forces for the mercy missions into enemy territory.

In Tokyo during that afternoon, Admiral Soemu Toyoda sent out an order to all fleet commanders:

FURTHER POSITIVE OFFENSIVE OPERATIONS AGAINST THE UNITED STATES, GREAT BRITAIN, THE SOVIET UNION AND CHINA WILL BE SUSPENDED PENDING FURTHER ORDERS.

That message was picked up by American intelligence and flashed to Washington. Undersecretary of War Robert Lovett called Secretary Stimson right away to inform him of the Japanese action. Stimson, suffering from a recurrent illness, left later that day for a rest in the mountains. For him the issue was resolved. For the leaders in Tokyo, the issue was in serious doubt.

TEN

August 12—Day of Crisis

Just before 1:00 A.M. on the twelfth, the answer from America arrived by shortwave radio from San Francisco. It had been eagerly awaited by both peace and war factions in Tokyo. At the Foreign Office, men worked furiously at translating the Byrnes message, while in another building on top of Ichigaya Hill, Army officers who listened to the English broadcast raged helplessly at their inability to decipher it. Since the Imperial Army had very few men capable of speaking the enemy's language, it was forced to proceed very slowly in translating the text into Japanese. The diplomats at the Foreign Office had much less trouble.

Premier Suzuki's secretary, Sakomizu, read the first rough draft handed to him. The message made these points:

> . . . from the moment of surrender the authority of the Emperor and the Japanese Government to rule the state shall be subject to the Supreme Commander of the Allied Powers who will take such steps as he deems proper to effectuate the surrender terms.
>
> The Emperor will be required to authorize and ensure the signature by the Government of Japan and the Japanese Imperial General Headquarters of the surrender

terms necessary to carry out the provisions of the Potsdam Declaration. . . .

The ultimate form of government of Japan shall, in accordance with the Potsdam Declaration, be established by the freely expressed will of the Japanese people. The armed forces of the Allied Powers will remain in Japan until the purposes set forth in the Potsdam Declaration are achieved.

Sakomizu was crushed by the apparent severity of the language. He quickly called his friend, Shunichi Matsumoto, Foreign Minister Togo's aide, and the two men sat down in the pre-dawn darkness to interpret James Byrnes' words.

To the two statesmen, the American reply was discouraging and inconclusive. It neither promised the Emperor's sovereignty nor explicitly denied it. It merely stated that he would be subject to the Supreme Commander, "who will take such steps as he deems proper to effectuate the surrender terms." Sakomizu and Matsumoto were confused by this clause but alarmed by another: "The ultimate form of government of Japan shall, in accordance with the Potsdam Declaration, be established by the freely expressed will of the Japanese people." In this sentence, the Foreign Office spokesmen could see justification for continued warfare by the military, who would interpret it as certain indication that the Allies meant to remove the Emperor from office.

Over breakfast, the discouraged Foreign Office aides discussed what to do. Matsumoto saw only one choice: "Let's push it through in its present form."

Sakomizu nodded. "Maybe it will work."

As another hot day broke in Tokyo, the two men rode quickly to talk with their superiors. Sakomizu confronted a sleepy Suzuki and convinced him quickly that the Byrnes note was acceptable. Without bothering to read the rough translation, the aged Premier assured his brilliant secretary that he would recommend its approval by the cabinet.

Matsumoto had little trouble with Togo. The frustrated Foreign Minister, depressed at the continued arguments about surrender, realized the pitfalls inherent in the Byrnes note, but agreed with his assistant that there was no other option left. It had to be forced through.

Sakomizu and Matsumoto returned to their offices somewhat relieved. It appeared that they had stolen a lead on the war party by coordinating policy and tactics for the next crucial debate.

They were wrong. While they went back to work, other men plotted to undo their actions.

On the same morning, young officers at the War Ministry were in the office of General Umezu demanding that he denounce the American proposal. At Naval Headquarters, Admiral Toyoda was besieged by impassioned men who urged that he publicly reject the contents of the note. The senior officers were in an impossible situation. Each had been willing to continue the war until urged by the Emperor to negotiate Japan's surrender. Now their subordinates were insisting that they back away from positions assumed under the Imperial mandate. To make matters worse, General Anami, the man who could calm troubled aides with a word, was nowhere to be found. His office reported that he was out on an unspecified mission. Admiral Toyoda and General Umezu tried to ride out the storm of protest until the War Minister returned.

Korechika Anami had not gone directly to his office that morning. Instead, he went to the official residence of Premier Suzuki. Accompanying him was an unlikely compatriot, Baron Hiranuma, whose sympathies toward the peace faction had nearly disappeared as he worried about the fate of the Emperor. Byrnes' note convinced the baron that Hirohito was in grave danger, and as a result, he had joined hands with his former foe, General Anami, in order to block unconditional surrender. The two men had embraced each other in a last-minute effort to thwart the Foreign Office. In Premier Suzuki, they felt they had the weak man in the enemy camp. Shortly after Secretary Sakomizu had convinced the Premier to agree to the American demands, Hiranuma and Anami cornered him. Isolated from his advisers, the tired Suzuki was no match for the marshaled arguments of men determined to upset the drift to peace.

Reverting to the terms he had originally supported, Anami immediately demanded, "The provisions referring to troop disarmament and occupation zones must be included in any agreement with the Allies."

Hiranuma repeated an urgent warning: "The Emperor may suffer greatly if the terms are not drastically revised."

On this point, Suzuki was vulnerable, for like all Japanese, he revered the Throne and would gladly die for it. When his visitors stressed again and again the importance of Hirohito's position, the Premier's mind reeled with the implications of being party to the dissolution of the Imperial House. As Anami and Hiranuma left, Suzuki promised them that he would not give ground on the question of the Emperor.

General Anami went immediately to another appointment. He met with Mikasa, the Emperor's youngest brother, the so-called Red Prince. Mikasa was a nonconformist, whose family never got accustomed to his "socialist" outlook, his concern for the rights of the masses. To court advisers, Mikasa was a rebel.

Anami hoped to convince the Prince to intercede with his brother and block the surrender. He miscalculated badly. Mikasa listened politely to the War Minister and then turned on him brutally. "Since the Manchurian Incident, the Army has not once acted in accordance with the Imperial wish. It is most improper that you should still want to continue the war when things have come to this stage."

Scolded like a child, Anami bowed out of the room. He was crushed beyond comment. Mikasa's words had cut deeply and would stay in his mind. Riding back to his office with his aide, Colonel Hayashi, the general kept repeating the Prince's words in disbelief. They marked the second personal attack on him in the last three days. Earlier, in front of several officers, his brother-in-law Takeshita angrily had told him to commit suicide if he agreed to surrender. At that time, Anami confided to his secretary: "Takeshita said such cruel things to me. Since I am nearly sixty years old, I do not think it would be difficult for me to die. Perhaps it would be difficult for a young man like you but . . ." The general's voice broke and he could not go on. Now, Mikasa's rebuke only added to his inner turmoil as he rode back to the seething corridors at Ichigaya.

There, the young officers had already forced General Umezu to go to the Emperor. Accompanied by Admiral Toyoda, the general stood before the ruler of the Japanese people and lodged a protest. Obviously under a great strain, the two senior officers urged prompt and unequivocal rejection of the American terms. Hirohito watched them closely and felt that they were mouthing the words, as though directed by an unseen force. He thanked them for their concern and dismissed them.

Within minutes, the Emperor summoned his adviser, Marquis Kido, to help him analyze the dismaying trend developing at military headquarters. If Umezu and Toyoda were under such apparent pressure, unrest among Army and Navy personnel must be intense and dangerous. Hirohito's suspicions were well founded. At noontime, the conspirators at Ichigaya surfaced to prepare for a rebellion.

They came to General Anami in his office where the War Minister had just returned from his shattering experience with Prince Mikasa. Takeshita, Hatanaka, Inaba and other men crowded into his presence to talk of the *coup d'état*. Colonel Sato, one of Anami's aides, immediately sensed their intent and spoke sharply to Major Hatanaka: "Don't be so hasty about a coup." Hatanaka lost his temper and screamed, "Badoglio! You're nothing but a duplicate of that traitor!" Sato rushed at the raging Hatanaka but Anami quickly intervened. He jumped between the antagonists and put out his hands. "Come now," he said, "military men must trust each other."

A heavy silence followed, until Anami gently suggested, "Takeshita, come to my home later. I will be happy to talk to you about it then." With that remark, the War Minister walked out of the room to a cabinet meeting. He had forestalled a discussion and avoided a lengthy confrontation, but he knew that sooner or later he would have to meet this band of unhappy men and talk of their plans for a *coup d'état*.

Anami was in an acutely difficult position. The men under him demanded that he defend what was left of the nation. Those above him accused him of trying to destroy any chance for peace and a future for the nation. He could not please both sides in the struggle. Though Anami was against unconditional peace, he was also against insurrection. Knowing that his army might erupt under him at any moment, he was trying to lull the junior officers into inaction while he worked out the best possible peace terms. In that way he could prevent his impetuous aides from disrupting negotiations. Anami hoped that his course of action would avoid bloodshed in the next hours and days.

The full cabinet met at 3:00 P.M. Anami and his new ally, Baron Hiranuma, listened intently as the text of the San Francisco broadcast of the Byrnes note was read. Premier Suzuki cautioned everyone that it was an "unofficial" version and that mistakes could have been made in translation. Then he asked for opinions. Anami and Hiranuma picked up where they had left off that morning with Suzuki. They reiterated their fears for the Emperor. Anami repeated his demands for additional conditions.

Foreign Minister Togo, edgy after days of tension, lost his temper. He snapped caustically, "To add issues at this moment would make the Allies wonder at the integrity of the Japanese Government and at its sincerity in negotiating at all."

His rage mounting, Togo rose from his chair and walked to the door. "Acting like this is contrary to reason," he shouted. Then, nearly at the end of his endurance, he slammed the conference room door behind him.

Trembling with anger, Togo picked up the phone in the next room and called his assistant, Matsumoto, who quickly sensed a crisis and warned him to adjourn the meeting before a vote could be taken. For want of a better solution, Togo agreed and went back through the oaken door to join his colleagues. He was just in time to receive a final blow.

Anami and Hiranuma had done their work well that morning. By concentrating their attack on Premier Suzuki, they had hammered at the weakest spot in the opposition's armor. The aged man had been shaken by the possibility that the Emperor would meet disaster if the Allies' terms were accepted.

When Togo walked back into the room, he heard Suzuki reciting the arguments of the war party. The Premier was backing away from surrender. Appalled at the change in Suzuki's position, Togo rushed to intervene before irrevocable damage was done. Controlling his voice, he interrupted: "Your words are worthy of careful consideration, but at the same time, Japan should not continue the war irresponsibly without paying any attention to its outcome."

Togo kept on talking to avoid losing the initiative. "Unless there is some prospect of victory, Japan should negotiate for peace. I therefore propose that the meeting be adjourned and that the question be reopened after the official communication from the Allies has been received."

There was an awkward silence. Someone in the room agreed and men started getting up to leave. Togo's tactic had won Japan a temporary reprieve. Anami and his followers had suffered another defeat.

Foreign Minister Togo could not calm down. Incensed at Suzuki, he went looking for him and found him in an anteroom. The

Premier stood helplessly as the bespectacled Togo shouted scorn at him. Too tired to argue, confused by the factional disputes erupting on all sides, he offered no defense for his actions. Togo stormed out of the room determined to resign and let others fight for peace. Disgusted with Suzuki, frustrated by the pigheadedness of Anami and Hiranuma, he was quite at a loss as to what to do next.

In late afternoon, he stopped first at the Foreign Office where aides implored him to go home and sleep on the question of resignation. Then he went to see Marquis Kido at the palace. After explaining the disastrous series of events at the cabinet meeting, Togo warned Kido that he must deal with the vacillating Suzuki before the peace coalition fell apart.

Meanwhile at the Foreign Office, Shunichi Matsumoto's long day had not ended. Busy since before dawn, when he and Sakomizu had first translated the radio message from San Francisco, he had manned the Foreign Office all day while his superior, Togo, fought with friend and foe at the cabinet meeting. Now, in the twilight of August 12, he sat behind a desk thinking of a way in which to give the diplomats more time to patch up their defenses.

Matsumoto reached for the phone, dialed the Telegraph Section of the Ministry, and spoke to the duty officer. He was explicit in his directions: "Watch for any Allied messages that come in this evening. If they do, stamp them received as of tomorrow morning. Above all, keep them secret." The duty officer agreed. Matsumoto hung up and sank back into his chair, hoping that his little scheme would give Togo and the other statesmen enough time to reorganize. In this fabricated limbo, the architects of peace might gain the upper hand. Matsumoto went home elated at his deception.

At 6:40 P.M., James Byrnes' note to the Japanese Government was received in the Telegraph Section by the duty officer. He promptly marked it received as of 7:40 A.M. the following day and filed it away.

Another message which came in shortly afterward further justified Matsumoto's concern over the state of affairs. The telegram was from Suemasa Okamoto, Japanese Ambassador to Sweden, who for two days had been trying to gauge Allied reactions to the impending surrender. Okamoto was desperately anxious to alert his countrymen to a grave peril.

THE AMERICANS ARE HAVING A HARD TIME HARMONIZING THE OPINIONS OF THE ALLIES—RUSSIA AND CHINA WANT THE EMPEROR OUT—GREAT BRITAIN ADVOCATES TEMPORARY RECOGNITION OF THE EMPEROR—THE LONDON TIMES IS AGAINST THE EMPEROR SYSTEM.

Okamoto added the obvious warning. Unless Japan accepted the original offer, President Truman might be weaned away from his position. The deadlock in Tokyo must be broken and quickly.

At 9:30 P.M. the Premier of Japan entered Kido's office in answer to an urgent summons. Suzuki listened as the Marquis lectured him on the day's misadventures. Kido minced no words: "If we do not accept the Allied position now, we will be sacrificing hundreds of thousands of innocent people to the continued ravages of war. . . . Furthermore it is His Majesty's wish that we advance on the basis of the views held by his Foreign Minister." Knowing his man well, Kido concentrated on Suzuki's overriding concern about the Emperor. By allaying the Premier's fears about delivering Hirohito to the enemy, he hoped to dissipate any lingering doubts in Suzuki's mind.

Once again the old admiral promised to stand fast against the opposition, to push through the surrender. Kido saw him to the door and returned to his room convinced that the peace faction was intact for the next crucial hours.

While diplomats and generals haggled over the issue of war and peace, Japanese civilians continued to die in clusters. Fires still raged in Nagasaki. On the twelfth, disaster teams were still threading through the wreckage looking for survivors. On all sides they found the dead.

Three sailors who entered the city as part of a search team saw buildings along the road smoldering, though not in actual flames. Just over a mile from Ground Zero, many dead lay beside the road. The bodies showed evidence of multiple burns and wounds about the head and extremities. From this distance inward toward the blast center, the number of cadavers increased markedly. These bodies were roasted black. Some of them seemed still alive. Others had swollen grossly, causing their stomachs to rupture onto the ground. There was no foliage anywhere. Everything was covered with a deep brown coating. A putrid, decaying smell clogged the nostrils and made rescuers gag and retch.

Survivors were being sent to surrounding towns for treatment. Hundreds of them had been brought to Omura Naval Hospital. The appearance of the patients was horrifying. Their hair was burned, their clothing torn to pieces and stained by blood, and the naked parts of their bodies were all burned and inflamed. Many had jagged pieces of glass and wood driven into their bodies. Few resembled human beings.

A strange thing began happening to survivors by the third day after the bomb: they started to die in increasing numbers. After being treated for burns and wounds, the people should have been able to pick up their lives and continue with the task of rebuilding. But instead they wasted away and became part of the mounting death statistics.

Doctors were at a loss to understand the mystery. Both in Nagasaki and Hiroshima, now nearly a week into the atomic age, patients walked into hospitals and died before the disbelieving eyes of physicians and nurses. One officer exclaimed to a companion: "These cases are entirely different from the injuries which have so far been seen. The patients you treated yesterday have died one after another."

The other man was outraged: "That's nonsense!" But it was not. The patients were not victims of ordinary bombs. They were dosed with gamma rays, which were destroying their insides and, like a time bomb, preparing to claim them after several days had passed.

They exhibited distressing symptoms of diarrhea and vomiting, lack of appetite and anemia. Their blood streams were being ravaged by radiation. As the days went on, more and more "survivors" fell down and died. The two cities faced a new unseen enemy.

While the small fires continued to burn day and night as families disposed of their relatives, the insidious *Genshibakudansho*, the "atomic bomb sickness," added fresh corpses to the unending rows about the wastelands. And still the leaders talked on in Tokyo about continuing the war.

On the night of the twelfth, in Peiping, China, a small group of soldiers tried to make themselves comfortable in the top floor apartment of a private home. Earlier that day, they had jumped from a plane into a field and then come by truck and train into the walled city on a delicate assignment.

Ripping off stolen enemy uniforms, the men quickly mounted a radio aerial on the roof and began sending a coded message back to OSS headquarters at Hsian.

Major Jim Kellis, leader of the team, reported that he and his men were now based in the home of General Mung, commander of Chinese mercenaries working for the Japanese Army. Mung had agreed to collaborate with the Americans and had smuggled the OSS agents into the heart of Japanese territory in order that they might be in position to act quickly in case Japan surrendered. Jim Kellis was actually living next door to a building that housed a section of the Japanese General Staff in North China.

After the message was sent, Kellis ordered the aerial struck. Then he and his men settled down to wait for some word of peace in the Far East.

ELEVEN

The Mounting Peril

General Anami could not sleep. Aware that his side had been temporarily thwarted by Togo's intervention in the cabinet meeting, he cast about for a new device, a stratagem to block unconditional peace. While the citizens of Tokyo slept on into August 13, the general conferred with aides at his residence. He finally ordered his aide Colonel Hayashi to leave on an important errand.

The colonel drove to the home of General Umezu and confronted the Chief of Staff at 4:00 A.M. Hayashi apologized for waking him, then said: "It is requested that the Emperor's decision be changed through the efforts of senior members of the Army. The Emperor has no confidence in Field Marshal Sugiyama. Therefore, the War Minister is contemplating having Field Marshal Hata make an appeal to the Emperor. What do you think of that?"

The question put Umezu in a difficult spot. Clearly Anami was asking for approval of a device to delay surrender. If Umezu disagreed, the onus of guilt could fall on him. He walked about for a few moments, then turned to Hayashi, and said, "I'm sorry. I support the acceptance of the Potsdam Declaration."

Hayashi rushed back to Anami with these fateful words and the War Minister was shocked into silence. His valued ally Umezu appeared to be deserting him. Anami felt desperately alone as he went to bed for a brief, merciful rest.

Within a few hours he was awake and on his way to see the Marquis Kido, who received Anami warmly and ushered him into his study. The two men were old friends. Both had worked for the Emperor as young aides in the household of the Imperial Palace. Kido had no illusions about the general's uncomfortable position in these last days. He fully realized Anami's dual role: first, to win the best possible terms for the Emperor and his army; second, to keep that army quiet until he accomplished his primary mission. It was the most difficult job Kido could imagine at that moment.

Anami opened the conversation by complaining, "No self-respecting nation could possibly accept the Allied terms."

Kido was ready for this argument and replied: "There is no way out. The Japanese have sued for peace. The Americans have given the terms. For Japan now to add conditions to conditions would result in certain rupture of negotiations and a renewed ferocity to the war. Look at it from the American position. What would they think the Japanese were plotting if, at this late stage, they put new rules into the game? If the Emperor changed his mind and rescinded the peace proposal, the Allies would consider him a fool or a lunatic."

Anami remained unconvinced. "Pessimism never yields good results. We should make one last effort to achieve better terms."

Kido said, "We must abide by the wishes of His Majesty. We must accept the Allied reply in its present form."

Anami started to smile. "I understand your position very well. I knew you would say something like that." Then he stopped for a brief instant before voicing the thought that nagged at him constantly: "But the atmosphere in the Army is so tense." He did not elaborate, just rose from the chair and said goodbye to Kido, who gazed sadly after the general as he went out to another appointment.

Anami was determined to avoid his young aides as long as possible. So far, Takeshita, Ida, Hatanaka and the others had not been able to sit down with him and discuss the coup. Time was slipping by and yet they could not get the key man to endorse their rebellion. While they fretted at the War Ministry, the general went directly to a meeting of the Big Six.

There he found the peace faction once more united. A restful sleep had improved Togo's mood and given him a fresh perspective on his duties. Suzuki was chatting amiably with everyone. Puffing on his cherished cigar, he had reversed his previous day's arguments and now resolutely championed the acceptance of the Byrnes note and the Potsdam Declaration. Admiral Yonai, whom Anami disliked intensely, maintained his rigid posture in favor of immediate surrender.

General Anami and his cohorts, Umezu and Toyoda, clung to their insistence on conditions. Umezu was no longer a diehard, as Anami well knew from the early morning conversation with Hayashi. Yet in public, the gruff Chief of Staff supported his superior against the diplomats. Anami had little else to feel cheerful about that morning. The Big Six were still hopelessly split. At noon the group adjourned for lunch and a later cabinet meeting.

If Anami had troubles with his own officers, his antagonist in the peace group, Admiral Yonai, was equally distressed by the machinations beneath him at the Naval General Staff. At noontime on the thirteenth, the Navy Minister finally lost his temper. He had been advised that Admiral Toyoda had complained of the Japanese capitulation to the Emperor just the day before, and he deeply resented this insubordination. He had also learned that the Vice-Chief of Staff, Admiral Onishi, the Father of the Kamikazes, had spoken disparagingly to various cabinet members about Yonai's own will to fight. If Yonai was annoyed at Toyoda, he was incensed at Onishi, who was engaged in a campaign of character assassination.

The Navy Minister fumed for twenty-four hours and then decided to have a face-to-face meeting with the two offenders. As a precaution, Yonai asked his assistant, Admiral Zenshiro

Hoshina, to stay as a witness to the encounter. Hoshina was to record significant dialogues and act as a bodyguard in case of any physical danger. Both Yonai and Hoshina feared the volatile Onishi whose reputation for rashness was almost legendary. The warrior was like an unstable element, capable of a violent reaction to a situation.

Shortly after noontime, the offenders marched into the Navy Minister's office and saluted. Ramrod straight, caps held in their left hands, the two men waited for some word from their superior. Yonai let them stand in awkward silence.

Finally he looked up and spoke sharply: "The behavior of the General Staff is execrable. If you have anything to say about me, why don't you come and tell me about it personally?" His voice rising, Yonai rushed on: "Such an impudent attitude is shameful. Do not do anything like that again."

Toyoda never moved a muscle. Onishi bent his head and began to sob.

Yonai continued: "And what is the idea of recommending momentous decisions to the Emperor without ever consulting me? For my part, I am not meddling with the this and that of what you are doing at the Naval General Staff. To have behaved as you have done is inexcusable."

Toyoda remained impassive. Onishi cried loudly, tried to apologize, lost his voice, and stopped. Yonai ordered them out. The two admirals marched through the door, one unchastened, the other heartbroken.

Yonai and Hoshina were both puzzled and thrilled. Neither had anticipated such a reaction from Onishi. To have cowed such a man, even temporarily, was a signal victory for the peace faction. Yonai went off happily to the afternoon cabinet meeting, which proved far different from the stormy one on the preceding day.

Kantaro Suzuki continued to espouse acceptance of the Byrnes note. No longer did the Premier mouth the words of the war party. The breach in the ranks of the peacemakers had been successfully closed to further exploitation.

Foreign Minister Togo, still discouraged by the opposition to his policies, nevertheless was fortified by the change in Suzuki's demeanor. He continued to argue relentlessly with Toyoda, Umezu and Anami, but was able to hold his own temper in check throughout the meeting.

For several hours the two factions sparred for position, for an opening. It was hopeless. The same conditions were imposed by the military, the same objections to them raised by the statesmen. Each side had become rigidly committed to its own cause.

During a break in the negotiations, General Anami stepped into the next room to call his office at Ichigaya. Standing there waiting for someone to answer, he realistically knew that he could not salvage anything at the conference table. Yet he had to keep up a pretense to his officers. Anami spoke reassuringly to the man on the other end of the phone: "Yes, everything seems to be going our way. They're coming around to my way of thinking." As he hung up, he turned to gaze into the astonished face of Secretary Sakomizu who was curled up in a chair nearby, catching a few moments of rest. Anami grimaced, then smiled. "It's better to let sleeping dogs lie, don't you think?" Sakomizu recovered his poise quickly and nodded agreement as he watched the War Minister walk back to argue hopelessly against surrender. The Secretary was suddenly filled with admiration for the general who was deliberately deceiving his aides.

As the rebels on Ichigaya Hill continued to dally, the debate began again in the cabinet room. Suzuki demanded a vote from the full cabinet. Since Toyoda and Umezu did not belong to this body, the Premier hoped to isolate Anami. He failed. Though twelve men sided with Togo, two others, the Justice Minister and the Minister for Home Affairs, agreed with Anami. One man could not decide what to do.

An impasse had been reached. Suzuki adjourned the meeting with the warning that he would once again seek the advice of the Emperor.

As General Anami left the room, he knew that the final hours of the struggle were at hand. When the Emperor spoke again, it would be too late to avert unconditional surrender. In the meantime, he had to face the conspirators gathering around him like jackals.

The rebels sought Anami out at his official residence. At 8:00 P.M. ten of them tried to solicit his final approval of a coup. Takeshita was there. So was Inaba. Hatanaka came with Jiro Shiizaki, a longtime friend.

Hatanaka brought a rumor of a plot against Anami's life. He and others had heard that peace advocates planned to kill the general if he continued to oppose the Potsdam Declaration. Anami scoffed at this story and turned to talk to another officer, Colonel Okikatsu Arao, senior officer of the Military Affairs Section at the War Ministry. Arao was now a spokesman for the plotters. As such, he was in a most uncomfortable situation. Convinced that Anami would never support a rebellion, Arao nevertheless wanted to maintain the respect of the men working under him. For their part, his subordinates trusted the burly, intelligent colonel, who was a natural leader of men and therefore an obvious choice to speak for the rank and file.

Arao himself believed that Anami had decided months before that the war was hopeless. As far back as the fall of 1944, he had accompanied the general on an inspection tour of the Home Islands and heard him say that it was impossible to defend Japan from invasion. In May of 1945, when Anami had ordered the release from prison of Shigeru Yoshida, a friend of the peace faction, Arao had sensed that the general was preparing for the inevitable day of surrender. Yet on the evening of August 13, he stood in front of the War Minister and spoke of a revolution. The hard-pressed Arao handed Anami a piece of paper, containing the outlines of the projected coup. The general took it, read it quickly, then listened with his eyes closed as Arao elaborated on the details.

The rebellion was set for 10:00 A.M. the following morning. General Mori had already been approached and had promised to think about it. Even if he refused, the coup could proceed because most of his regimental commanders had agreed to act. Marquis Kido and Premier Suzuki would be imprisoned and the Emperor placed in a form of protective custody. The Eastern District Army would be a big stumbling block unless General Tanaka joined the rebels. He would be approached as soon as Anami consented to lend his name to the plot.

The fateful moment had arrived. On this man's answer hung the fate of millions. Anami asked: "Are you sure that you've thought of everything? It seems to me that your groundwork is a little vague. There are too many things still to be accomplished." He concluded, "The plan is very incomplete." Still he did not say definitely whether he was for or against the basic idea of revolt.

The rebels begged for an answer. Anami told Arao to come to his office at midnight to discuss it further. Then he walked with the officers to the front porch. They were both discouraged and optimistic. Anami had not given quick approval as they had hoped but neither had he flatly rejected their plan. Anami waved them down the stairs and then added a note of caution: "Be careful, since they may be watching you tonight. Perhaps you had better return in separate groups instead of a single mass." The rebels broke up and left quietly.

No one was watching them but Anami had good reason for saying what he did. Earlier in the week he had warned both General Mori and the secret police commander, Okido, to be on the lookout for trouble from the ranks.

Inside the house Colonel Hayashi was furious with his superior. By not vetoing the plan, Anami had implicitly encouraged the plotters. When Anami came back in, Hayashi spoke his mind: "You've given those men tacit agreement to their plans. You should say no definitely. It's silly even to talk of a coup because the people won't support it."

Anami listened thoughtfully, then shrugged and said, "Perhaps you're right. I'll talk again to Arao."

Hayashi felt that Anami was letting his men take unfair advantage of him and wanted to protect him from the intrigues. He doubted the War Minister's political sense and questioned whether he should therefore even be the War Minister. He considered Anami an admirable person, rare among military men, but felt that those same qualities hindered his judgment of officers he liked. Now these officers were taking advantage of the relationship to foster a conspiracy, and Anami did nothing positive to crush the incipient danger.

Tojo, Anami's predecessor, would have moved ruthlessly against the rebels. But Anami could not act against his own men, and as a result, they would spend the rest of the evening of August 13 making plans for revolt on the next day. Anami would have to change his tactics or the explosion would take place on time.

At midnight, the general was at his office where Arao joined him. Remembering Hayashi's instructions, Anami told Arao that he doubted the coup would succeed. Again he avoided forbidding the conspirators to proceed with action.

After Arao left, Anami went to Hayashi and explained, "I told Arao what you said but I wonder if he will interpret it to mean that I am against the coup?"

Hayashi murmured, "I wonder."

By two o'clock on the morning of the fourteenth, Anami was in bed. The other leading figures in the government crisis were also trying to get some rest before renewing the interminable struggle. Foreign Minister Togo had spent several hours in heated argument with General Umezu and Admiral Toyoda. During their discussion, Admiral Onishi, recovered from his dressing-down by Navy Minister Yonai, had burst in and demanded that Japan fight to the very end, to the death of all of the inhabitants of the nation. Togo let him ramble on, then flatly rejected his plea.

Premier Kantaro Suzuki slept like a drugged man. At eighty, he could not keep the pace maintained by Anami and others. His body ached with fatigue, his mind was numbed by the constant strain of debate and intrigue. Within hours, he would have to go once again to the Emperor of Japan for help, and the thought galled him. Somehow Suzuki felt he had failed His Majesty and yet he could not think of another way out of the dilemma. August 14 had to bring a climax.

In the fading hours of the thirteenth of August, a radio message had gone out from American Naval Headquarters in Washington to all units. From the Palaus to Hawaii, from Australia to the fast carriers standing just 150 miles off Honshu, Admiral Ernest King advised, "This is a peace warning." All strike forces were cautioned to refrain from attacking the enemy in the next hours. Washington was giving the Japanese a few final hours to get their house in order. Beyond that time, assaults would be renewed.

At three o'clock on the morning of the fourteenth, an American colonel, Ray Peers, was trying to get some much-needed rest in his quarters in Kunming, China. He was awakened by Colonel Richard Heppner, who had just received a message from Wedemeyer in Chungking ordering the OSS to put the mercy missions plan into effect. Heppner was not ready and needed help.

Peers had compiled an extraordinary record as leader of Detachment 101, a guerrilla outfit in Burma. Now he was assigned to China as Deputy Strategic Services Officer, in charge of clandestine operations south of the Yangtze River. For one month he had been surveying his new command, getting acquainted with the problems associated with it. He never anticipated any like the one now handed him.

When Heppner outlined the mission, Peers said, "Move the teams up to Hsian right away."

Heppner brought him up short: "But we don't have the teams, we have had to use all of our personnel in new operations behind the Japanese lines. So that's the problem. What do you suggest?"

Peers, a man of action, quickly assumed charge of the project. As dawn broke, he began to screen all available people for the dangerous jumps into Japanese territory. He had very little time left.

TWELVE

August 14—The Final Word

In Tokyo, events moved swiftly on the morning of the four-teenth. After only three hours sleep, General Anami breakfasted with Field Marshal Hata, just arrived from Hiroshima, where his headquarters had been destroyed. He had come to report to the Government on the effects of the atomic bomb. Hata told Anami that the entire city was gone, that the bomb was inhuman. How-ever, he offered one bit of consolation. He said he believed the weapon was ineffective on anything dug in underground. Since it evidently was exploded in the air, properly entrenched defenses could survive unscathed.

The harried War Minister seized on this remark, telling Hata: "Be sure and mention this to the Emperor when you see him. Tell him that the bomb is not so deadly." Anami was grasping at any shred of hope.

From this meeting, Anami went to Ichigaya. At 7:00 A.M. his men converged on him. Because Takeshita and the others planned to move at 10:00 A.M., they had to have Anami's guar-antee of cooperation within the hour. To speed matters further, they had told generals Tanaka and Mori to come to Ichigaya that morning for a special conference. By this time the rebels were frantic.

The general was prepared for them. Realizing that the peace group might move quickly for another Big Six meeting with the Emperor, both he and Umezu had asked that the conference be delayed at least until 1:00 P.M. Between now and then he had to thwart the rebels. Almost immediately he made his most important move.

He took Colonel Arao down the hall to Umezu's office. There Anami bluntly asked the general, "Will you back a coup?"

Umezu sat behind his desk and looked at his friend. Then he turned his gaze on Colonel Arao and said: "Absolutely not. There's no chance of it succeeding. For one thing, the people won't follow you." Umezu's voice became scornful. "Forty percent of the factory workers have left their jobs already. We could never carry on the war under these conditions."

Anami looked at Arao, who could say nothing in the face of such determined opposition. By the time they left the office, the coup was falling apart. Anami, who knew of Umezu's attitude before the meeting and who was certain there was absolutely no chance of his Chief of Staff lending aid to the rebels, had led Arao into a baited trap. The colonel went to a telephone to report the bad news to his collaborators. For Arao, the onerous task of acting as spokesman for his colleagues was over.

While the coup foundered at the War Ministry, the peace faction was galvanized into action. Koichi Kido was the catalyst. For several days, the B-29's had waged a campaign of enlightenment as well as destruction over Japan. Millions upon millions of leaflets fell from bomb bays as the Twentieth Air Force attempted to inform civilians that the war was hopeless. The Americans hoped this cascade of paper would foment public opinion toward insisting that the carnage cease. They reasoned that the Government would thus be pressured more quickly into acceptance of the terms of surrender. But the plan, though skillful, was fraught with dangers. If enough troops read the information, if they became aware for the first time of the disastrous turn of events, if they suddenly grasped what was going on in the cabinet meetings in Tokyo, then quite possibly they would take things into their own hands.

At 7:00 A.M., a servant brought Kido a slip of paper that had fallen into his garden. It was an Allied leaflet and it told the whole story. Kido was appalled. A sense of impending disaster rushed over him, and he knew that decisive action must be taken that day before the troops put two and two together.

He called the palace and asked for an immediate audience with the Emperor. At eight thirty Kido arrived in his presence and broke the news. Hirohito sensed the danger immediately and urged Kido, "Do whatever you wish to speed the end of this war." Kido suggested calling a last conference of all principals to demand surrender that day.

Leaving the library, he met Premier Suzuki, who coincidentally had come at that time to ask for the Emperor's help in getting a decision. Kido asked the old man if he had called the Big Six into session. Suzuki looked anguished: "I am having a hard time. The Army wants me to wait until 1:00 P.M. while the Navy asks me to postpone it without setting a specific time." Suzuki seemed at a loss as to what to do next.

Yet he made an unusual request and asked Kido if it would be possible for them to meet jointly with the Emperor and settle basic strategy for the day. Holding a dual audience with the Ruler was almost never done. But these were extraordinary times and Kido knew the Emperor would agree. They met with him at ten o'clock; out of the meeting came a surprising tactic, which threw the other members of the cabinet into a frenzied haste and caught the war party completely off guard.

Emperor Hirohito sent out a summons for his cabinet ministers to meet with him at ten thirty, in less than half an hour. The message caused absolute chaos. All over Tokyo, officials put down telephones and frantically rushed about to dress in proper attire. On this unusual occasion they were not required to wear formal clothes. Nevertheless, the resulting confusion in offices verged on the hysterical. Private secretaries lost their ties, shirts were exchanged, collars were closed by men trying to look more presentable before their Emperor. By car, they converged on the palace for a momentous confrontation.

They gathered in the library, a one-story building. They had entered it through an air-raid shelter in the entrance hall and now made their way to a flight of stairs leading to the underground conference room. Single file, the elite of the Japanese Government walked down the wet mat-lined steps between walls dripping with moisture. At the bottom of the stairway they turned right and walked to an open door, twelve inches thick. Beyond it was the council room where eleven of them had met with the Emperor on the night of August 9.

The air was clammy as they seated themselves in two rows of chairs in front of the familiar narrow table, now covered with a beautiful gold brocade cloth. Beyond the table was a solitary chair, straight-backed, with arms on both sides. Behind the chair was a six-fold gilded screen. Other than these furnishings, the room was starkly bare.

Twenty-four people sat waiting for the Emperor of Japan. In the front row were Yonai, Suzuki, Togo, Umezu, Toyoda and Anami. Surrounding them were assistants and secretaries. Baron Hiranuma was in attendance. So was Secretary Sakomizu, who was terrified. In his superior's hands lay the power to bring off this meeting. It was up to Premier Suzuki to guide the conversation and circumvent any opposition. Sakomizu feared that the old man would fail badly.

For days Sakomizu had worried about Suzuki, and his fears seemed to be justified. The Premier had not been able to force through the Emperor's initial surrender request of the ninth. At eight o'clock on this very morning, Sakomizu had gone to Suzuki to ask if he had prepared a proclamation for the Emperor to read at the cabinet meeting. Suzuki had no idea that he should have written one. Sakomizu was furious. He became even more incensed when Suzuki told him that he did not even have a speech prepared in case the Emperor called a meeting that day. Now, at ten thirty, Sakomizu felt his worst premonitions were about to be confirmed. The old man was sure to botch the whole plan. At the most important hour in his life, he would fumble his way through the agenda and lose the initiative so carefully built up these past days.

An eerie quiet prevailed, broken once or twice by nervous coughs. Anami sat in full military uniform, staring impassively at the door beside the gold screen. At 10:55 it opened and the Ruler of the Japanese Empire walked into the room. He was dressed in a military uniform. He wore white gloves. Hirohito moved to the simple wooden chair and sat down. His audience rose and bowed as he came in. Now they sat down and waited. Suzuki was the first to speak.

The aged Premier rose and faced Hirohito. After apologizing for calling upon him once more for guidance, Suzuki launched into a recital of the difficulties which had brought the cabinet to an impasse. In the back row, Sakomizu listened. His sweating palms betrayed his intense excitement as he heard the eighty-year-old warrior seize the reins of leadership and forcefully lead the discussion.

There was no doubt that the Premier was in complete command of the situation in this crowded room. Suzuki spoke without notes, yet his presentation was cogent and compelling. After outlining the problem, he turned to the generals and admirals and asked them to state their arguments once more. Anami and Umezu were so choked with emotion that their speeches were only confused and ineffective. It remained for Admiral Toyoda, the man without a fleet, to defend the war party against its detractors. He spoke brilliantly.

Toyoda stood before his Emperor and his peers and launched a last defense of the Japanese military. His points were the old ones: "The Emperor's sovereignty must be maintained. . . ." "Japan must not be occupied. . . ." "The clause referring to the government eventually being 'determined by the free will of the people' is most dangerous and will undermine the entire Japanese tradition. . . ." Having argued his faction's position better than anyone in the room, he sat down.

Feet shuffled and twenty-four men waited for the next move. Suzuki asked the Emperor to speak.

Hirohito leaned slightly forward in his chair and began:

"If there are no further views to present, I will present mine. I would like to have all of you agree with me. My view is still unchanged from that which I expressed at the conference on the ninth.

The Emperor was already having difficulty speaking. He began to sob out phrases, to pause and control his voice, then to continue. Everyone was visibly affected. Men started to sob quietly.

"I have studied the terms of the Allied reply and have concluded that they constitute a virtually complete acknowledgment of the position we maintained in the note dispatched several days ago. In short, I consider the reply to be acceptable." At this point, the Emperor broke down. His gloved right hand moved up under his glasses and wiped his tear-filled eyes. Then he continued:

"I appreciate how difficult it will be for the officers and men of the Army and Navy to surrender their arms to the enemy and to see their homeland occupied. Indeed, it is difficult for me to issue the order making this necessary and to deliver so many of my trusted servants into the hands of the Allied authorities by whom they will be accused of being war criminals. In spite of these feelings . . . I cannot endure the thought of letting my people suffer any longer. . . ."

Hirohito was almost incapable of further speech. His chest heaved as he struggled to finish. In the hot room, tears mingled with sweat on many faces. The Emperor concluded:

"It is my desire that you, my Ministers of State, accede to my wishes and forthwith accept the Allied reply. In order that the people may know of my decision, I request you to prepare at once an Imperial rescript so that I may broadcast to the nation.

"I am afraid that members of the armed forces will be particularly disturbed. If requested by the War and Navy Ministers I will be willing to go anywhere to talk personally with the troops.

"It matters not what happens to me but I wonder how I can answer the spirits of the ancestors if the nation is reduced to ashes with great sacrifice of life.

"Therefore, as the Emperor Meiji once endured the unendurable, so shall I and so must you. If there is anything more that should be done I will do it. If I should have to stand before a microphone, I will do so willingly.

"Finally, I call upon each and every one of you to exert himself to the utmost so that we may meet the trying days which lie ahead."

He stopped suddenly, groping in vain for more words. In the silence, all knew that the war was really over. It was done. Prime Minister Suzuki slowly approached the Emperor, bowed deeply, and humbly apologized. Hirohito rose slowly and walked back through the door he had entered less than an hour ago. He had delivered his nation to the enemy.

Few of his audience saw him go. Instead of rising to bow before the Emperor, most sat crying into their hands. Two men slid onto the floor. On elbows and knees, they cried uncontrollably. The tiny room was filled with sorrow as grown men expressed their grief. Rivals sobbed beside each other. Enemies comforted each other. Japan had lost its honor.

One by one, the bereaved filed up the long stairway into the bright sunlight. Only they knew the tragic truth. No one else in the country was aware of it. Now came the most awesome task, delivering Japan to the enemy without inciting the military, which might go wild at the news.

Anami, however, was still plagued by his conscience. Had he done enough for his country? Should he insist on one more all-out attack on the Americans to show his country's strength and possibly make the enemy pause and reconsider the terms?

As the conference broke up, he asked his secretary, Hayashi, to follow him into the bathroom. There, he spoke plaintively: "There is one last piece of advice I want to ask of you. The Imperial decision has been issued, but according to intelligence sources, there is a large American convoy outside of Tokyo. What do you think of the idea of proposing peace after striking the convoy?"

Hayashi was dismayed at this thinking and immediately said: "Your idea is absolutely mistaken. In the first place, the Imperial decision to terminate the war has been issued, and in the second place, even though there is a rumor of a large American convoy south of Tokyo Bay, there has been no confirmed report from the air patrol units. Therefore, it is a mistake to think of such a thing."

Anami protested no more. In fact, he seemed to want this response from Hayashi. He wanted to be told that he had done his best, that there was nothing left to do. Even as he got solace from Hayashi, the general's brother-in-law Takeshita was on his way to him with more talk of rebellion.

Anami and the others went directly to a last cabinet meeting. The members met to formally ratify the Emperor's request. There was no more opposition. Anami, Umezu and Toyoda seemed almost relieved to have the issue decided. No one protested.

After the abortive interview with Umezu that morning, Colonel Arao had told his friends that the coup appeared hopeless, and it had been put off indefinitely. Then later that morning, two subordinates of Takeshita went to Umezu's office to plead one last time.

The general was a harried man that day. Not wanting to be unkind to the officers, he merely tried to point out the practical side of the matter: "I am not absolutely opposed to the idea of a coup. However, you men must realize that it has no chance of succeeding." Yet the two officers went away under the delusion that Umezu would back them if they could somehow pull off the rebellion.

This information went the rounds in the Ministry and once more extremists dusted off the operational plan for seizure of power in Tokyo. Before noon, news of the impromptu Imperial conference with the cabinet had reached the Ministry. Shortly thereafter Takeshita headed across town to Suzuki's official residence.

He found the War Minister in an anteroom off the main conference room. The cabinet had just adjourned after approving the Emperor's decision. Takeshita came right to the point: "The men still want to follow you and now we think Umezu will go along with us. Will you reconsider?"

Anami quickly shook his head. "No, I will not. It is too late. The decision has been made in the other room."

Takeshita gasped at this news. "Then resign your position and that will make the Emperor's action worthless." Normally in Japan if the full cabinet did not agree, an Imperial rescript was invalid. And if Anami quit, the cabinet would automatically dissolve.

Anami appeared to hesitate, then said, "Yes, that might be a solution. Get me some paper." He walked around the room. Takeshita waited for his next remarks. Anami came back to him and shook his head. "No, it's too late for that. I'm going back to the Ministry and tell the men the news." He put on his hat and walked out to his car in the driveway. Takeshita, now convinced that the war really was over, followed him to the Ministry building.

The Ichigaya Heights headquarters was the scene of a strange mixture of emotions by the time General Anami arrived there. Word of the impending surrender had seeped out to field grade officers and their reactions were predictable. Most of them sat crying or staring at the walls of their offices. Some shouted noisily through the corridors that the war should go on. In some offices, papers were pulled out of the cabinets and burned as men prepared for the day of the enemy's arrival.

In his office, the Vice-Chief of Staff, Torashiro Kawabe, pondered a brazen move. A die-hard militarist to the end, Kawabe believed right up to this day that the Army should fight on the beaches. But now he realized that further opposition was senseless and he wanted only to make sure that the surrender would be carried out according to plan. He knew that the highest ranking officers in the Army were gathered in another room on the same floor and wondered if he ought to seal the bargain by asking them to sign a pledge of allegiance to the rescript terminating the war. To that end, he composed a simple document: "The Army will act in accordance with the Imperial decision to the last." He walked to the room with Vice-Minister of War Wakamatsu, who had seconded his plan.

Just outside the conference room the two waited to be called into the presence of the elite in the Imperial Japanese Army. Inside, sitting around a table, were Umezu, stolid, scowling, finally convinced that the right thing had been done that morning; Doihara, who had helped begin the ill-fated adventure years before in Manchuria and had become the first Japanese mayor of Mukden; Hata, whose headquarters in Hiroshima had disappeared just eight days before; and Sugiyama, the field marshal, just a spectator in these recent hectic days.

The two went in to present their paper, which was intended merely to guarantee that no leader would have second thoughts about the Emperor's decision and break away from the majority. When Torashiro Kawabe told the generals what he wanted, he did so with some fear that they would take offense at his obvious insinuation. But the fight had gone out of them and they no longer wanted to carry the burden. Umezu signed quickly and one by one the others affixed their signatures to the simple document. General Anami walked in at the last moment, looked at the paper, and signed it without a murmur.

At two o'clock in the afternoon, section leaders and field officers crowded into Conference Room Number One where Anami stood morosely behind a desk. Visibly affected as he asked for quiet, the War Minister then spoke to the hushed group: "A meeting has just been held in the Imperial presence and His Majesty has rendered his final decision in favor of terminating the war. The Imperial Army must act in complete accord with this decision. Japan will henceforth face difficult times. Even though you may have to sleep on the ground and eat stones, I ask you—one and all—to do your utmost to preserve the national polity."

Anami had spelled it out with brutal clarity: The rebels were too late; the decision had been rendered; forget the revolt. The general had ended his show of paternal interest in the plans of his aides. Now he was telling them to stop the nonsense once and for all.

Hatanaka uttered a mournful wail and burst into tears. Colonel Ida looked accusingly at the War Minister and said, "Why have you lost your resolve?"

Anami closed his eyes and seemed to be exerting great effort to control his emotions. Then he answered: "I could not refuse the Emperor any longer. Especially when he asked, in tears, to bear the pain no matter how trying it might be. I could not but forget everything and accept it." He gazed at his subordinates in an attempt to get their understanding.

Angry men left Conference Room Number One and vowed that it was not too late, that they would prove Anami wrong. The coup would succeed without him. One of the dissidents was Kenji Hatanaka, Anami's protégé. Almost immediately he set out on a bicycle for the headquarters of the Eastern District Army, a key group to the success of a revolt.

As this desperate young man went about his chores, the rest of the world was becoming aware that the deadlock in the cabinet had been broken. A radio operator on Okinawa wrote down a radio message beamed in English from Tokyo by Domei News Agency at 2:49 P.M.:

FLASH FLASH TOKYO AUGUST 14—IT IS LEARNED THAT AN IMPERIAL MESSAGE ACCEPTING THE POTSDAM PROCLAMATION IS FORTHCOMING SOON.

The message did not come as the day passed, but the United States knew that the end was near and issued instructions accordingly.

On Okinawa, units of the Eleventh Airborne Division continued landing. On August 11, they had been alerted in the Philippines to move out immediately for the Ryukyus. From Lipa Airfield in northern Luzon, planes flew northwest in a continuous stream toward Yontan and Kadena airports on Okinawa. By now most of the division was bivouacked on the island. All units were advised that Japan was the next stop.

In the Pacific Ocean, Halsey's heaving warships still prowled off the shores of Honshu and Shikoku. An air strike was held up as planes loaded bombs on the flight deck.

In base headquarters at Oppama Airfield south of Tokyo, Japanese fighter pilots gathered at the summons of their commandant. The officer appeared to be ill as he stood shakily before them using his desk as support. None of the pilots was prepared for what he told them:

"The surrender orders may be announced at any moment. . . . Order must be maintained at this base. There may be hot-heads who will refuse to accept the decision to surrender. . . . Remember—and never forget it—His Majesty's orders come before anything else."

The men were absolutely stunned. Though they knew the war was tearing Japan apart, they had not expected the end to come in this way, on this day. The pilots went out the door and across the field in shock, disbelieving and yet knowing the awful truth.

On Tinian, far to the south, B-29's again were being loaded for another night of destruction over the Home Islands, against the possibility that the Japanese would not surrender. Two cities were marked for fire bombing that night, the night of the fourteenth. The Americans were taking no chances on letting the Japanese reconsider.

◆ ◆ ◆

Soviet tank columns slashed across the flat plains of Manchuria against increasingly disorganized resistance as the Soviets rushed to acquire real estate and put in claims for postwar rights.

At Hsian on the edge of the Gobi Desert, Gus Krause was alerted to expect thirty-six OSS men bound on a special mission. He had no idea what they intended to do.

Krause had problems of his own. He sent a telegram to Kunming outlining the latest intelligence estimates from his own men in the field. He knew that the Japanese were about to collapse. He also knew something else, something that promised to shatter all dreams of peace in the Far East.

NOW APPEARS ALL FIELD TEAMS FACE CONFLICT WITH COMMUNISTS IN TRYING TO CARRY OUT ORDERS TO OCCUPY CITIES ON JAP SURRENDER AND SEIZE RECORDS. TEAMS IN POCKET SAY REDS BAR ENTRANCE INTO HANKOW, PENGPU, AND SUCHOW. LEOPARD FACES REDS ON WAY TO TAIYUAN. KELLIS FINDS SOME REDS NEAR PEIPING. LION HAS TANGLED WITH REDS. HOUND REPORTED 100,000 REDS NEAR HIS AREA. REQUEST INSTRUCTIONS ON WHAT ACTION TEAMS SHOULD TAKE. SUGGEST THAT IF TEAMS MUST FIGHT REDS TO CARRY OUT ORDERS THEY BE WITHDRAWN TO HSIAN. SINCERELY FEEL TEAMS SHOULD NOT RISK THEIR LIVES IN CONFLICT WITH REDS. FEELING IN NORTH CHINA IS CIVIL WAR WILL START IMMEDIATELY AFTER JAP CAPITULATION. PLEASE ADVISE SOONEST.

In Tokyo, Kenji Hatanaka arrived at Eastern Army District headquarters. He went to General Seiichi Tanaka's office to ask the general for his support in an uprising. Tanaka listened to the young major as he expounded on the necessity for action: "The government and the military leaders have decided to terminate the war—a decision which I cannot accept as things stand now. My idea is that we should establish ourselves within the palace, sever communications with the outside, and give assistance to the Emperor in a final effort to retrieve the situation. I have already gotten in touch with the Imperial Guards Division and have made the necessary arrangements. I would like you to take part in the plan."

Tanaka was aghast. He thundered at Hatanaka: "Go back to your barracks and stop this ridiculous scheme. Do what you're told and accept what your leaders say. The war is over."

Hatanaka stormed out of the office and went ahead with his next step. Shortly after four o'clock, he appeared at the room of Lieutenant Colonel Masataka Ida, another of Anami's protégés. Hatanaka and Ida were close friends. Ida was the weaker of the two, the more easily moved. Hatanaka counted on this fact. He repeated the speech he had given earlier to Tanaka. But Ida had changed his mind about the coup and turned him down flat. He declared it was "too late for such an adventure."

Hatanaka took it surprisingly well. "All right, I'll do my best and leave the rest to Providence." They parted cordially.

The major kept raking over the ashes of the fire of rebellion. It looked impossible to get any cooperation as the actual surrender neared, but he was persistent.

Convinced that rebellion was no longer a major threat, the Kempei Tai secret police relaxed their guard. Since Takeshita, Ida and other senior officers appeared to have lost heart, Colonel Tsukamoto and his superiors paid little attention to Kenji Hatanaka as he frantically sought support.

THIRTEEN

The Rebellion

Early on the evening of the fourteenth, Major Kenji Hatanaka's search for supporters brought success. Jiro Shiizaki, a colleague at the Ministry, had always supported him. Another who finally agreed to participate was Major Hidemasa Koga, the son-in-law and next-door neighbor of the deposed Premier Hideki Tojo. Father of an eleven-month-old boy, he now served in the Imperial Guards Division, which protected the Emperor.

For the past two months, Koga had worked long days constructing a new air-raid shelter for the Imperial family. When it was finished the young major stood at a personal crossroads. Because of the pending coup, he was torn between his friendships with other officers and concern about his own family.

On the afternoon of the thirteenth, the handsome cavalry officer had gone to Tojo's home to see his family. Mrs. Tojo saw him ride up on a motorcycle and run to the door. He burst in and went to the general's study at the left of the entrance hall. Since General Tojo was occupied with a guest, Koga went on into the back of the house where his wife and child waited.

He scooped the baby up in his arms and asked his wife to follow him into the family air-raid shelter. There he spoke urgently: "I want you to go to Kyushu with the baby. You'll be safer there with my family." His wife listened quietly as he added forcefully, "I want you to go as soon as possible." He held the baby close, then put him down. Moving to his wife, he asked, "Do you have my hair and nail clippings?" She was startled because, in Japan, these things are left to relatives by the dead. When she nodded he continued: "There are times when one must do one's duty. I can't avoid the troubles ahead." He embraced her and quickly broke away. On the way to the front door, Mrs. Tojo appeared with a box of sweets. Thanking her, he looked into Tojo's study once more. Seeing the general still engaged, Koga merely waved and hurried out the door. He had been home only ten minutes.

When General Tojo came out of his study, he knew from the stricken faces of his wife and daughter that his son-in-law was in trouble. His wife asked him to talk to Koga before he got into bad trouble. Not aware of what was happening at the War Ministry, Tojo decided to go there and find out the reason for Koga's strange actions. He called for a car and went off to Ichigaya.

When he returned at about nine o'clock that night, he seemed pleased. After officers had briefed him on the general situation, he had found Koga and talked persuasively to him about the future. He warned him to think carefully before involving himself in a coup. The son-in-law promised to stay calm, and Tojo left feeling that Koga would behave. He was wrong. Other forces were also working on the youthful patriot. Under extreme pressure from fellow officers at the palace, Koga joined the revolt.

Major Hatanaka had been talking to officers in the Imperial Guards Division for several days. He sensed that they would be sure to follow him if he could prevail on the commanding general, Mori, to cast his lot with the rebels. Though Mori had so far resisted all overtures, Hatanaka planned one last appeal to him.

He definitely could count on Jiro Shiizaki and Koga. Other officers in the Guards Division were easily swayed. Hatanaka felt encouraged enough to proceed. He got on the phone and began calling conspirators into action.

Later, at ten o'clock that evening, he and Jiro Shiizaki went to see Colonel Ida in his bedroom at the War Ministry in the hope of persuading that vacillating officer to help his friends. Ida was morose, brooding over the past day's events. He had decided to commit suicide. Earlier he had gone around to his co-workers at the Ministry urging them to do likewise. Now he lay in bed staring into space.

Hatanaka burst in upon his reverie. "Ida, all the members of the Imperial Guards have agreed with us except General Mori. Koga is too young to persuade him, so come and talk to him."

Ida sat up straight. He thought for a moment, and then asked: "What will you do if I can't convince him, I mean, if he doesn't agree with us? What will you do then?"

"If Mori doesn't agree with us, I'll give up the coup, but we should at least try."

Ida was torn. His friendship with Hatanaka went back several years, and he was very fond of the ascetic-looking officer. They had spent much time together during the war and had even joined in discussion groups under a certain Professor Haraizumi, a man of great influence on the younger element at the War Ministry. Haraizumi preached on the nature of the Emperor system and on the obligations of the military in fostering and nurturing that way of life. He felt it was the sworn duty of the officers to uphold the Emperor and to carry out Imperial orders unhesitatingly. Now Hatanaka was asking Ida to upset the expressed wishes of the Emperor.

The rationale was simple. Because men around Hirohito had forced his hand, the younger officers were only seeking to rid the government of this subversive group. If the Emperor had been beguiled by men like Kido and Suzuki, the military did not have to honor a proclamation from the Throne. It made sense to Hatanaka and his followers, and now they wanted Ida to come with them.

Colonel Ida excused himself and went out to talk with others in the War Ministry. When he came back, he tried to reason with

Hatanaka: "It's difficult to convince even our group of friends around here. It will be more difficult to persuade General Mori." He repeated his first question: "In that case, what will you do?"

Shiizaki broke in: "I'm sure God will help us. We must attempt a coup."

Hatanaka added, "If Mori doesn't agree with us, I'll kill him."

Ida was shocked. His fears rising, he then asked about General Tanaka, another in the group of generals the rebels needed.

Hatanaka airily dismissed this issue. "It's not positive yet but if the Imperial Guards Division goes, all of the Army will follow us. Of that I'm sure."

Ida instinctively felt the danger of the situation but he did not want to desert his old friend. Though he knew that the coup was beginning on forlorn hopes, he gave in and agreed to go to General Mori. Hatanaka smiled happily as the two shook hands.

The one man who held the absolute power to make any coup succeed was involved at this time in drafting the Emperor's speech to the people, to be given on the following day. Closeted with the cabinet, General Anami was engaged in a running verbal battle to soften the language of the declaration. Even at the end of the war, Anami was trying desperately to salvage the reputation of his army, to shift the blame for the country's defeat away from his men. His overriding concern was for the Emperor's safety, but as the last moments of the struggle approached, he was determined to word the proclamation so that the stigma would not fall on the Army.

When the cabinet discussions were finally over late in the evening, Anami was tired and utterly despondent. Burdened with a general's grief at surrendering his forces, at turning over his country to the enemy, he went to say goodbye to a man he deeply admired: Admiral Suzuki. Dressed in his braided and bemedaled uniform and wearing white gloves, Anami carried a box of cigars to the old man. He presented this gift and said, "I should have given you every assistance in this war, but I am afraid I have caused you a great deal of trouble instead."

Suzuki immediately grabbed the general's hand, and the two leaders stood looking at each other for a long moment. The Premier realized that Anami was offering his friendship, and was deeply moved by the gesture. "I fully appreciate your painful position," the old man said. "I have not yet lost hope for the future of Japan."

Anami agreed with that thought, then bowed and walked from the room. Tearfully, Suzuki watched the door close.

The War Minister left for his official residence near the center of the city. His public life was ended. The formalities had been concluded and he could lay down his sword and title.

When Anami reached home, his servants noticed his somber mood. He went straight to his first-floor bedroom and ordered some sake wine and cheese brought in. Stripping off his coat, he sat down on a tatami mat and wrote with a brush on a large sheet of paper. The room was quiet, the atmosphere tranquil. Outside the house the air was sultry, the streets empty.

Shortly before midnight, the now-committed Ida arrived at the headquarters of the Guards Division just inside the walls of the Imperial Palace grounds. The building was crowded with soldiers running and shouting through the corridors. General Mori was inside his office talking to his brother-in-law, Colonel Shiraishi. Ida waited in the hallway with his fellow conspirators. Shiizaki was there. So was Koga. So was Major Sadakichi Ishihara, an officer just recently transferred to Tokyo. A highly emotional man, he wholeheartedly supported the coup.

Hatanaka joined the group just as Mori announced that he would talk to them. It was twelve thirty on the morning of the fifteenth when the small group of officers crowded into Mori's room to confront their commanding officer. The fate of their coup might hinge upon his answer. Mori was in a terrible position.

Ida, acting as spokesman, asked the general for his cooperation. Mori began a monologue on his own philosophy of life, and avoided a direct answer. He was obviously stalling.

Hatanaka listened for a few moments, then impatiently turned toward the door. Interrupting Mori, he said, "Ida, I must go out as I have something to do. Please look after my affairs while I am away." He disappeared, leaving Ida to spar with the general.

Hatanaka hurried over to the War Ministry to talk with Colonel Takeshita, who had already given up his attempt to convince Anami to lead an uprising. After the news of the surrender, Takeshita had retreated to his own quarters and begun drinking. With his fellow officers, he tried to forget the calamitous events of the afternoon. At 12:45 A.M., Hatanaka baited him once again:

"The second regiment has already entered the palace grounds with their colors and will occupy the Imperial Palace at 2:00 A.M. All the regimental commanders have agreed with us. Everything is going well."

Takeshita listened as the excited Hatanaka continued: "Right now we are talking with Mori. He'll agree soon, so please help us."

He looked at Takeshita pleadingly but the colonel hastened to dissuade him: "It's too late. We would need the agreement of four generals, Anami, Tanaka, Mori and Umezu. That's impossible now." In effect, Takeshita was saying the revolt was doomed.

The two argued over this point for some minutes. Then Hatanaka broached the one favor he wanted of Takeshita: "When the coup at the palace is a success, ask Anami to come in with us. Go and ask him to do that." Takeshita agreed to at least talk to his brother-in-law, and Hatanaka went back to the palace grounds optimistic about the possibilities for that night.

Takeshita left his quarters hurriedly and rode to the official residence of the War Minister, where Anami sat in his bedroom. The brothers-in-law greeted each other warmly. After writing two letters, Anami had sat down before a low table and started to drink from a small cup. Takeshita began to tell him of the situation at the palace but sensed that the general's mind was on other things. He stopped in mid-sentence.

His suspicions were confirmed when Anami said, "I'm think-ing of committing suicide." He spoke matter-of-factly as though he had mentioned the weather;

Takeshita nodded. "I thought you would. But couldn't you wait until later?"

Anami shook his head vigorously. "No, my mind is made up." He went on to say that he had thought of waiting for a few days till the anniversary of his second son's death, but had decided not to. "Besides, this is the anniversary of my father's death and it would be fitting to join him now."

The two men toasted each other with sake and talked of their families and personal affairs. It was 1:45 A.M.

In the center of the city, the deadly debate continued. Ida and General Mori had talked now for over an hour and the general had so far evaded a commitment. At one thirty Hatanaka rejoined the discussion, which now took its final, fateful turn.

Mori had run out of arguments. He looked across at the assembled rebels and suggested one last alternative: "I understand your position perfectly. Frankly, I am moved by your arguments. Now I'll go over to the Meiji Shrine and ask God's will." This was his final escape route, chosen to delay the conspirators and fight for time. Since he was known for his very religious beliefs, it would be perfectly normal for him to want to meditate before making any decision.

Mori watched the men across from him for a reaction. Beside him, Colonel Shiraishi shifted uncomfortably as he watched Hat-anaka and the others weigh the remark.

Mori himself broke the silence. "Ida, why don't you go and ask my aide, Mizutani, what he thinks of the plan." Ida rose from his chair and walked out the door. Left in the room were Mori, Shiraishi and just two rebels. Hatanaka, dripping with sweat from his hurried trip across town, stood before Mori's desk. At his right was another officer, a Mister X, whose identity cannot be revealed even today because of what happened in the next moments.

Hatanaka had wasted several hours of valuable time trying to plead with Mori. It was 2:00 A.M. and his patience had run out. He asked the general for a definite statement. Mori had none.

The two rebels acted almost simultaneously. Hatanaka pulled a revolver out of his holster and fired into the body of Mori. His companion ripped his sword out of its scabbard and slashed downward through the general's left collarbone. Mori was dead in seconds. As his body slid off the chair onto the floor, the horror-stricken Shiraishi leaped up to grapple with the murderers. The man with the sword saw him coming and cut viciously at his head. The blade caught Shiraishi on the right side of his neck and continued through to his left ear. As his body toppled forward onto the floor a huge geyser of blood spurted out from the trunk and spattered the room. Held to the torso by one shred of skin, his head lay at an angle to the rest of the body. The killers looked down at the bloody corpses for a moment and then walked out into the hall.

Hearing the gunshot, Ida rushed up to Mori's room, where he met Hatanaka coming out, holding the revolver in his right hand. Hatanaka's face was clouded with sorrow. In a trembling voice he tried to explain: "I had no time to argue so I killed him. I couldn't help it." Hatanaka looked at his friend for sympathy.

At that moment, Colonel Mizutani grasped Ida's hands in his and urged him to go at once to General Tanaka for support. Ida hurried to the headquarters of the Eastern District Army. The rebel who had decapitated Shiraishi left the palace to seek support from units in the Tokyo suburbs.

Hatanaka recovered his composure and instructed his men to issue orders forged with General Mori's seal. It was 2:15 A.M. With Mori gone, Hatanaka could seize the palace and move to the next objective.

He had learned that the Emperor was going to report to the nation at noon that day. It was rumored that Hirohito had made a recording which would carry his voice to the people and advise them to lay down their arms and obey the will of the Imperial House. Hatanaka had to find that record and destroy it before it was too late. The most important task before him now was to ascertain its hiding place and seize it. Since the record must be somewhere inside the palace grounds, the rebel leader planned to interrogate members of the Imperial Household.

The phonograph disc was indeed just a stone's throw away from Hatanaka. It had been cut shortly before midnight in the Administration Building in the middle of the palace compound. Hirohito had arrived there at 11:25 P.M. and had been greeted by several officials from NHK broadcasting station. As they watched, the Emperor spoke into a microphone. When he finished his short speech, the recording was played back. Hirohito was dissatisfied with the quality and insisted on making two more. When the final recording was made, he returned to his residence. At 12:05 A.M., the Emperor was in bed.

The record was given to Yoshihiro Tokugawa, the Court Chamberlain, who took it to his own room in the Administration Building and placed it in a wall safe. Then he went out to the switchboard to check for any air-raid warnings in the area. Satisfied that everything was all right, Tokugawa relaxed and entered into a conversation with the broadcasting people who were finishing up their chores before leaving.

At 12:50 A.M. he was informed that the Emperor was asleep. At the same instant a conditional air-raid alert sounded. Tokugawa was not concerned that bombs would fall on Tokyo that night, so he went to his room and fell asleep. By 1:30 A.M. the building was quiet.

Within thirty minutes General Mori died and the rebels went into action. The radio officials, who had finally packed up their equipment and started for home, were stopped at the palace gate. Soldiers shepherded them to a small building near the main entrance where they joined others already scooped up in the dragnet put out by Hatanaka.

By 2:15 A.M., seventeen people were being forcibly held in a small room. Their fate was uncertain.

Across from the palace grounds, in the heart of Tokyo, Colonel Ida was getting nowhere in his fight to win over General Tanaka. When Ida came into the Eastern Army Headquarters, he found that officers there already knew about the coup; Major Koga had called a few minutes before, tearfully begging for support. He had been almost unintelligible as he sobbed out his plea. Now, when Ida repeated the same request for help, he was refused with a flat "Absolutely not."

Ida was shaken, and his own resolve began to diminish. Officers at Tanaka's headquarters convinced Ida to try to dissuade the rebels. He agreed and left for the palace. It was 2:45 A.M. The first breach in the rebel ranks had occurred.

By now, the palace grounds were filled with noise and excitement. Because of the air-raid alert, all lights had been shut off, and flashlights stabbed through the blackness as soldiers hurried about in unfamiliar surroundings. Inside the Imperial Household Agency, Chamberlain Tokugawa was rudely awakened by an assistant, who whispered: "The buildings are surrounded by soldiers." Tokugawa leaped up and ran outside with a flashlight. In the corridor, he came upon a group of servants running downstairs to the "Safe Room," an air-raid shelter in the basement. He immediately thought of Marquis Kido, a prized target for any plotters against the Government, and gave orders for his assistant to go to the Marquis' room and bring him down to the underground sanctuary.

Upstairs, Kido had already found out about the coup. Dozing in his study, he had been awakened by an aide who pounded on the door and begged him to go to the resident doctor's room to hide from approaching soldiers. The almost timid-looking Kido balked at such deception and said he would stay and face the consequences. When the aide insisted, the Marquis finally agreed and went with him. Moments later, he hurried back to his own room, ran to his desk, tore up state papers within reach, and flushed them down the toilet. Then he looked for a way to avoid the rebels.

At this point, Tokugawa's urgent summons reached him and he went down to the great vault in the basement. He walked into the stifling, airless room shortly after three o'clock and began to pace the floor with other members of the Imperial staff.

Kido was furious at this attempt to upset the surrender but was convinced that it would come to no good. He reasoned that word of surrender had already gone out to the United States, and that the Emperor's voice would so inform the people tomorrow. The soldiers could not win. Dripping with sweat, the bespectacled Marquis listened as the excited rebels searched for the phonograph record. If they should find him in the cellar, he would die quickly.

Meanwhile, Major Hatanaka had no new information as to the whereabouts of the recording. None of the seventeen men imprisoned near the main gate would say anything about it. As he stood in the woods near the Emperor's residence, his disillusioned compatriot Colonel Ida approached him out of the darkness. The sad look on his face warned Hatanaka what to expect. Ida spread his hands and blurted out: "I tried to persuade Headquarters but I couldn't. In fact they were quite cool to me. Hatanaka, withdraw these troops or you'll have to fight the entire Eastern District Army."

The rebel eyed him calmly and answered: "I'm not afraid to fight. We have occupied the Imperial Palace and the Emperor is in our custody. Moreover, we have hostages including Shimomura, the Chief of the Cabinet Information Board. We have nothing to worry about."

Losing his temper, Ida shouted, "Nonsense! It is impossible to run the Guards Division without General Mori and he is dead. So don't be stupid." As Hatanaka bridled at this remark, Ida quickly shifted his attack. "Withdraw the troops before dawn and together we'll take the responsibility for the coup. My dear Hatanaka, tomorrow morning this will all be a dream. People will forgive us and pass it off as midsummer madness."

Hatanaka bit his lower lip, as he always did when frustrated. His disheveled hair was matted on his sweating brow, his uniform was soaked from exertion in the humid August weather. Ida waited for the pale, almost feminine-looking rebel chieftain to answer. Hatanaka finally said, "Go and ask Anami what I should do. I'll wait for your return." The two parted in the moonlit forest clearing.

With Ida off seeking Anami, the chief conspirators, Hatanaka, Shiizaki and Koga, met at three thirty to plan their final strategy. The record was not yet in their hands. Koga ordered a soldier to bring in the manager of the broadcasting station. That terrified man told Koga the record was somewhere in the Imperial Household Agency just a short distance away. Immediately the search centered on that building, where Marquis Kido cowered in an underground shelter and wondered what his fate would be.

As flashlights played about the wooded areas of the palace enclave, Hatanaka strove to keep the rebellion going. Ida had left believing that the rebels would surely disband shortly, but Hatanaka had second thoughts. Though time was running out for him, he might just be able to find the record before dawn. With that in his hands, the surrender could be thwarted. Otherwise he had little cause for cheer. Ida no longer was an ally. General Tanaka would not be talked into giving support. No word had come from Anami. Even within the palace walls, dissension was breaking out among regimental commanders who had sided with the conspirators.

One of them, Colonel Haga, had gone along with the plan because Hatanaka assured him that General Anami was coming to the palace to personally persuade Hirohito to reconsider the decision to surrender. When Anami did not appear by three o'clock, Haga became suspicious and confronted the ringleaders. "Where is Anami?"

Hatanaka stalled for time. "I'll make a call and see if he's on his way." After he left, Major Koga walked into the room and Haga continued his questioning. No one had told him of Mori's death. Koga could not carry on the deception and confessed: "General Mori is dead and we want you to take charge of the Guards Division."

Haga was stunned at the news. "Who killed him? Why? I'm sure you know the story."

Koga proceeded to tell him everything.

By four o'clock Hatanaka was losing his grip on his men. His soldiers were bedeviled in their search by the protracted shutdown of electricity in the Imperial Household Agency. Flashlights illuminated very little in the cluttered rooms of the huge building. Soldiers repeatedly passed by the door leading to the small group of men huddled in the cellar. In that refuge, Kido and the others spoke in whispers as the noise of rebellion ebbed and flowed around the corridors. They were soaked with perspiration and parched by thirst. But at least they were alive.

Few of the sleeping citizens of Tokyo were aware of the palace crisis, though the stillness was occasionally broken by gunfire. In his bedroom General Anami could hear firing from the direction of the palace, and said to his brother-in-law Takeshita, "For that also, I will offer my life." He had sat for the last three hours talking and drinking. Takeshita mentioned that the general was possibly drinking too much to perform the traditional suicide with a knife. Anami reassured him that he would have a steady hand. "The wine will make my veins dilate better and the blood will flow more freely. There is nothing to worry about," he said. Anami continued talking about his family.

Across from the palace, about a quarter mile away, Kempei Tai headquarters too was well aware of the situation at the palace. Makoto Tsukamoto, the colonel who had been recalled from Formosa only a short time before, was sleeping when gunfire sounded. Kempei officers wanted to call out their own troops to march against the rebels but Tsukamoto feared such action would only cause further bloodshed. If the military police tried to disarm a hot-headed, fully armed force, the greatest slaughter might occur.

Because of his visit to the War Ministry on the eleventh, Tsukamoto knew that Colonel Ida must be involved in the violent
demonstration. He resolved on two courses of action. First, the
Kempei soldiers would be maintained in a state of readiness to
prevent a spread of the revolt beyond the Imperial compound.
Second, he could send for Colonel Ida's father to speak with his
son and talk him out of the coup. A messenger was dispatched to
the countryside while Tsukamoto held on in Tokyo, awaiting the
arrival of the mediator.

By this time, Ida himself had become a mediator. Rebuffed by
General Tanaka, he had already told Hatanaka to disband his
men by dawn. At 4:00 A.M. he arrived at the single-story bun-
galow of the War Minister to speak to Anami about the situation
at the palace.

He found Anami and Takeshita in the bedroom and immediately guessed what was about to happen. Anami had wrapped a
white cloth about his abdomen and put on a white shirt given to
him by the Emperor. Ida burst into tears and cried, "Let me die
with you." Anami walked over to him and slapped his face hard,
then slapped him again several times. The two fell into each other's arms and wept. Straightening up, Anami gazed at his young
protégé. "Live on after me and serve your country." He patted
the colonel's shoulder and asked him to sit and drink some wine.

Together with Colonel Takeshita, the men toasted each other
and talked quietly for half an hour. At four thirty, Takeshita was
called out to speak with a messenger who had arrived at the front
door. Ida got up and said goodbye to his commanding officer who
smiled sadly at him. Filled with grief, Ida went outside the house
and waited for a car to pick him up.

Inside, Anami moved quickly. He had wanted to die outdoors
on the ground in the manner of repentant sinners. But, since too
many people were around, he chose the only other alternative.
He walked out into the corridor, knelt down, and cut open his
stomach from left to right.

Takeshita found him a few seconds later. The general was still conscious and in terrible pain. Yet he was able to plunge the dagger into his neck just below the right ear. He remained kneeling in a spreading pool of blood.

For a moment Takeshita's instinct for the rebellion revived and he forgot his brother-in-law's agony. Running out onto the lawn, he found Ida and said, "Anami has committed *seppuku*. I can get his seals to use in the coup."

Ida was shocked. In disgust, he snorted, "Don't be silly," and Takeshita dropped the issue.

Behind them on the blood-soaked floor, General Anami writhed in pain. When some of his men approached him, Anami summoned his voice and croaked, "Get out of here. Get out." Within minutes the stricken general fell across the threshold of his bedroom and lay on his face.

Ida went on to the War Ministry while Takeshita went back to the room.

He was joined by Colonel Hayashi, Anami's secretary, and for a time the two watched the great body in its death throes. Then a phone rang. While Hayashi went to answer it, Takeshita rushed to Anami, picked up the dagger, and pushed it back into the neck wound. Still Anami did not die. Takeshita took the general's jacket, spread it over the huddled form on the floor, and then stepped back to watch in silence. The only sound was the heavy breathing of the unconscious War Minister. Minutes passed and the tableau remained frozen. Anami was dying hard.

While Anami bled, violence was being done elsewhere in the name of the Emperor. As in 1936, when soldiers hunted down men who opposed their plans, squads of fanatical men had gone out into the warm summer night to track down and slay men they thought were betraying Japan. There was no concerted plan. Hatanaka and his men at the palace had been in contact with various officers around Tokyo, and a loose scheme had been discussed. But the soldiers who walked the streets of the capital this night struck out at the officials of the Government in haphazard fashion. At widely separated points in the city, they moved in to kill.

The primary target was Premier Suzuki, the man held most responsible for the surrender. The first warning of danger came to Secretary Sakomizu as he lay in bed at the official residence of the Premier. He was exhausted after the ordeal of the Emperor's conference and the late-night wrangling over the wording of the surrender message to the Americans. At 11:30 P.M., he had gone to his room. Thirty minutes later, the Palace called to say that the Emperor had made the recording to be broadcast later that day. The last job was done.

Sakomizu's rest was interrupted once again by the arrival of another member of the Foreign Ministry, who discussed with him various problems associated with the text of the communiqué to the Allies. When that was done, Sakomizu went to sleep.

At 4:00 A.M. the chatter of a machine gun brought him to a puzzled alertness. The gunfire was outside the building and was accompanied by raucous shouting. The rebels thought they would find Suzuki inside, but earlier that night the old man had gone to his suburban home to get some well-earned rest. Sakomizu thought immediately of Suzuki and told an aide to call him. Fortunately, just two days before, a telephone had been installed in the Premier's private home.

The aide waited breathlessly as it rang several times. When the sleepy voice of the Premier answered, he blurted rapidly, "Your Excellency, soldiers are now attacking the Ministry. When they don't find you here, they'll come after you at your home. You must get away."

The cold chill of remembered nightmares seized the aged Premier. Only nine years before, his sleep had been rudely shattered by another band of fanatics such as these, and he had lived in dread since. As he thanked the man for calling, Suzuki wondered what he would do. He put down the telephone and stood listening. Then he ran to his bedroom and woke his wife, who followed him out the back door. The old warrior slipped out and ran hurriedly down an alley toward his chauffered automobile.

Within fifteen minutes, soldiers entered the house and confronted a terrified maid, who told them that the Prime Minister
was not home. The soldiers searched the rooms and then poured
gasoline around the kitchen. A match was dropped onto the floor
and a rush of flame leaped high. When the maid tried to pour water
on the blaze, an officer pushed her aside and threatened to kill her.
She retreated from the house as it burned brightly in the darkness.

Premier Suzuki rode in the dilapidated car through the quiet
streets of Tokyo with his aged wife and two servants. Looking
back, he could not see any pursuers nor could he see flames.
After about an hour he reached his sister's home and collapsed,
exhausted, into a chair. Assassins had missed him again.

They had also just missed Baron Hiranuma. At that moment
the aged statesman lay cowering behind furniture in a building near his blazing home. Outside, soldiers stood around the
inferno, laughing in the belief that their quarry had just been
consumed in the fire.

Back at the palace, the rebellion foundered. The phonograph record still remained in its hiding place. Chamberlain Tokugawa,
righteously incensed at this invasion of Imperial property, was
finally seized by some of Hatanaka's men at about 4:30 A.M. The
Chamberlain was so angry at the effrontery of the rebels that he
shouted, "Your actions tonight are deplorable." For this remark, a
soldier punched him in the face.

Tokugawa was questioned for thirty minutes on the whereabouts of Marquis Kido and the precious recording. Beneath his
feet the Marquis paced the floor of the vault and wondered how
long he could remain free. Tokugawa told the officers nothing,
denying any knowledge of the record's hiding-place in a loud
voice so that his own people would understand what to say to the
searchers. At 5:00 A.M. he was set free. From watching the troops
running around the rooms and listening to their conversation,
Tokugawa got the impression that they were losing heart, that the
spirit of the revolt was fading. He guessed correctly.

Hatanaka's authority had collapsed. Only shortly before, Colonel Haga, the man who was supposed to take control of the Guards Division, lost his temper with the ringleaders. Heartsick at the news that General Mori had been shot down, Haga realized that he had been duped, and screamed, "Get out of here." Koga, Ishihara, Shiizaki and Hatanaka got out. Koga and Ishihara were disconsolate. Both of them had been appalled when Mori died, and since then nothing had gone right. Ishihara, in particular, had become almost hysterical as the night wore on, and was of little help.

Hatanaka had one last card to play. He took several men with him and raced to the broadcasting studios of NHK, the government radio station. There he went to Studio Twelve and pointed his gun at Morio Tateno, a radio announcer on duty.

"Let me speak on the radio at the five A.M. news hour."

Tateno refused, saying, "You have to get the permission of the Eastern Army Headquarters." Because of the air-raid alert, the Army automatically took control of radio broadcasts.

The furious Hatanaka berated Tateno, who could do nothing but repeat the statement. No one could go on the air without sanction from General Tanaka.

As the two stood there arguing, the telephone rang. Hatanaka picked it up. General Tanaka's office had traced him to the radio station. Hatanaka identified himself and listened quietly as the voice on the other end urged him to give up the rebellion. The disheveled ringleader stood with the receiver in his left hand, the revolver in his right. Finally he broke in: "I want only five minutes. We want to let the nation know what the young officers think." When the voice on the phone refused his request, Hatanaka hung up.

He was defeated. There was nothing else he could do to stop the surrender. As he stood in the studio, the Japanese reply was on its way to Switzerland. Harry Truman was sitting in his office at the White House waiting patiently for some word. General Anami, Hatanaka's beloved leader, lay on the floor of his bedroom bleeding to death. The Emperor slept on, undisturbed by the frenzied search for his recording. Hatanaka fought alone.

He wiped tears from his eyes and walked out the door of the studio, muttering to his aides, "We did our best. Let's go back to the palace."

Hatanaka's forces had broken up while he was away. General Sei-ichi Tanaka, commander of the Eastern District Army, had come to settle the crisis. After hearing reports from his officers, he had decided to make a personal appearance on the palace grounds to persuade the troops to disband. On the way there, Tanaka sat back in his seat, his eyes closed, his mind burning with indignation at the young officers who had perpetrated the incident. As the car sped around to the main gate, Tanaka wondered where to begin his delicate job of diplomacy. He finally settled on the First Guards Regiment as a likely trouble spot.

His choice was fortunate, for that large unit was just about to join with Hatanaka. Troops were marching out the gate in full battle dress as Tanaka's automobile pulled up.

The general leaned out of the window and shouted, "Oh, it's you, Watanabe," to the regimental commander, who was fastening his helmet as he walked down the steps of his headquarters. "I'm lucky to be on time. Your orders are false. Call back the troops."

Whether or not Watanabe knew the truth, he immediately obeyed the general's command. His soldiers returned to quarters and the very last reinforcements for the rebels put down their guns and were dispersed to barracks.

Tanaka went on to stamp out the fire. He found one of the hapless conspirators, Major Ishihara, and put him under arrest. "You fellows have really done it," he shouted. He heaped invective on the distraught officer, who cringed, wild-eyed, under the attack. Colonel Fuwa, Tanaka's assistant, sat on Ishihara's left and watched him closely because he feared that violence might erupt at any minute. The rebel was trembling, hysterical, capable of striking at his tormentors. As Ishihara was led off to jail, Tanaka turned away from him in disgust.

The general walked on through the wooded grounds and spoke to knots of soldiers, urging them to break up the gathering and go back to their barracks. He cajoled, threatened, prodded and ordered. The troops were sullen, tired and frustrated. But they listened and the momentum swung to Tanaka's side. As the first streaks of morning appeared in the sky, the rebellion petered out. The coup was dead.

In the bedroom of the War Minister, Anami's life flickered. He had been unconscious for over two hours, yet his breathing continued in an irregular, noisy manner. His body moved about on the floor, thrashing, writhing in the welter of blood from his wounds. Men came and went. They stared at the figure in silence. Some cried. All were transfixed as they saw a proud man attempting to die.

As Anami's life ebbed, another military man made a decision. Far to the southwest of Tokyo, at Oita Airbase, the duty officer, Lieutenant Tanaka, made a telephone call to Captain Takashi Miyazaki, aide-de-camp to Fleet Commander Admiral Ugaki. He informed the sleepy officer that Ugaki planned to take his own life by flying a suicide mission against the American ships off Okinawa. As commander of the Kyushu kamikaze forces, the admiral felt it proper to follow the example of his own men and dive into an enemy vessel. With the war ending, he had no desire to live on.

Miyazaki dressed hurriedly and raced across the runway as sunlight broke through the darkness. He arrived at the admiral's quarters in a hillside cave. The fortunes of war had driven him into this primitive lair, which served as both office and bedroom.

Ugaki lay fully dressed on a cot. Miyazaki stood before him and collected his breath before speaking. "The duty officer tells me you have ordered a sortie of carrier bombers. May I ask your plans, sir?"

The admiral smiled up at him, knowing full well that Miyazaki already knew what he intended that day. He said nothing, just continued to smile.

In Tokyo, Hirohito woke up at twenty minutes before seven. Only then was he informed of the drastic developments of the long night. He asked that General Tanaka be brought in to report on the coup. That redoubtable warrior was supervising the last stages of the withdrawal of dissident elements from the compound. At 7:00 A.M. he met a member of the Household staff on the palace grounds; he presented him with his calling card, and inquired as to the Emperor's health. Assured that he was well, Tanaka offered, "The rebellion is over."

And it was. Peace came once more to the spacious acreage in the center of Tokyo. Early risers going to work on the fateful morning of August 15 could not possibly imagine the drama that had gripped the sacred ground in the past hours. On the surface everything looked normal. But in the forests lurked three men who would have turned the city into a battleground had they succeeded in their plan. Hatanaka, Shiizaki and Koga had so far eluded arrest but they knew their hours of freedom were numbered. Tanaka let them stay out of sight, assuming that they would probably commit suicide.

At the War Minister's home, nothing had changed. Anami still clung to life. He had been unconscious for nearly three hours. When Colonel Shinaji Kobayashi, from the staff of General Sugiyama, came to see the dying man, he was sickened at the prolonged struggle he witnessed. Though others had wanted to speed Anami's death, none actually dared interfere. Kobayashi acted immediately. He ordered everyone from the room except one military physician, to whom he gave explicit instructions. The doctor agreed and opened his medical kit. From it he drew a hypodermic needle. He approached the thrashing form, bent down, and inserted the syringe in an arm. General Korechika Anami died in seconds.

When assistants cleansed the body, bloodstained papers that had lain under Anami for hours were revealed. One read:

Believing firmly that our sacred land shall never perish, I—with my death—humbly apologize to the Emperor for the great crime.

Anami had offered himself in payment for the mistakes of the Army.

FOURTEEN

Peace on Earth

As General Anami's men prepared his body for cremation, half a world away the President of the United States was standing in the Oval Room of the White House. The office was a bedlam as photographers snapped pictures of the group centered around Truman's desk. Generals, admirals, statesmen, all listened as the Chief Executive, cool-looking in a summer suit, read from a paper.

"I have just received a note from the Japanese Government in reply to the message forwarded to that Government by the Secretary of State on August 11. I deem this reply a full acceptance of the Potsdam Declaration which specifies the unconditional surrender of Japan. In the reply there is no qualification. . . ."

The man who had insisted on qualifications lay dead on a bedroom floor in Tokyo. While his servants mourned, America went wild with joy.

In the villages, towns and main cities, emotions spilled over into a reckless pursuit of pleasure. Times Square was choked with a surging mob of carefree human beings, who kissed and laughed, drank and made love in the midst of bright lights blazing again after a long war.

In the nation's capital, crowds milled around the White House and waited for Truman to appear. He did so, and made a short speech to the masses lining the railings. They cheered his every sentence, then applauded him as he moved back inside to call his mother in Independence, Missouri. The excited throngs spread to the downtown area and proceeded to lose their inhibitions. Soldiers jumped into passing cars to kiss unprotesting women. In front of the *Washington Post* newspaper building, a soldier and a girl got out of a taxi and started to take off their clothes, to the encouragement of an enthusiastic group of well-wishers shouting, "Take it off!" "All the way!" "'Atta girl!" The couple stripped completely, then dressed in each other's clothes; the girl put on shorts, pants and shirt while the soldier struggled into bra, panties, slip and dress, to the applause of the bystanders. Then the two exhibitionists jumped into the cab and were swallowed up in the dusk.

Though few cities could claim such ardent demonstrations of joy, the pattern of behavior was similar in many places. That night the G.I. was king and he knew it. The police in most places tried to be as inconspicuous as possible. Their orders were to maintain some semblance of peace but to avoid excessive controls.

In San Francisco, more control was desperately needed. In this city surrounded by Navy installations, the news of surrender had come just before four o'clock in the afternoon. The Navy immediately took over. Sailors got drunk and civilians joined them. By evening the celebration was out of hand.

Car after car was stolen and driven by crazed men who tore recklessly through the busy streets. Several people were struck down and killed while the motorists drove on, oblivious to the horror behind them. Young women found that being out among celebrating countrymen could be disastrous. People stood by horrified as at least six girls were forcibly thrown to the sidewalks, held down and repeatedly raped. No one moved to their aid. Policemen watching the assaults looked the other way, afraid to confront the liquor-sodden servicemen. Windows were smashed in the downtown shopping area, liquor stores were looted clean. A pedestrian walking down a side street was hit on the head by a basketful of bottles loosed from an upper-story window, and died of a fractured skull. Well into the morning hours, San Francisco continued in the grip of rioters who knew no authority. During the nightlong celebration of peace in that city, twelve people died.

In Manila, Filipinos groped about in the ruins of their once beautiful city. Laid waste only months before by the savage block-by-block defense of the trapped Japanese, the capital of the Philippines was slowly being rebuilt by the energies of its people who, more than any other, knew the horrors of war in the Pacific. Among the shouts of joy that day were the muted sobs of those mourning their dead still beneath the ruins.

On the outskirts of the city stood Bilibid Prison, the infamous home of countless American and Filipino captives during the Japanese occupation. The sighs of these hopeless souls still haunted its cavernous interior. So many had wasted away there in body and mind in the grim days after Bataan. So few had survived.

Now, in August 1945, Bilibid housed as prisoners the former captors, Japanese soldiers. Little by little since February, these emaciated remnants of General Yamashita's huge army had been flushed from hiding places in the formidable hill country; now they wandered around the courtyards and corridors of Bilibid in a continual daze. Though happy to be alive and eating sufficiently well, they felt that they could never go home again. Since capture was a disgrace, most of the prisoners thought their families and friends in Japan would treat them with contempt if ever they set foot in the Home Islands. They were the living dead.

The surrender news came in a paper brought into the jail by a soldier. The Japanese crowded around an interpreter, who read the startling information to a growing group of prisoners. Some stared at him disbelievingly. Others broke down into loud sobbing and wandered away into the cool shadows of the yard. It was almost too much to comprehend. They could go home, but to what?

North of the prison, in the remote fastnesses of Luzon, the American foot soldier still held his rifle ready. For months the

Thirty-second Division had pursued the stubborn enemy through the jungle and mountains, trying to beat the last resistance out of him. The Thirty-second had been killing Japanese for three long years. By August of 1945, the end was in sight, but the killing went on.

At 8:00 A.M. on the fifteenth, Truman's surrender announcement came through to the soldiers on Luzon. The Japanese were not informed. Two hours later, they rushed the command post of Company A, 128th Infantry Regiment, and killed one more American. In the afternoon, another unit was cut off temporarily by a determined assault on its position in the hills. When the news of the surrender was passed up to them, one G.I. observed caustically, "Yeah, the war's over. It's all over this goddamn hill." The sound of artillery fire punctuated his remark.

Off the coast of Japan, the fast carriers of Bull Halsey's fleet prepared to renew the attack on the morning of the fifteenth. The order for a temporary lull in bombing activity had expired. At 6:15 the last of 176 planes had taken off from the pitching decks for sweeps against targets in the Tokyo area.

Just then an urgent message crackled into the radio room: CESTCPAC: SUSPEND ATTACK AIR OPERATIONS X ACKNOWLEDGE.

Halsey ordered his signal officer to contact the departed aircraft. Seventy-three of them were raised by radio and recalled to the fleet. The other 103 planes were over the mainland, strafing, bombing and fighting off 45 Japanese planes which rose to the last challenge of the Pacific War.

Another message arrived for Halsey on the bridge!

CEASE OFFENSIVE OPERATIONS AGAINST JAPANESE FORCES X CONTINUE SEARCHES AND PATROLS X MAINTAIN DEFENSE AND INTERNAL SECURITY MEASURES AT HIGHEST LEVEL AND BEWARE

OF TREACHERY OR LAST MOMENT ATTACKS BY
ENEMY FORCES OR INDIVIDUALS.

The thousands of men in the Third Fleet knew now that the
war was truly over.

When the pilots returned from the Tokyo raid, they were
elated. On the *San Jacinto*, they rushed from their planes to
tell how they had shot down twelve enemy fighters. Nobody
paid any attention to them. Men kept saying, "Who cares?"
Like children with a great story to tell, the pilots raced around
from officer to officer to recite the impressive story of the dog-
fight over Japan. No one was impressed anymore. The war was
over.

In Tokyo, the Emperor had scheduled a meeting with his top advisers for ten o'clock in the morning, but because of the rebellion
of the preceding hours, it was postponed until 11:15.

Major Hidemasa Koga walked through the forest into the headquarters of the Guards Division, where General Mori's body lay
in state. Koga had been revolted when this gracious, fair officer
was shot dead by Hatanaka. For the rest of the night, he had
wandered in a daze, unnerved and disillusioned by the violence
he had witnessed in the name of the Emperor. His concept of a
coup did not include murdering loyal soldiers. He had been party
to a terrible wrong.

Koga gazed down at Mori lying in the wooden coffin. Kneeling at the general's feet, he placed a pistol to his own chest, pulled
the trigger, and died on the floor beside his commanding officer.

Outside the Emperor's palace, two men were seen distributing
handbills to strolling pedestrians. One man was on a horse, the
other on a motorcycle. They were Hatanaka and Shiizaki, who
had emerged from the wooded area inside the compound to explain their actions to the public. They stopped people and forced

leaflets on them. Then the two disappeared again into the forest of pine trees near the Double Bridge Gate.

Shiizaki knelt down on the ground and drew out a ceremonial dagger. Facing toward the interior of the palace grounds, he ripped open his stomach and fell unconscious to the grass.

Hatanaka stood a short distance away. His attempt to obstruct the peace had failed miserably. A gentle man by nature, he had resorted to extreme violence and killed a man mourned by many. Balked at every turn, he had no recourse but to follow Anami and the others in death.

Hatanaka raised the pistol with which he had murdered Mori nine hours before. He placed it between his eyes and pulled the trigger. His fragile features dissolved in blood.

Passers-by heard the report of the gun but passed on without stopping. The morning sun warmed the grass around the palace and glistened on the red stains spreading under the trees.

FIFTEEN

The Emperor Speaks

In the morning newscast on August 15, the Japanese people were told that the Emperor himself would speak to them at noon. It was an unprecedented break with tradition. Never before had the Emperor talked personally to them. The people had never heard his voice.

As the sun rose to the mid-point, in schools, factories, private homes and military bases, everyone gathered around radios or loudspeakers. Very few had an inkling of what they were about to hear.

At Oppama Airfield southwest of Tokyo, air force personnel lined the runways. Standing at attention among them was Saburo Sakai, whose distinction as Japan's greatest fighter pilot went back to the early days of the war when he and his comrades ruled the skies as far south as New Guinea. Now, across the airfield, smoke rose from a trash fire where papers were being burned to prevent their falling into the hands of the enemy.

At Oita Airfield, Admiral Ugaki was dressing in his cave. All morning long his fellow officers had tried to dissuade him from flying the last kamikaze mission. He had said to a close friend, "This is my last chance to die like a warrior. I must be permitted that chance." His radio too was turned on as noon approached.

On the other side of Kyushu, in Nagasaki's Urakami Valley, a few radios still functioned. In a schoolyard a crowd was grouped within range of one loudspeaker. Not far from them, corpses still lay about, blackened and ballooning up grotesquely in the heat. Thousands of flies feasted on the remains. The stench was intolerable. Daily more of the original survivors were dying from the invisible work of radiation.

At one minute before twelve o'clock, radios everywhere blared the final strains of "Kimagayo," the Japanese national anthem. Then an announcer stated that the next speaker would be the Emperor of Japan. All traffic stopped. Most subjects bowed their heads. An unnatural hush invaded the cities and villages.

"To our good and loyal subjects," the Emperor began. "After pondering deeply the general trends of the world, and the actual conditions obtaining in our Empire today, we have decided to effect a settlement of the present situation by resorting to an extraordinary measure." The voice was high-pitched, thin and reedy, quavering slightly as though under strain. "We have ordered our Government to communicate to the Governments of the United States, Great Britain, China, and the Soviet Union that our Empire accepts the provisions of their Joint Declaration."

The language was court Japanese—a stilted, archaic form strange to many of his listeners. Comprehension of his purpose was slow in coming as he next set about exonerating his country for the debacle of the war:

"To strive for the common prosperity and happiness of all nations as well as the security and well-being of our subjects is the solemn obligation which has been handed down by our Imperial Ancestors, and which we lay close to heart. Indeed, we declared war on America and Britain out of our sincere desire to ensure Japan's self-preservation and the stabilization of Southeast Asia, it being far from our thought either to infringe upon the sovereignty of other nations or to embark upon territorial aggrandizement.

"But now the war has lasted nearly four years. Despite the best that has been done by everyone—the gallant fighting of military and naval forces, the diligence and assiduity of our servants of the State, and the devoted service of our one hundred million people, [and here, in dealing with the defeat of the military, the Emperor was delicate to an extreme] the war situation has developed not necessarily to Japan's advantage, while the general trends of the world have all turned against her interest." With this, he moved on to another topic:

"Moreover, the enemy has begun to employ a new and most cruel bomb, the power of which to do damage is indeed incalculable, taking the toll of many innocent lives. Should we continue to fight, it would not only result in an ultimate collapse and obliteration of the Japanese nation, but would also lead to the total extinction of human civilization. Such being the case, how are we to save the millions of our subjects, or to atone ourselves before the hallowed spirits of our Imperial Ancestors? This is the reason why we have ordered the acceptance of the provisions of the Joint Declaration of the Powers."

Those who had not fully understood his opening statement now heard it confirmed. Around the radios, in the streets, people wept. Sobbing, their faces in their hands, they strained to hear the words of solace that followed.

"We cannot but express the deepest sense of regret to our Allied nations of East Asia, who have consistently cooperated with the Empire toward the emancipation of East Asia. The thought of those officers and men, as well as others who have fallen in the fields of battle, those who have died at their posts of duty, or those who have met with untimely death, and all their bereaved families, pains our heart night and day. The welfare of the wounded and the war-sufferers, and of those who have lost their homes and livelihood, are the objects of our profound solicitude. The hardships to which our nation is to be subjected hereafter will certainly be great. We are keenly aware of all ye, our subjects. However, it is according to the dictate of time and fate that we have resolved to pave the way for a grand peace for all the generations to come by enduring the unendurable and suffering what is insufferable."

Having first justified, then commiserated, in conclusion Hirohito warned:

". . . Beware most strictly of any outbursts of emotion which may engender needless complications, or any fraternal contention and strife which may create confusion, lead ye astray, and cause ye to lose the confidence of the world. . . . Unite your total strength to be devoted to the construction of the future. Cultivate the ways of rectitude; foster nobility of spirit; and work with resolution so ye may enhance the innate glory of the Imperial State and keep pace with the progress of the world."

With this, the voice stopped.

The shock was felt in various degrees and various ways all over Japan. For the first time in twenty-six hundred years the Japanese people would bow to a conqueror. Some were stunned to a point of incredulity, particularly in outlying areas where there was difficult radio reception and less general ability to understand the Emperor's unfamiliar mode of speech. In the cities too there was disbelief. In Sendai, for example, the people were so certain of continued fighting that they could not absorb the meaning of the broadcast. Two or even three days later, many there were still in doubt, and went about in a kind of dream that shielded them from the hard reality.

Others responded with immediate grief or fear. In Osaka, Mrs. Katsuko Oiyama recalled that she was so upset that she and her daughter "went right to bed and cried all day." A child in Kobe remembered hearing at school that the Americans "would squeeze our throats and kill us and make holes in our ears and string wires through them." She burst into tears of fright.

At Oppama Airfield, the solid ranks of airmen broke. Nearly all of the men were in tears.

The sobs of the people in the schoolyard crowd in Nagasaki were mingled with the noise of the many American planes still circling the stricken valley to photograph the phenomenon below.

In their grief and shock and fear, most civilians in Japan

simply retreated into their homes to await the enemy. The military, however, were far from passive. In the hours after the Emperor's speech, truckloads of drunken soldiers careened through the downtown section of Osaka, shouting that the war would go on. Bottles of liquor crashed onto the streets as they vented their frustrations at the world. Pedestrians merely watched them.

Hundreds of subjects congregated in front of the Imperial Palace that afternoon to pray and offer continued allegiance to the Divine Ruler. It was an orderly group, filled with sorrow. Scattered through the crowd were sobbing army officers who had come there with one purpose in mind. Pistol shots rang out and uniformed men toppled to the pavement. Nobody screamed or ran. People just moved away from the corpses and left the plaza in front of the palace.

Immediately following the Emperor's broadcast, Suzuki's cabinet resigned in a body. The old man had done the job he had been assigned to do. From April to August, he had ridden the mounting wave of tension that gripped Japan and had managed to maintain his balance despite several slips that had nearly ruined the precariously built foundations of peace. The venerable admiral had performed the most onerous task ever given to a Japanese, and thereby rescued his countrymen from complete annihilation. For this he had nearly died at the hands of fanatics. For this he would remain a hunted man for months, unable to sleep in his own bed, hounded from sanctuary to sanctuary, until finally, some time after the United States Army occupied his nation, the hunters tired of the chase.

The new Premier was of royal blood, an uncle of Hirohito. Prince Higashi-Kuni, whose behavior in his youth had scandalized the court, was not an ideal choice for the position, at least not in normal times. Considered by associates an arrogant man, he possessed limited talents, less than brilliant intellectual attainments. Nevertheless, he served one very important function in August of 1945. As a member of the ruling family, he was a direct link to the throne, a rallying point for the people, a deterrent to those who would continue resisting the Emperor's proclamation. The new Premier was the figurehead who could control the population in the crucial days ahead.

Years earlier, well aware of the dangers involved in war with the West, Higashi-Kuni had tried to impress upon his military friends the rashness of Japanese aggression. Posted to the Army as a general, he had violently opposed the coming crisis with the United States. When the disaster of total war engulfed the nation, he resigned himself to inevitable defeat. Finally, as it came, the Prince stepped forward willingly when Hirohito asked for help. He took up Suzuki's title and set about restoring a measure of calm to a troubled nation.

At Fukuoka, scene of the massacre of American fliers only four days before, officers at Western Army Headquarters listened to the Emperor's broadcast and then made plans for the afternoon.

A meeting was held and an order read: "There will be an execution of enemy fliers. The fliers are being executed because they are being held responsible for indiscriminate bombing . . ." The man who read the directive added, "The executions will be kept secret."

One vital reason impelled the Japanese to act against the remaining B-29 crew members in detention at the headquarters. The Americans knew too much. They could testify that other POW's had been alive a few days before the war ended but had suddenly disappeared from sight.

In the middle of the afternoon, another procession went down the road to Aburayama. In the back of a truck, sixteen American airmen sat surrounded by guards. None of the prisoners knew the war was over.

In the field where eight fellow prisoners had been slaughtered four days before, they were stripped and formed into a ragged line. The commander of the Japanese execution squad stood nearby with his girl friend, invited to watch the spectacle. When he shouted an order several of his men closed around the first victim. They took him into the woods at the edge of the field and fell upon the defenseless man with swords.

The brutal scene was repeated again and again on the dwindling group of captives, who were dragged individually or by twos and threes into the trees and cut into pieces. Unlike the previous "organized" deaths of fliers, this day of killing was an orgy, a frenzied destruction of human beings. Shouts of triumph rose from the throats of the excited Japanese, who ripped and slashed the prisoners in the secluded forest.

While crowds of happy people roamed the streets of New York, San Francisco and New Orleans, sixteen Americans were dumped into hastily dug pits across the Pacific at Aburayama. They were unrecognizable. The men who killed them went back to headquarters to burn any records pertaining to the whereabouts of the victims.

At Oita Airfield, the last kamikaze attack of the Pacific war was about to be launched. It was close to five o'clock in the afternoon. Admiral Matome Ugaki had listened carefully to the Emperor's message. He had said goodbye to his associates in a brief ceremony where the traditional sake cups were drained by all. He had made his preparations for death. Finally he had stripped all insignia and braid from his uniform. Now he walked out of his hillside home toward the apron of the runway.

Captain Miyazaki, resigned to his superior's decision, raced up to him and asked to go along on the mission. Ugaki rebuked him gruffly: "You have more than enough to attend to here. You must remain." Miyazaki burst into tears. The admiral walked on.

When he reached the parking area, he was dumbfounded to see eleven naval fighter-bombers lined up ready for takeoff. Rear Admiral Tokiyushi Yokoi, Ugaki's chief of staff, approached the group leader and asked him if the men intended to follow Ugaki to Okinawa. He said they did.

Ugaki was deeply moved. "Are you so willing to die with me?"

Twenty-two right hands flashed into the air as his flyers saluted him. Visibly moved, the admiral went to the lead plane and signaled for takeoff. Eleven motors coughed and caught, then roared loudly over the flat terrain. Just as the first plane moved onto the runway, Ensign Endo, whose place Ugaki had usurped, vaulted onto the wing and squeezed into the rear seat beside the admiral. They smiled at each other as the aircraft moved down the field. One by one, the ten other ships revved their engines and moved off into the shimmering heat of the August afternoon. In moments, Oita was quiet. The waiting began.

Flying time to Okinawa was a little more than two hours. At twenty-four minutes past seven o'clock, the radio in the control tower at Oita airfield came to life. Ugaki delivered a final message to his men:

"I alone am to blame for our failure to defend the homeland and destroy the arrogant enemy. The valiant efforts of all officers and men of my command during the past six months have been greatly appreciated. . . ."

Static garbled most of the statement from here on. The last clear words reported that the planes were diving.

Ugaki and his men were never seen again. The United States Navy had no record whatsoever of any suicide attacks on its ships that day. Where the mission went, no one ever learned. Admiral Ugaki left only an epitaph and an unsolved mystery.

That afternoon, the body of General Anami, in full-dress uniform, was brought from his official residence to an office building on top of Ichigaya Hill. It was placed in a small room to lie in state between the corpses of Hatanaka and Shiizaki, which had been found in the pine forest near the palace. Fellow officers visited the three caskets and bowed in prayer. A stream of grieving soldiers shuffled through the room and cried bitterly.

At twilight Anami's body was taken from the building. A straggling line of mourners followed the coffin bearers across the top of the hill and down a slope to a freshly dug hole. Over the hole an iron grating had been placed. The casket was laid upon it, and twigs and sticks were heaped over and under it. Cans of gasoline were poured over the wood.

In the soft light of the summer night, onlookers watched as a colonel struck a match and tossed it toward the corpse. With a *whoosh*, flames leaped up and out. The widow and five-year-old son of the general stumbled back from the pyre and stood staring. The soldiers saluted.

The cremation lasted into the darkness of August 15. The torch shone from Ichigaya Hill for hours and then dwindled.

When his wife and son moved away from the glowing pyre, they were followed by officers who would now turn to the painful duty of dismantling General Anami's army.

Within hours after Emperor Hirohito's broadcast the enemy contacted Tokyo. For the first time since December 7, 1941, the United States military spoke "in the clear" to the Government of Japan.

FROM: Supreme Commander for the Allied Powers
TO: The Japanese Emperor
The Japanese Imperial Government
The Japanese Imperial General Headquarters
ITEM [I] HAVE BEEN DESIGNATED AS THE SUPREME COMMANDER FOR THE ALLIED POWERS (THE UNITED STATES, THE REPUBLIC OF CHINA, THE UNITED KINGDOM AND THE UNION OF SOVIET SOCIALIST REPUBLICS) AND EMPOWERED TO ARRANGE DIRECTLY WITH THE JAPANESE AUTHORITIES FOR THE CESSATION OF HOSTILITIES AT THE EARLIEST PRACTICABLE DATE.
IT IS DESIRED THAT ABLE [A] RADIO STATION IN THE TOKYO AREA BE OFFICIALLY DESIGNATED FOR CONTINUOUS USE IN HANDLING RADIO COMMUNICATIONS BETWEEN THIS HEADQUARTERS AND

YOUR HEADQUARTERS. YOUR REPLY TO THIS MES-
SAGE SHOULD GIVE THE CALL SIGNS, FREQUEN-
CIES AND STATION DESIGNATION. IT IS DESIRED
THAT THE RADIO COMMUNICATION WITH MY
HEADQUARTERS IN MANILA BE HANDLED IN ENG-
LISH TEXT. PENDING DESIGNATION BY YOU OF
ABLE STATION IN THE TOKYO AREA FOR USE AS
ABOVE INDICATED, STATION JIG NAN PETER [JNP]
ON FREQUENCY ONE THREE SEVEN FOUR ZERO
KILOCYCLES WILL BE USED FOR THIS PURPOSE.
UPON RECEIPT OF THIS MESSAGE, ACKNOWLEDGE.

MacArthur

SIXTEEN

Delayed Reactions

In the early light of the morning of the sixteenth, a military truck drove slowly through the deserted streets of Tokyo. It bounced over the rough pavement and jostled a pine box lying in the rear. Inside the box lay the cramped body of the warrior Onishi, the founder of the kamikazes.

The admiral had taken his own life the day before as an act of expiation for his failure to avoid defeat. In the last hours of war, he had tried desperately to avert surrender. His attempts had been met by scorn, rage and ill-concealed hatred on the part of those he had accosted.

After hearing of the Emperor's final decision, Onishi had retreated to his official residence and committed hara-kiri. Refusing all help, he had lain on the bloody floor for nearly eighteen hours. When death came at last, he was gripping the hand of a friend. Now his body was being taken to a crematorium but his spirit was less quickly disposed of.

Also on the morning of the sixteenth, two men came to the huge headquarters building on Ichigaya Hill. Colonel Ida's father had been found, and Colonel Tsukamoto of the Kempei Tai was bringing him to see his son.

Ida himself had spent a miserable twenty-four hours since deserting his fellow plotters in the abortive revolt. Shaken by the deaths of Mori, Anami and the others, he had returned to his home on the fifteenth and contemplated suicide. For most of the day he had lain in bed. At 6:00 P.M. he had said goodbye to his wife and told her to claim his body the next day at the War Ministry. Then he had gone to Ichigaya and prayed before the caskets of Anami, Shiizaki and Hatanaka. He had cried bitterly and determined to die as they had.

When Tsukamoto and Ida's father entered the War Ministry, the supposed widow had arrived just ahead of them, ready to claim her husband's body.

From an office down the corridor, loud laughter sounded. Colonel Arao emerged walking beside another officer. It was Colonel Ida.

At the sight of him, alive and smiling, his wife flew into a rage. "You said you were going to kill yourself. You have no courage."

As the woman continued to scream at him, Ida smiled broadly and said, "Arao and others have talked me out of it." He tried to convince her that he was not a coward, but to no avail. Through the halls of the War Ministry, the matter of family honor resounded. Ida finally turned from his embittered wife, his father, his friends, and walked away. He preferred to go on living.

In Peking, China, OSS Major Jim Kellis had also heard the Emperor's broadcast. Realizing that it was important to move quickly, he told Chinese "puppet" general Mung that he wanted to see the ranking enemy general in Peking as soon as possible. On the morning of the sixteenth, a Japanese colonel drove up to Mung's home, where Kellis was staying, and delivered a note. General Takahashi would like to see the American major at his convenience. Immediately Kellis dressed in the uniform of the United States Army and walked out to his appointment.

At Japanese headquarters, he was ushered into the general's office. Takahashi rose and exchanged salutes with Kellis. The American spoke:

"I am Major James Kellis, acting as liaison officer for General Wedemeyer. I have come here to effect the prompt release of Allied prisoners in the area."

Takahashi listened, then smiled and said, "Welcome to Peking. I will cooperate with you completely."

The two men sat down and began to go over details of repatriation. Kellis and his team of OSS personnel had surfaced exactly on time.

Northeast of Peking, a single B-24 bomber rode high over the fields of Manchuria. It had come from far to the southwest, from Hsian. There, just after midnight on the sixteenth, Major Gus Krause, the OSS commander of that outpost, had said goodbye to six men as they climbed into the squat, four-engined plane for the long trip to the Hoten Prison Camp at Mukden, Manchuria. Krause had been apprehensive as he waved to the parachutists, for he knew that his own men, like Jim Kellis stationed behind the Japanese lines, were better trained to accomplish such a mission without trouble. He felt that Operation Cardinal, this attempted rescue of POW's, could easily end in disaster.

The B-24, carrying an extra gas tank in its belly because of the length of the flight, wobbled up into the night and climbed heavily into the star-filled sky. The members of the mercy team settled down in the rear and fell asleep.

Major James Hennessy commanded the group. He was nervous but dared not show it. Major Robert Lamar, a combat doctor, was also nervous but managed to nap in the cold interior of the plane. He was the only man aboard who had ever jumped from a B-24. Three enlisted men dozed in the cramped quarters. They were Sergeants Edward Starz, Harold Leith and Fumio Kido, a Nisei interpreter. Another member of the team was a Nationalist Chinese guide, Major Cheng-Shi-Wu, who was not happy about the idea of dropping into the midst of the Japanese Kwantung Army.

As sunlight streamed into the plane, the pilot called Lamar to the cockpit. He told the doctor that only two passes—one for the men and one for the equipment—could be made over the jump zone because of the fuel situation. Lamar went back to alert his group, and instructed them once more on the problems of leaping out of the bomb bay of the B-24.

At the Hoten camp, POW's gathered in the courtyard for their regular morning recreation period. The prison housed over seventeen hundred men who had managed to survive for years by pitting their inner strength against the privation and humiliation of a Japanese concentration camp.

Ingenuity born of desperation had kept their spirits and bodies reasonably sound. Enlisted men had become master thieves, capable of filching almost any food or equipment from under the noses of their captors. When the Japanese made the mistake of having prisoners unload trucks or railroad cars, sometimes over half of the merchandise on board disappeared into pockets, up sleeves, or down the inside of pants. The Japanese were always mystified at the resultant discrepancies and sometimes tried to beat the truth out of innocent-looking captives. They invariably failed to get to the source of the looting.

A brisk black-market business was conducted with susceptible guards, who would bring delicacies into the camp in exchange for watches and other valuables. An over-the-wall trading routine was established between enlisted men and local civilians, and food was sold at tremendous prices to Allied officers. Cigarettes brought five dollars a pack.

Prisoners received some news of the war from papers smuggled into the camp at a price. The reports in them reflected a steady Allied advance toward Japan, but few at Hoten realized how greatly it had accelerated.

In the second week of August, the situation in the Mukden area was tense. Large fires were visible outside the prison. Intermittent machine-gun and rifle fire was heard in the distance as Russian armies pressed closer. Guards had been doubled at the camp itself, and Japanese officers seemed to be in a highly excitable and ugly mood. The Allied prisoners read these signs and realized that something big was about to happen. Local peasants added substance to the mounting rumors by reporting that the town of Mukden itself was a scene of rioting and martial law.

General George Parker, a senior American officer, was terribly concerned about his men. When the Japanese issued orders to the prison bakery to prepare an extra supply of "travel bread," he deduced that some part of the camp population was about to be moved. Parker was appalled at the thought, for he knew that a march at this point could only result in the death of many of the undernourished and exhausted POW's.

On August 16, in the yard of the compound, several Americans lounged in the warm sun. When a plane roared over, they looked up curiously. When parachutes spilled out into the sky, the prisoners got excited. Jumping up, they asked each other what it could mean. Someone suddenly said, "Say, I remember back at Fort Benning they used to use those colored chutes." The yard at Hoten Camp came alive.

Major Lamar had been first to go through the hatch of the B-24. At a signal from the jumpmaster, he plunged forward and down into the Manchurian morning. Behind him, five other bodies hurtled through the hole in the belly of the bomber. Sergeant Ed Starz was the next to last out. When his chute opened, he relaxed a bit and looked below to see where he would land. The intended drop zone, a golf course, was nowhere in sight. Instead, the mercy team was drifting into a vegetable field. As he braced for a landing, Starz noticed several people running away from the area. When he hit, he rolled, stopped, and quickly unbuckled his reserve chute. Then, dropping his harness on the ground, he ran to the rest of the team, all of whom had landed safely.

Major Hennessy stood in the middle of a cabbage patch and made a fast decision. He, Leith, Lamar and Kido would head down a nearby road toward the prison camp while Starz and

Major Cheng remained to gather the equipment now being dropped by the B-24 on its last pass.

As the OSS men talked, a happy crowd of Chinese approached them. Obviously in good humor, they clapped their hands as more parachutes floated down from the bomber and scattered supplies over the landscape. One peasant told the group that the men seen running from the field were Japanese soldiers, who by now must have reported the "invasion" to higher authorities.

Hennessy wasted no time. He took his three men toward the road to camp. Starz and Cheng stayed with the equipment which the Chinese spectators had begun to collect for them.

On the road the four Americans headed briskly toward the prison. Five minutes passed, then ten. Hennessy and the others seemed to be alone as they walked along.

They were not. Up ahead, a company of Japanese troops appeared, running at double time. Hennessy ordered a halt. The Japanese slowed, then came on warily.

Fifty feet away, a sergeant shouted something which Kido translated: "He says to kneel down." The four Americans went to their knees. The Japanese moved in among them and made menacing gestures with their bayoneted rifles. They were particularly interested in the Japanese-American Kido.

The sergeant commanding the enemy unit asked, "Who are you?" When Kido translated, Hennessy said, "Tell him we are Americans here to bring aid to the prisoners at Hoten. Tell him that the war is over." Kido repeated this to the Japanese, who simply sneered. Hennessy realized that the Japanese had no idea the hostilities had ended and murmured: "Oh, God."

It began to rain. The Americans stayed in the road on their knees while the Japanese sergeant walked about, undecided, confused. His men stood poised with rifles pointed down at the OSS men.

Hennessy finally asked if they could move under some shelter. The Japanese noncom listened to the translation, hesitated, then ordered the captives to stand up. They were escorted to a nearby factory outbuilding where they stood under an over-hanging roof.

When the Japanese sergeant found out that two other Amer-icans were back in the field collecting supplies, he sent Major Lamar and two Japanese soldiers after them.

Sergeant Ed Starz and Major Cheng had spent nearly thirty minutes watching the Chinese peasants pick up the equipment. Seated inside a small building, the two agents ate watermelon and wondered when the Japanese would come for them. Cheng kept assuring Starz that everything would be all right. Starz watched the peasants and waited expectantly. Suddenly the band of work-ers scattered. One of them shouted to Cheng, "The Japanese are coming." Then he too ran away.

Cheng reacted violently. He tried to climb through a rear win-dow of the building. Starz ran toward him, grabbed at his collar, pulled him back into the room and told him to act like a man. Together, they walked to the door. More than thirty Japanese soldiers were coming straight toward them, armed with rifles, bayonets, swords, poles, and poles with knives fastened to the ends. Starz breathed deeply and went forward to meet the enemy. Cheng followed.

The two OSS men were quickly surrounded by bayonets. An officer with a pistol in his hand approached and took off Starz's belt and revolver. Starz asked if he could speak English. The officer could not. Starz's jacket, pants and shorts joined the other articles on the ground. He was left standing in his shoes and undershirt. Cheng too was stripped.

The order was given: "Kneel down." They knelt, and were then forced to face a stone wall. Starz looked back over his shoul-der and saw one of the Japanese pulling his sword from its scab-bard. He tensed for what was to come. Nothing happened. He looked again over his shoulder and saw the tip of the sword still touching the ground. Fascinated, Starz watched the sharp point, waiting for it to sweep up in an arc and flash into his neck. It stayed where it was. As the seconds dragged by in the cabbage patch, Starz began to think he might survive.

Through Cheng, the Japanese told the men to turn around. They were allowed to sit on a bench with their backs resting against the stone wall. They saw three men come into the field, one of them Lamar, fully clothed and smiling, the other two Japanese, fully armed and sullen. Lamar motioned for Starz to get up. As the sergeant rose, bayonets were pushed toward his face and he sat down quickly.

Lamar was suddenly seized and stripped down to his shorts. When he started to protest, one of the Japanese smashed him in the mouth. He was prodded over to the bench and seated beside Starz. As the Americans began to talk to each other, Cheng was put between them to stop all contact. Again a ring of steel closed in on the captives. They sat and stared back at the weapons.

Soon the Japanese patrol leader made another move. Because of the rain, he prodded the three men into the building where Starz and Cheng had previously taken shelter. By now, more Japanese officers had arrived, and Cheng attempted to explain the purpose of the mission. At Lamar's urging, he asked that he and his companions get their clothes back. The enemy soldiers considered the proposal for a few minutes and then made a significant gesture. The OSS team was allowed to dress.

At this point Lamar produced a paper signed by General Wedemeyer. It stated that the purpose of the paratroopers was to bring relief, not to fight. The Japanese thought the note was terribly funny. It seemed that they had no idea that Japan had surrendered, that the war was over. Nevertheless, a subtle change took place. In a few minutes, cigarettes and watermelon were passed to the prisoners.

Outside, a Japanese officer rode up on horseback and said something to the guards. Five minutes later, another officer arrived and went straight to the OSS team. He began to apologize for their detention and said that news of the surrender had just reached Mukden. Hands were shaken all around.

Still the Japanese remained cautious, in case the news of surrender proved false. Starz, Lamar and Cheng were blindfolded and taken outside. They were guided to a truck and put in the back, where Hennessy, Leith and Kido joined them shortly. The reunited team was driven to military police headquarters.

For the first time all of the men were treated cordially. Sake and hot tea were served. Better yet, a bottle of Johnny Walker Scotch was broken open and shared. Even Sergeant Kido was treated courteously.

He had been having a difficult day. At one point in his detention, the Japanese had begun to beat him, though most of their abuse was verbal. The Nisei confused them. At military police headquarters, Kido overheard an officer speaking on the telephone: "We have an American-born Japanese here. What do we do with him?" Though Kido's status remained perplexing, they finally allowed him to interpret and present Hennessy's views.

For over an hour, the American unit sparred with a collection of enemy colonels, who grew progressively more friendly over the flowing Scotch. At one point, a Colonel Kamata lamented the fact that he would have to commit suicide the following morning because he was responsible for the death of several escaped prisoners. No one attempted to dissuade him. The relaxed conversation drifted into random observations about Manchuria and the Japanese Kwantung Army, with only occasional further references to the Americans' mission.

While they chatted together, another truck drove up. The Americans were taken to the main prison camp, this time without blindfolds.

At the camp, strange things had already begun to happen. Guards were suddenly more friendly. Six Allied men had been suddenly released from solitary confinement, one of them after living in the "hole" for over one hundred days. Within the camp, General George Parker had noticed these signs of thaw and wondered at the reasons for them.

Hennessy and the others were taken to the office of the commandant, Colonel Matsudo, who received them graciously. While the mercy team talked, they could see prisoners outside, straining to understand just what was going on inside the room. News of the six strangers filtered quickly to every corner of the compound. Some men connected them with the parachutists earlier in the day. Most assumed that they were merely more prisoners for Camp Hoten.

Matsudo refused to allow the OSS team into the barracks. He asked instead that the mission stay overnight at a local hotel. In the meantime, he would cable Tokyo for further instructions. Hennessy protested vigorously, but Matsudo refused to give in. Though the atmosphere was not dangerous, the opposing sides had reached another impasse.

Late in the afternoon, Hennessy agreed to wait until morning to see the Allied prisoners. Matsudo in turn promised to evacuate his own men from the prison as soon as possible and turn over its administration to the Americans. On this note of compromise, the meeting was adjourned.

Prisoners trying desperately to get a clue from the proceedings at the headquarters building saw Sergeant Harold Leith raise his hand to them and make an OK signal with his thumb and index finger. They heard Sergeant Kido sound a piercing whistle in their direction. These signs of confidence sustained them during a long night, in which few of the Allied captives slept well.

In Japan, a second message from MacArthur was received before the first one had been answered. The Allied High Command called for a delegation of Japanese to proceed at once to the Philippines for conversations. MacArthur wanted the Japanese to deliver all secrets about Japan's armed forces and to receive Allied plans about the occupation.

No one in Japan wanted to go. Though anxious to comply with the requests from the Supreme Commander, officers in the Army and Navy gagged at the thought of going to the camp of the enemy and laying bare the national defenses. General Umezu, as Chief of Staff, was the logical man to head the delegation, but he absolutely refused to participate. The choice then fell on Lieutenant General Kawabe, his second in command. Kawabe too loathed the idea, but he accepted the job and chose his staff. Fifteen men, representing the Foreign Office and the military, were picked to make the trip. Several ran away immediately to the mountains rather than face the unpleasant and degrading task. Their places were quickly given to new men. Plans went ahead for takeoff on the following day.

On the same afternoon—August 16—station JNP in Tokyo answered MacArthur's first message. Communication Number One to the conqueror was polite and helpful.

> HIS MAJESTY THE EMPEROR ISSUED AN IMPERIAL ORDER AT 16 O'CLOCK ON AUGUST 16 TO THE ENTIRE ARMED FORCES TO CEASE HOSTILITIES IMMEDIATELY.
>
> IT IS PRESUMED THAT THE SAID IMPERIAL ORDER WILL REACH THE FRONT LINE AND PRODUCE FULL EFFECT AFTER THE FOLLOWING LAPSE OF TIME:
>
> A. IN JAPAN PROPER 48 HOURS
>
> B. IN CHINA, MANCHURIA, KOREA, SOUTHERN RE GIONS EXCEPT BOUGAINVILLE, NEW GUINEA, THE PHILIPPINES SIX DAYS. . . .
>
> WITH A VIEW TO MAKING THE AUGUST WISH OF HIS MAJESTY REGARDING THE TERMINATION OF THE WAR AND THE ABOVE MENTIONED IMPERIAL ORDER THOROUGHLY KNOWN TO ALL CONCERNED, MEMBERS OF THE IMPERIAL FAMILY WILL BE DISPATCHED AS PERSONAL REPRESENTATIVES OF HIS MAJESTY TO THE HEADQUARTERS OF THE KWANTUNG ARMY, EXPEDITIONARY FORCES

IN CHINA AND THE FORCES IN THE SOUTHERN
REGIONS RESPECTIVELY. THE ITINERARY, TYPE OF
AIRCRAFT, MARKINGS, ETC., WILL BE COMMUNI-
CATED LATER. IT IS ACCORDINGLY REQUESTED
THAT SAFE CONDUCT FOR THE ABOVE BE
GRANTED. . . .

Yet even as the Emperor slowly deactivated the Japanese war
machine and tried to smooth the way to peace, obstacles were
put in his path. The plans for Kawabe's mission were plagued
by growing fears that a plot was afoot to destroy the planes that
would carry the sixteen delegates to the Philippines the next
morning. It was rumored that the delegation would be attacked,
possibly from Atsugi Airbase, just after taking off from Tokyo.

To die a warrior's death, even at the hands of their countrymen, seemed to many of the delegates preferable to the dishonor-
able chore ahead of them. But they also knew the importance of
an orderly transfer of power. Even Captain Toshikazu Ohmae of
the Navy, who only two days earlier had been among the more
fanatical die-hards, was determined that the process must not be
jeopardized, that the surrender must be consummated without
trouble.

Late on the sixteenth a message mentioning "internal problems" was sent to Manila, requesting a forty-eight-hour delay of
the mission. MacArthur's headquarters agreed to postponement
till the nineteenth.

The leader of the defiant group at Atsugi Airbase was a Navy
Captain, Ammyo Kosono, a man totally committed to further
prosecution of the war. For the past several weeks he had worked
desperately to prevent defeat.

A highly capable aerial tactician, he had been given command at Atsugi in order to guard against B-29 flights over
Tokyo. As he watched his finest men go down in flames during the summer months, Kosono became increasingly alarmed

about his nation's chances for survival. Powerless to stop the bombers' attacks, he concentrated his hopes on defeating an enemy invasion, and thus salvaging at least a conditional peace. To that end, he exhorted fellow officers to maintain a spirit of optimism and faith. Most laughed at him. Enraged, Kosono decided that such weak-minded men must be purged from positions of influence.

On August 7 he asked Admiral Onishi to get him transferred to Naval General Staff Headquarters. When Onishi seemed inclined to grant his wish, Kosono plotted further to stage his personal reforms from within. Three days later, his plans were abruptly interrupted by news of the Emperor's peace offer through Switzerland. The shock of this development temporarily immobilized him. His transfer to the General Staff would surely be discarded, and he would have to revise his tactics.

Forty-eight hours later he was back in action, trying to persuade senior naval officers to continue the war. In discussion after discussion, his proposals were met only with scorn. But Kosono did not give up. Day and night, he schemed and plotted with those junior officers who were favorably inclined to his strategy. By the second week of August, he had convinced a sizable group of young men to join him at Atsugi. To forestall the prospect of open warfare between Navy factions, on August 14 he visited Admiral Kudo at Marine Force Headquarters in Yokosuka.

When Kosono burst into the room, Kudo was about to have lunch. Sensing immediately that he was dealing with a desperate and distraught man, the cautious admiral handled his visitor with great tact.

Kosono explained the problems he had been having in past days with Navy men who objected to his plan for continuing the war. He then came to the point of his visit:

"I don't want to fight my own countrymen. My enemy is the Army of the United States only. Please don't send any soldiers to fight me at Atsugi."

Admiral Kudo listened to his guest and then calmly assured him, "Kosono, that will never happen."

Kosono returned to his fighter command to prepare for renewed hostilities with America. When he arrived, his aide informed him that the Emperor had just held a second meeting in the air-raid shelter to demand that the cabinet accept the Potsdam Declaration. This news staggered the exhausted captain who had spent nearly seventy-two hours in ceaseless pursuit of support.

Late that afternoon, he went to bed. A recurring touch of malaria compounded his poor physical condition and forced him to send for a doctor, who noted that Kosono had a high fever and appeared near collapse. Although the doctor prescribed bed rest, the overwrought commander got up early that evening and sought out several senior officers around Tokyo to enlist their support. Surprisingly, this time he received encouragement from nearly everyone, and he went back to Atsugi convinced that he would prevail over the "traitors" around the Emperor.

The next day, the fifteenth, after listening to Hirohito's recorded broadcast, Kosono mounted a wooden platform near the Atsugi runway and addressed the rows of pilots standing stiffly at attention:

"I realize that, by the Government's acceptance of the Potsdam Declaration, the Japanese army forces are demobilized. However, since that moment, there has begun a national war, which means defense of our country by the individual. If you want to fight with me, stay here. If you don't, you can go back to your homes. I'll fight on with absolute certainty of victory."

Kosono marched off the platform, leaving behind hundreds of airmen struggling to make a last painful decision. When he walked through camp a few hours later, he noticed the renewed spirit of the men and felt that they would stand by him.

Within the next twenty-four hours, leaflets hurriedly printed by the Atsugi warriors began to fall on Tokyo. They clearly stated Kosono's case:

Government officials and senior statesmen who were caught in an enemy trap have enticed the Emperor to issue the message ending the war. It was a terrible thing to do. The Emperor is a God. There is no such thing as surrender in Japan. There is no surrender in the Imperial forces. We, as members of the Air Force, are sure of victory.

There was an immediate reaction from the Government. On the afternoon of the sixteenth, a black limousine swept into the Atsugi base. From its fender flew the standard of Admiral Teraoka, Kosono's superior in the Tokyo military district.

Realizing that Teraoka's visit was anything but a social call, Kosono posted three armed officers outside his office before greeting the admiral. Then, at Teraoka's request, he led the way to a secluded room where they could speak privately. Teraoka demanded that the rebellious captain explain his actions. Kosono was happy to comply:

"The Emperor wants to sacrifice himself to save the nation. He is just like a father who wants to bear the blame for his son's wrongdoings. As a son, can you stand to see him do that? We must fight." Kosono kept talking as the admiral watched him closely. "The Emperor's declaration about the end of the war proved to me that he has an affliction in his mind." At this statement, Teraoka nearly interrupted, but Kosono quickly continued: "We must make an effort to get rid of his affliction. It is our duty."

Teraoka was incensed at the reference to the Emperor's mental state but refrained from pursuing the point. Instead, he warned the agitated Kosono: "Remember, there is a very slight difference between being loyal and disloyal. In these present conditions, be careful of what you do." He then strode briskly from the room and walked through a cordon of Kosono's supporters who stood with swords in their hands.

Within an hour Teraoka reported Kosono's statements to Admiral Yonai at the Naval Ministry. That devoted servant of the Emperor was also enraged at the references to Hirohito's mental capacity, and marked Kosono down as a dangerous element to be dealt with summarily. He invented and discarded a number of plans to deal with the situation, then finally came to a decision which he hoped would resolve it peaceably. He went to Prince Takamatsu, the Emperor's brother and a close friend of Kosono, and asked him to call the rebel captain directly. Takamatsu did so, but Kosono refused to listen to him. His plans for a coup continued.

At midnight that evening, Kosono was still laboring at his desk over the final aspects of his grandiose scheme. Suddenly his fingers began to tremble violently. The spasms increased, out of control. He jumped up and screamed at the top of his voice. His secretary was struck dumb by the spectacle. As Kosono retreated to a corner, the terrified secretary bolted out to summon a doctor. On their return, the two men found the sweating captain squatting on a cushion, mumbling the names of ancient gods. It took the efforts of both men and an injection of morphine to quiet him.

Though Kosono had a period of rationality the following day, it was short-lived. Men sent by Admiral Yonai to talk with him that afternoon found him trussed in a straitjacket. From Atsugi Airbase he was removed to the Nobi Navy Hospital. For Ammyo Kosono, the war was over at last.

On the morning of the seventeenth, after a pleasant night at the Yamato Hotel in Mukden, OSS Major Hennessy and four of his team were driven to the Hoten camp. One man was missing from the group. Major Cheng-Shi-Wu had deserted his friends. Frustrated the day before in his effort to escape, he had finally managed to merge into a crowd of Chinese spectators after leaving the prison for the hotel.

At the camp the team met the senior Allied officers and then circulated among the joyous men. In the confusion, one voice shouted clearly, "Hiya, fellas, it's all over. We're here to bring you home." Pandemonium took over the yards and barracks.

Starz, Leith and Kido were bombarded with questions: "Who is this guy Truman?" "What about this new bomb?" "Where the hell did you guys come from?" "What happened at Midway?" "How does penicillin work?" The prisoners would not let their rescuers alone for a moment.

Major Lamar sat down with a group of senior officers and conducted a briefing. The first question asked him was, "What is the stock quotation on U.S. Steel?" Someone at Mukden had retained a sense of humor during the long years of misery.

At the commandant's office, Hennessy received some upsetting news. General Wainwright was not at Hoten. He was detained in Mukden Camp Number Two at Sian, over one hundred miles away to the northeast.

Arrangements were initiated to send Major Lamar and Sergeant Leith up to Sian as soon as possible. In the meantime, Major Hennessy would get acquainted with his newly acquired territory.

In the midst of the babel in the Hoten compound, a chauffeured Japanese staff car drove up to the main gate. From the rear stepped a tall American soldier, Captain Roger Hilsman, who had come all the way from Burma for a special reason.

Weeks before, he had asked his former commanding officer, Colonel Ray Peers, to allow him to go on any rescue mission into Manchuria. Hilsman wanted to look for his father, a colonel captured in 1942 in the Philippines and last reported at Mukden. It was not known whether his father was still alive.

When Peers began to select men for the mercy missions, he remembered Hilsman's request and sent for him. Dressed only in jungle fatigues, the captain hitched a ride to Kunming but missed the first flight to the advance base at Hsian.

He was forced to linger a day at Kunming waiting for another plane. When he finally got to Hsian, he found he had missed again. Operation Cardinal had already gone on to Mukden.

On August 17 Hilsman got a ride on a B-24 going into the Mukden area. As it came over the airport, he could see a Russian fighter parked on the runway. When his plane landed and he jumped down on the apron, he saw a Japanese general engaged in conversation with a Russian officer. Hilsman went up to the two men and asked for transportation to the Hoten camp. The Japanese general put a staff car at his disposal.

Still dressed in his camouflage uniform, Hilsman leaped out of the car at the prison gate, ran inside, and asked the nearest man where he might find a Colonel Hilsman. The soldier stared at him, thought a moment, then said, "Yes, sir, that barracks there. Second floor." He pointed at a building.

The captain ran through the door and went upstairs. He scanned the beds and went up to one of them where a middle-aged man sat. The man was staring at him and murmuring, "My God, my God." Captain Roger Hilsman's search had ended.

SEVENTEEN

An Order From MacArthur

At dawn on August 19, Kawabe's Manila delegation assembled at the Navy Department building in Tokyo.

The small group drove out to Haneda Airport past vast acres of flattened city blocks. The morning was beautiful. A bright sunshine filled the skies and caused someone in the group to remark, "Perfect shooting weather." The kamikazes were never far from their thoughts.

Though Kosono himself was no longer a problem, there were other fanatics at Atsugi still capable of launching an attack. There were also other airbases in Japan with kamikazes less flamboyant, perhaps, than Kosono, but as disinclined to accept surrender as he. An elaborate secret plan had therefore been concocted for the flight. From Haneda, the mission would fly to Kisarazu Airbase, across Tokyo Bay on the Bose Peninsula. There they would change planes and go south approximately one hundred miles over the ocean before swinging west toward the Ryukyus. En route they would be met by a convoy of American fighters and bombers which would guide them from the southern tip of Kyushu to the American base at Ie Shima off Okinawa. From there they would fly on to Manila. The roundabout course cut the risk of kamikaze interception from the Home Islands. As an added precaution, at the time of mission takeoff, decoy bombers would head out from Tokyo in another direction.

At 6:00 A.M. the men took off across Tokyo Bay. They landed fourteen minutes later. Kisarazu was the main base of the Third Air Fleet under the command of Admiral Teraoka, the same man who had tried to reason with Kosono at Atsugi three days before. He greeted the delegates and invited them to join him in a meal. It had been prepared by cooks specially selected for the occasion, for Teraoka too feared mission sabotage, by poison.

When the time came to board the two planes lined up on the runway, Teraoka had wreaths of flowers brought out. He asked Kawabe to drop them over Okinawa to honor the memories of the more than 100,000 Japanese servicemen who had died there. Then the delegation filed in two sections into the waiting bombers. These were of the slow two-engined type known as "Bettys" by American pilots. On MacArthur's orders, both had been painted white and had a large green cross on each side of the fuselage. Each plane received eight members of the mission. As the officials settled into their places, the pilots opened their secret orders. Only then did they see the chart showing the route.

The Bettys roared down the runway and up into the brilliant light. In their rear seats the delegates were uncomfortable and tense. On Kawabe's plane, it was easy to look out at the sky because the sides were stitched with bullet holes from some previous encounter with American fighters. But Kawabe closed his eyes to everything around him and appeared to sleep. No one else slept, but none bothered to speak either.

One hundred miles out, the two planes turned and flew west, approximately parallel to the long southern perimeter of Japan. The men in the planes stayed relatively quiet. Kawabe still appeared to doze. Others followed his example.

At eleven o'clock, the mountains of southern Kyushu appeared on the right side. On this island the warrior race of Japan, the samurai, had emerged centuries before. On this same island today, descendants of the samurai, kamikazes, waited for the enemy occupation forces. There was no reason to believe they would wait peacefully. But then, those who could see out through the bullet holes in the lead plane's fuselage saw to their relief that heavy cumulus clouds had appeared. Interception by fighter planes would be most difficult.

At 11:15 A.M. the bombers were suddenly surrounded by fourteen planes coming up alongside to inspect them. Alarmed at first, the occupants of the Bettys soon saw that the strangers were two B-24's and twelve P-38's of the American Air Force. The two bombers were slightly ahead, the twelve fighters around, above and below. They performed acrobatics, diving past the white Bettys which lumbered along in the middle of this concentration of protective power. The threat from the kamikazes was over.

One hour and fifteen minutes later, the island of Ie Shima appeared dead ahead. A huge white cross marked the runway. The Bettys circled over the base and proceeded into the landing pattern. American aircraft were massed below, and for a brief moment, Captain Ohmae, in the lead plane, wondered if perhaps his pilot would forget himself and dive straight into them. But his fears were allayed as he heard the pilot's radio request for landing instructions. The pilot used the call sign "Bataan." MacArthur had thought of everything.

When the planes taxied up to the designated area, the delegates saw a large number of soldiers standing in a huge circle around the apron. A Nisei officer came to the door of the first plane and told them to move to a C-54 transport for the last leg of the journey to Manila. The sixteen men filed down the ramps into a blistering heat which seared their eyes. Kawabe looked particularly uncomfortable. Though American soldiers came close to snap pictures, no one spoke to the Japanese. There was complete silence as the forlorn group walked up to the huge four-engined plane.

They boarded the transport and sat down in far more comfortable circumstances than they had expected. They began to relax as they realized that the Americans meant them no harm. Some had thought they might be killed. Now all but Kawabe began to chat and laugh. Sour and gloomy, he sat looking out a window while the rest pulled their boots off and settled down. Out the windows they saw G.I.'s wandering around the Bettys and staring at the Japanese crewmen who stood sweating in their heavy flying suits.

At one thirty, the C-54 rose into the air. Its pilot, Colonel Earl T. Ricks, took it over the length of Okinawa to the south east, flying low to show the Japanese the vast strength concentrated on the island. Looking down from twelve hundred feet, the delegation was astounded at the arsenal displayed below. As the plane neared the southern tip of the island, a door was opened and Admiral Teraoka's bouquets of roses were tossed into the slipstream. They tumbled down over the last fortifications manned by Japanese soldiers in the war. Inside the planes sixteen men bowed their heads and offered silent prayers.

Lunch was served as the plane headed out over the water. A stewardess who moved among the Japanese caught their attention because of her blond hair which they found fascinating. The meal she and the stewards gave them consisted of bully beef sandwiches, cheese, hardboiled eggs, peanut butter, bread, cake, pickles and pineapple juice. Even the moody Kawabe ate.

The weather worsened while the plane was still quite a way from the Philippines. It pitched and rolled in the turbulence but moved steadily southward. The Japanese nodded and dozed.

Four and a half hours after taking off, the C-54 circled over the landing strip at Nichols Field southwest of Manila. Down below, an enormous sea of khaki stared up at the special plane as it swept down and onto the runway.

Kawabe led the way down the ramp from the transport. It was six o'clock in the evening of a humid day in Manila, and the sun still shone in the west. At the bottom of the steps, he halted before an American officer. Behind Kawabe other members of the delegation stopped abruptly on the steps. They noticed the quiet crowd of servicemen surrounding the plane in a vast semicircle. All the Japanese were uneasy. One of the Foreign Office representatives, Katsuo Okazaki, was particularly discomfited by the hundreds of cameras clicking, going off like machine guns. The Air Force representative, Colonel Masao Matsuda, stood stiff as a pole, staring straight ahead. Mindful of the thousands of eyes upon him, he rose to his full height and gazed over their heads at nothing.

At the bottom of the steps Kawabe stood, a short, rumpled figure, uncomfortable in his woolen uniform and his high collar. His sword dangled almost to the ground at his side. The spurs on his cavalry boots shone in the twilight.

The American who greeted him was no stranger to Japan and its people. He was Colonel Sidney Mashbir, the friend of Captain Zacharias and the author of those broadcasts to his friends in Japan in July. Looking casual in suntans and no tie, Mashbir said in fluent Japanese, "I have come to meet you." Kawabe saluted and Mashbir returned it. Then the Japanese put out his hand to Mashbir, who instinctively brought his own forward. At the last second, he realized that such a greeting was inappropriate, and jerked his hand back as though it were burned. His thumb swept over his right shoulder and pointed toward a line of waiting cars. Immediately understanding Mashbir's predicament, Kawabe withdrew his hand and walked stiffly on. The other fifteen delegates filed across the concrete as cameras clicked and whirred.

Bedraggled from the long flight, dressed in ill-fitting makeshift uniforms, the Japanese hardly looked like worthwhile foes. G.I.'s in the crowd wondered openly at the size and appearance of the enemy. Most of the opinions were good-natured. The procession was so forlorn that few servicemen could remember past bitternesses.

Behind Mashbir, another group of officers waited for the Japanese. In the center stood the very tall, brilliant General Charles Willoughby, head of General MacArthur's Intelligence Division. Willoughby was one of the inner circle, part of the small band of devoted men who formed a powerful buffer between MacArthur and the world outside. With the others, he had helped to foster the legendary aura that surrounded the pipe-smoking hero of many wars.

Kawabe walked into the first car and Willoughby stepped in behind him. Mashbir went around the car and got in beside the driver. Willoughby was friendly and asked the Japanese in what language he wished to converse. Kawabe replied, "German," which happened to be Willoughby's native tongue; he had lived in Germany until the age of twelve. Warmed by the American's pleasant manner, Kawabe felt the melancholia that had gripped him since morning begin to slip away.

Several cars were filled, and slowly left Nichols Field, heading toward downtown Manila. In one of them, a startled Japanese officer tried to think of something to say to an American Nisei interpreter, who barely let him get comfortable before asking: "When the Japanese attacked Hawaii, why didn't they land?" Still wary of Americans, the officer just stared back at him and kept silent all the way to the city.

The trip through the center of Manila was not pleasant for the Japanese. If the group was apprehensive about meeting the Americans, it had all the more reason to fear the Filipinos. Only six months before, Manila, "Jewel of the Orient," had been systematically burned to the ground by the desperate marines and sailors of the Japanese Navy, acting under orders to deny the capital of the Philippines to the enemy. During MacArthur's three-week siege in February 1945, Filipinos had died by the thousands as Japanese troops, inflamed by desperation and reckless abandon, had used them mercilessly. Mass rapes, multiple assaults on young women and little girls, had been perpetrated in streets and hallways. Columns of men and women had been doused with gasoline and set ablaze. Others had been tied together and bayoneted to death. In hospitals, nuns, nurses and patients had been stripped, raped and killed. Mutilated corpses had lain everywhere among the ruins. Manila had paid a terrible price for its freedom.

Now, as the delegation sped through the streets, Filipinos lined the route to stare at them. Stones flew out of the crowd. The air was filled with screams of "*Bacayaro!*"—"Stupid boy!"—to the Japanese, a vile epithet. Kawabe and the others looked neither right nor left as the citizens raged. Within minutes they arrived at the Rosario Apartments near the harbor.

The accommodations were surprisingly pleasant. Two men were assigned to each of the rooms, which were clean and adequate. Some had windows overlooking the magnificent bay, now crowded with ships against a setting sun.

Dinner was served in the dining room, where American officers sat and pointedly ignored the Japanese. The two factions ate in relative silence, separated by a few yards and a hundred battlegrounds.

When the time came to go to the meeting with the American instruction committee, the first trouble developed. Told that officers could no longer carry their swords with them, Kawabe and the others objected strenuously, saying that they should be allowed to wear them at least into the building where the meeting would be held. After consulting, the Americans agreed.

The Kawabe group was taken in the darkness to the City Hall, where the American delegation waited. Giving up their swords at the door to a second-floor conference room, they entered and sat down across from their conquerors.

The American leader was General Riley Sutherland, MacArthur's Chief of Staff. Sutherland—tall, thin, austerely handsome—was to speak for the Supreme Commander, who had no intention of sitting down with the enemy. The two men had been associated since the late thirties, when Sutherland had been assigned to the Philippines as a staff officer. One of his fellow aides had been Dwight Eisenhower, with whom Sutherland reputedly clashed several times. When the unhappy Eisenhower went home in 1938, Sutherland became MacArthur's right-hand man, protecting his privacy, detouring people and problems away from his door. He was a perfect second-in-command, serving his general well, acquiring a reputation for ruthless efficiency. He had been heard to say, "Somebody's got to be the bastard around here."

After introductions were made on both sides, the meeting began. Everyone was stiffly formal, conscious of the historical import of the moment. For the first time in its history, the sovereign nation of Japan was handing over its vital secrets, betraying its soul to an enemy. From this moment on it would cease to be independent.

Sutherland's voice was strong, his tone stern. He directed the Japanese to read the documents put before them, the instructions relating to the occupation and surrender. Soon a serious difference of opinion arose.

The issue in question was the American plan to land at Atsugi Airbase on August 23, in four short days. Kawabe was horrified at the proposal since he knew that conditions in Japan were still tense and that his people needed time to dismantle the still potent war machine. He objected strenuously, saying to Sutherland, "The Japanese side would sincerely advise you not to land so quickly. At least ten days are needed to prepare." As Sutherland listened impassively, he added, "Maybe you should know that we are having trouble at home with some of the kamikaze units. They delayed our trip, in fact." General Sutherland did not bother to answer. Instead he began to discuss the harbor facilities at Yokosuka, just inside the entrance to Tokyo Bay.

The original American plan called for small units of the Army and Navy to land on the twenty-third at Atsugi and in Sagami Bay southwest of Tokyo. On the twenty-fifth, the Navy would enter Tokyo Bay itself. MacArthur would land at Atsugi on the twenty-sixth as the Marines took over the Yokosuka naval base. The surrender would be formally signed on the twenty-eighth in Tokyo Bay.

Fearing a clash between still-armed Japanese soldiers and combat-hardened American troops, Kawabe's group continued to protest the speed with which the Americans intended to move. But Sutherland remained impervious, and next requested that the delegation break up into small sections to discuss various military questions. The Japanese were divided up into units according to their branch of service and the American officials proceeded to elicit information.

One by one, the vital secrets of the Japanese Empire were exposed to the enemy. Sutherland wanted to know how many divisions were emplaced around Tokyo. When told, he wanted to know how many marching days it would take them to reach the capital. He was told.

The number of planes available to the Japanese were listed. Airbases, gun emplacements, ammunition dumps, minefields, the basic components of warfare were spotted on maps of Japan.

The Americans wanted the exact location of all submarines, especially those carrying the deadly *kaiten*, the human torpedo, underwater counterpart to the kamikaze. Japanese naval personnel marked their positions at various bases on the coast of the Home Islands. Sutherland wanted assurance that none were presently on the high seas. He got it.

Every Japanese army division was pinpointed on large-scale maps. Every naval ship was marked for the enemy to locate.

As the hours went by, some stiffness went out of the meeting. Coca-Cola was served and cigarettes were passed out to the grateful Japanese. Smiles became more frequent as the American officers guided the emissaries from Tokyo through the emotion-ridden task of betraying their country's defenses. Admiral Forrest Sherman was particularly kind to his guests, who relaxed under his pleasant manner.

By four o'clock in the morning, it was done. The Japanese had handed over all their precious data to the foe.

General Sutherland made a concluding statement: "The Japanese side has furnished all the necessary information on the occupation. It is very eager to have peaceful occupation without any trouble. The United States side has the same desire but wants an early accomplishment of the occupation in agreement with the terms of the Potsdam Declaration. We do not want any wasted time. Therefore, we will make the landing date August twenty-eighth." Sutherland had conceded five days of grace to the Japanese to let them get things under control.

Kawabe was still not satisfied: "It is impossible to prepare within that time. At least ten days will be necessary. We do not want any trouble in the occupation." When Sutherland was adamant, Kawabe realized the futility of his own position. He offered one last comment: "You are the winners and so your decision is almighty, but to our way of thinking, there remains some uneasiness." The meeting ended on that note.

In the predawn darkness, the Japanese were whisked back to the Rosario Apartments where they had a prolonged discussion of the American demands. One thing was apparent. Someone should fly back to Tokyo immediately and alert authorities to the fact that Americans would be landing much sooner than expected. It was decided first to send a telegram to the Foreign Office and ask its advice.

While the wire was being sent to Tokyo, various documents presented by the Americans were examined. One of them was rather unusual and sent the blood pressures of the delegation soaring. It was a directive spelling out privileges to be accorded Occupation officers. Listed very carefully was the number of maids to be allotted to various ranks. Generals got three, colonels, majors, captains and commanders two, and the lowly lieutenant only one. In the midst of discussions about Japanese armaments, installations and other vital defense questions, the maid issue sparked a spontaneous protest in the delegation. Tempers flared as the tired, nervous Japanese raged at the offensive request. On the alert for some sign of American haughtiness, they found it in the maid issue.

Curiously, when the delegation left for Japan later that day, the maid-quota document was not in their baggage. It had been removed from the list of instructions they carried. Possibly the Americans had somehow learned of the objections Kawabe's group voiced in their private discussions.

After four hours of sleep, the Japanese were ushered to a breakfast of bacon and eggs and then taken to the City Hall for a last briefing. The August 28 deadline stayed as it was. Kawabe did not bother to argue any more.

Just before adjournment, General Sutherland handed Kawabe the draft of a surrender proclamation to be issued in the name of the Emperor. Prepared in Washington, it was now read aloud by an interpreter. Almost immediately members of the Japanese delegation tensed visibly. Kawabe's chin even began to quiver.

To some Americans in the room who were familiar with the Japanese language, the reason was obvious. In the Proclamation, pronouns normally used in connection with the Emperor's name had been omitted in favor of more common, less dignified terms. To the Kawabe group, the document was an insult to the Throne and the personage of Hirohito.

When the reading was over, Kawabe expressed his anxiety by slamming his hand down on the table. The meeting ended on this somber note.

Before boarding the plane for the return trip, Kawabe and Foreign Office official Okazaki accepted an invitation to a brief rendezvous with General Willoughby at the Rosario Apartments. There the Americans retrieved an awkward situation.

Aware that the original surrender proclamation contained serious errors, the Allied Translator and Interpreter Section in Manila had hurriedly drafted a new version containing appropriate Imperial references. This document was handed to Kawabe by Colonel Sidney Mashbir, who apologized on behalf of General Willoughby and told the Japanese to disregard the proclamation first given them at City Hall.

The Japanese were astounded and delighted at the switch in documents. On the way to the airport, they expressed their gratitude repeatedly. In this atmosphere of good will, goodbyes and salutes were exchanged at Nichols Field. At 1:00 P.M. the transport rose into a rain-filled sky and headed north to Ie.

Within nineteen hours the emissaries of two warring powers had met and discussed the pending occupation of a sovereign nation. The conqueror had been courteous, the losers on the whole impressed with the forebearance and general behavior of the victors. A good beginning had been made.

The flight to Ie was over four hours long. When the Japanese landed this time, there was no crowd to gaze at them. The two Japanese Bettys were there waiting for the delegation. However, one of them was found to have mechanical trouble, necessitating an overnight stay for eight members of the mission. Kawabe and seven others quickly took off in the other plane for the last leg of their arduous trip.

The eight delegates left on Ie prepared to spend a night in the enemy camp. They went to chow, and G.I.'s standing in line smiled at them and generally made them feel comfortable. Off in the distance, Colonel Matsuda noticed a battlefield graveyard, where Americans walked through rows of white crosses stretching for acres. Some knelt at markers and bowed their heads. The Japanese officer watched and was watched in turn as he stared at the field of dead men.

To the northeast, near the Japanese shore, the bomber carrying Kawabe to Tokyo labored on into the night. When the pilot looked at his instrument panel, he was shocked to discover the gas gauge was nearly empty. Checking it out, he found that a fuel line had sprung a serious leak. He confided his news to two naval officers, Captains Terai and Ohmae, who chose not to alarm Kawabe. As the eight men sat in the rear of the aircraft the pilot changed course to bring the ship closer to the coastline of Japan in case the fuel supply dwindled too quickly and necessitated a forced landing.

At eleven o'clock, the pilot told Kawabe that the fuel leak would force him to make an emergency landing somewhere on the coastline of Honshu several hundred miles from Tokyo. Though there was bright moonlight, the ocean below was dark and forbidding. The prospect of ditching was not pleasant.

The delegation's chief concern, however, was for the surrender documents. Kawabe wondered what the Americans might think if they were lost or destroyed. After consultation, the only possible expedient was suggested.

"Okazaki, are you still a good swimmer?" Katsuo Okazaki, the Foreign Office delegate, had been a champion swimmer, competing in 1924 in the Olympics in Paris. Now in his forties, he was being asked to guard the papers with his skill and his life. Recovering from his surprise at the question, he took them and tucked them inside his shirt.

As the plane bored in toward the coast, the pilot saw the outlines of a beach. He brought the Betty down low over the water till it was just skimming the waves. When it touched the crests, the passengers were tossed wildly about. The pilot gunned the engines and lifted the bomber slightly. It went a short distance, then settled in the water just a few yards from a smooth beach.

The top turret was flung open and the delegation tumbled out into knee-deep water. Only one man was hurt. It was Okazaki, the swimmer. He had smashed his head against the fuselage as the plane hit the surf, and lay dazed and bleeding until the others pulled him to safety.

The survivors assembled on the white beach under the brilliant summer moon. Off to the northeast, the sacred mountain Fuji stood out clearly. Stunned, soaking wet, and unable to determine their exact location, the delegates stayed on the beach forty-five minutes waiting for help to find them. Finally they moved on. A few people they saw in the vicinity only fled when hailed. Finally two fishermen stopped to listen, and guided them down a road toward a village. Police were called and a truck came to pick them up. The tired travelers were taken to an airbase where they slept fitfully for a few hours, then took off early in the morning in another antiquated plane.

In Tokyo the entire cabinet of Premier Higashi-Kuni waited in a state of extreme agitation. Knowing nothing of the forced landing, they had no idea of Kawabe's fate. When the general appeared, Higashi-Kuni embraced him and offered him the thanks of the country. Kawabe was too exhausted to appreciate the honor. He only knew that his distasteful job was finished.

EIGHTEEN

Violent Interlude

The news that Americans would be coming into the Tokyo area in only five days was terrifying to Japanese officials. They had good reason to worry.

Scattered reports filtering into command posts reflected a series of plots against the Government and surrender. American reconnaissance planes had twice been attacked by Japanese fighters since the truce of the fifteenth. Atsugi was still a source of trouble. Though Kosono had been dragged away to a padded cell, his men refused to leave the airbase. Their planes were still operational, their spirits still inflamed with the passions of misguided patriotism. Now Atsugi was the designated landing place for the first American units, and yet it was not under control.

Atsugi's defiant sentiments were shared by many young men in the armed forces of the Empire. Already a detachment of soldiers had moved on Tokyo from Mito, a city to the north, to start another coup. They had come by train to a wooded area known as Ueno Park and encamped for the night on its slopes and grass.

In downtown Tokyo, the Kempei Tai decided on a bold stroke to remove the threat to peace. Major Ishihara, one of the cohorts of Hatanaka and Koga during the attempted coup at the palace on August 14, was now released from his cell. Police had discovered that he was a close friend of the rebel leader at Ueno, and they hoped he would be able to dissuade his friend from rebellion. Ishihara had changed markedly in the past few days. Contrite over his role in the uprising, he was only too happy to cooperate with the Kempei Tai.

On the evening of August 17, he went to Ueno Park, arriving just a little before midnight. Standing among hostile soldiers, he called to his friend, "Okajima, where are you?"

Another officer rose in front of him and demanded, "What do you want with him?"

Ishihara repeated, "Okajima—"

The other man shot him dead.

When the rebel Okajima was summoned to view the body, he began to cry. His aide ripped out his sword, lunged at Ishihara's killer, and drove the weapon through his heart.

At that moment, Okajima lost his zest for a coup. When representatives of General Tanaka pressured him the next morning to disperse his men, he quickly agreed.

On the day after Kawabe returned from Manila, August 22, another crisis erupted on Atago Hill in Tokyo. A group of right-wing students, determined to resist the surrender, had been positioned in a building on top of the hill for several days; they had assembled an arsenal of ammunition and grenades. Already nervous over the pending Allied occupation, the police had quickly tried to quell the disturbance. On August 20, Kempei Tai colonel Makoto Tsukamoto walked up the slope to reason with the students. His pleas were ignored. Other police officials went to the top of Atago but were unable to disband the group. On August 22, armed men surrounded the rebels.

A call went out to Yoshio Kodama, entrusted by the Government with the handling of such incidents around the capital. Through driving rain, Kodama went to the scene in the afternoon. Both in the building and on the drenched slopes below there were enough guns in possession of rebels and militia to start the war all over again. Kodama rushed to talk to the leader of the student group and discovered he was a long-time friend, Yoshio Iijima. Iijima explained that the rebels believed the Emperor to have been forced by his advisers to surrender. When Kodama told him that he was wrong, Iijima was crushed. He and his friends broke down and cried.

When he recovered he asked, "Can we stay here at least till morning? Then we'll leave and cause no further trouble." Kodama promised to check with the police and left the building.

A steady rain had now changed to a torrential downpour. At the bottom of the hill Kodama talked with the chief of police, who told him he could not take the responsibility for allowing the insurgents to stay longer than six o'clock that night. He had already issued them an ultimatum, he told Kodama, ordering them off the hill. If the insurgents refused to withdraw, he would have to follow his orders and send his own troops up after them. Then he added, "If you get permission from headquarters I'll be happy to go along with their wishes."

Kodama ran back to the unhappy group at the top and outlined the problem. Iijima explained his reason for staying until morning: "We wanted to choose some men to die for their responsibility in this affair." The pitiful group had decided to punish itself for its own indiscretion. Kodama begged them to delay their decision until he got back.

Once more he ran down the hill in the driving rain, and once more he talked with the chief of police, who shouted over the fury of the storm: "I want to avoid any unnecessary sacrifices. I hope your efforts will succeed. Hurry back." Kodama raced off in a car to Metropolitan Police Headquarters to get an extension on the six o'clock deadline, now only thirty minutes away.

At three minutes to six, he returned armed with the power to negotiate with the rebels. As he got out of his car and looked up through the rain, he heard the reports of pistols being fired. They were followed almost instantly by an awesome series of shattering explosions which turned the top of Atago into a spreading column of black smoke. Kodama ran up the slope along with the police.

When the police prematurely fired, the young men had linked themselves into a chain, and pulled pins from grenades. They lay sprawled on the ground, their entrails spilling out, their blood carpeting the grass. The leader, Iijima, his arm blown off, lay with his lungs shredded and exposed. Weeping from shock, Kodama knelt down beside him and washed his face with rain water as police began to collect the pieces of bodies that littered the grass of Atago.

FROM THE JAPANESE IMPERIAL G.H.Q.
TO THE SUPREME COMMANDER FOR THE ALLIED POWERS
RADIOGRAM NO. 19 (AUG. 22)
    . . . IN SPITE OF OUR UTMOST EFFORTS TO AVOID CALAMITIES OF WAR, THE SITUATION IN CHINA HAS NOT BEEN IMPROVED AND THE ACTIVITIES OF IRREGULAR FORCES . . . ARE CAUSING SERIOUS DIFFICULTIES IN THE CESSATION OF HOSTILI-TIES. . . .

Both in Japan and on the fringes of the Empire, trouble continued to plague the attempts at orderly surrender.

On the evening of the twenty-third of August, another important meeting was held in Tokyo. The time had come to choose a man to meet the first Americans to land in Japan, and Japanese officials were anxious to select the proper delegate for this most delicate assignment. Upon this initial confrontation on the soil of Honshu itself might rest the character of the entire occupation.

In the heavy downpour which again drenched Tokyo that day, one man drove to the conference hopeful of being chosen for the job. Lieutenant General Seizo Arisue, the ambitious Chief of Intelligence for the Imperial Army, knew that his countrymen had to choose a high-ranking officer for this extraordinary post. Supremely confident of his own abilities, he believed that his experiences with ranking American officers before the war would stand him in good stead when the first Americans arrived and occupation began. But he had no doubt that his nomination would be challenged. He had many enemies among Foreign Office personnel, and they would probably try to prevent his selection. Arisue, a bantam-sized figure, enjoyed the prospect of a fight. A huge cigar clenched in his teeth, he got out of his limousine and walked into the midst of his enemies.

His surmise had been correct. The Foreign Office spokesmen quickly revealed their hostility. Harsh words filled the air when his name was brought up for consideration. He was called a Fascist, a friend of Mussolini, and therefore eminently unsuited for the sensitive chore of greeting MacArthur. Premier Higashi-Kuni was particularly outspoken in supporting this objection to him. Arisue hastened to take up the fight.

He could not deny that he and Mussolini had indeed become close during the period he had spent in Europe as part of his training. However, Arisue argued, just because he admired the Italian leader, it did not necessarily follow that he was a Fascist at heart.

The argument dragged on for some time, with Arisue striking back at his detractors. Perhaps because of his defiant stand, perhaps because there was nothing more positive against him than guilt by association, supporters rallied to his side at a late hour, and General Arisue won out over the faction at the Foreign Office. He was instructed to go to Atsugi Airbase the next day, August 24, to prepare for the arrival of the Americans within forty-eight hours.

When the cocky, bemedaled officer left the building and walked through the still pelting rain, he was both elated at his personal victory and appalled at the monumental challenge before him. Atsugi was a cauldron of intrigue, caused by dissident elements. It was also a badly damaged airstrip, in pitiable condition to receive the conquerors. Arisue went to bed wondering whether he could, in fact, cope with the responsibilities he had fought to assume.

At twelve o'clock the next day he had further reason to doubt. Before leaving the meeting the night before, he had requested seventy men to be present at the noon hour to go with him to the airfield. Just ten arrived at the appointed time.

General Arisue led a small caravan of cars down the dusty road to Atsugi past long columns of Japanese soldiers going the other way. Fully armed, they had been ordered to quit the area to avoid conflict with the approaching Americans. Tanks, artillery pieces and men moved steadily to the north and east as the small procession of black cars headed southwest to Atsugi and a rendezvous with the invader.

To Arisue the spectacle was unreal. His Japanese Army was leaving the field without having engaged the enemy. Unbeaten units were retreating from the beaches and defenses to which they had been assigned. Only the black limousines were traveling in the direction of the pending confrontation. Somewhere to the south, the enemy of recent years and days was preparing to fly into an airfield in strength and take control of his country. Seizo Arisue smoked his cigar in silence as he neared the airport.

When he arrived he saw that the base was a shambles. Hangars had been blasted apart by American bombs. Runways were pitted from frequent attacks. Not one of the bullet-ridden planes littering the field had a propeller.

Less than twenty-four hours before Arisue's arrival, soldiers sent by Imperial General Headquarters had arrived from Tokyo to dismantle the engines and prevent any kamikazes from making last flights against the enemy. This action had precipitated a vicious battle between the Navy personnel based there and the Army visitors. With fists, pistols and pieces of furniture they had fought for the right to control Atsugi. Rooms in the barracks had been demolished, and walls and chairs were smeared with blood. But now the kamikazes were gone. Arisue went to work.

During the evening of the same day, the exhausted general was sitting near an open window going over the status of the work details. Suddenly a loud commotion sounded outside the barracks building. He poked his head out and yelled, "What the hell is going on?" There in the moonlight two soldiers were engaged in a deadly duel with swords. They had reached an impasse over the fact of surrender and had decided to settle the issue by fighting to the death outside General Arisue's window. Their battleground was badly chosen. With the awesome responsibility of greeting the Americans before him, Arisue had no time for personal grievances. He roared through the stillness at the two combatants, who were so startled that they dropped their swords and slunk away in the darkness. General Arisue returned to his desk and a bottle of beer.

Back in Tokyo, General Seiichi Tanaka was sipping calpis—his favorite soft drink—with his aide in a room next to his office in the Dai Ichi building. He had spent the last twenty-four hours completing paper work. During the afternoon, his second son, Toshimoto, had come to visit him and the general had sent him away brusquely, saying, "Don't disturb me tonight. I'll be busy with a guest."

The day before, Tanaka had been at home for a few quiet hours with his wife and the rest of his family. He played with his grandchildren and read poems in his bedroom. When he said his goodbyes and left the house under an umbrella, his wife handed his aide a revolver, whispering, "Please give this to him."

A proud man, Tanaka had been bothered for months by the deterioration in Japan's situation. He was a sensitive intellectual, more apt than most to suffer inner conflict over such a calamity. The general's background was unlike that of most military leaders in Japan. For three years he had attended Oxford University where he had studied the works of Shakespeare. For one year, 1930, he had served as military attaché at the Japanese Embassy in Mexico City. In both places he was exposed to the more liberal philosophies of Western society. Yet in the last days of the war, Seiichi Tanaka's Oriental heritage rather than his Western education dominated his thinking.

When he assumed the command of the Eastern Army group, he was entrusted with the defense of the Tokyo district. Yet he had watched helplessly as American planes flattened a different section of the capital on each raid. The raid of May 25, which partially destroyed the Emperor's palace, had plunged him into complete despair. As sworn protector of Hirohito, Tanaka had wanted to atone for the misfortune by killing himself. Only the personal intervention of the Emperor had dissuaded him.

Unable to forget the enormity of the crime against the Throne, Tanaka continued to brood through the summer months. The attempted coup in the palace on the day of surrender was the final blow. He was shocked and hurt at the audacity of the young officers who besieged the Imperial enclave and killed others to thwart the expressed wishes of the Government. Though he succeeded in dispersing the rebels, he humbly apologized to the Emperor. Hirohito saw his agitation and expressed both appreciation for the general's actions and hopes that Tanaka would continue to work for the nation.

Tanaka had done so. After the fifteenth, he continued with the demobilization of his troops and was instrumental in resolving a number of anti-surrender outbreaks in the capital. Now the Americans were about to land in his own area of supervision—the ultimate insult to his honor. His last public statement was made to a rebellious student group at Kawaguchi: "I am telling you as the commander of the Eastern District of Japan that Japan was defeated. We must demobilize. I know what is going on in your hearts but we must all think of His Majesty.

"You men all have bright futures. It is you who must lead Japan from now on. Begin again. The atom bomb has changed the state of war completely. It is the will of God that we abandon the long history of the Japanese Army. New generations will come. Please make an effort to construct a new nation."

The young men before him and the general himself were crying when he finished.

Now, on the evening of August 24, he sat talking with his aide. The calpis he loved was followed by tea. As he finished it, he said fondly to the junior officer, "You have devoted your life to me," then rose abruptly and went into the next room. His aide sat alone for about ten minutes, his eyes filled with tears. Then a soldier came to him and told him Tanaka wished to see him.

When the aide came to the doorway of the general's office, he saw Tanaka sitting in an armchair, in full dress uniform. The two men stared at each other for an instant. Then Tanaka pulled the trigger of his pistol and tore his chest apart.

Carefully arranged on the desk beside him were his last bequests and mementos. There were six letters, his military cap, a pair of white gloves, and a gorgeous sword presented to him by the Emperor. Behind these stood a small statue of the Emperor Meiji, a cigarette case, two sacred books on Buddhism, an eyeglass case with eyeglasses, and a set of false teeth.

The general's last message to his family was simple: "All of us devoted ourselves to His Majesty as military men but now I feel terrible that Japan has been defeated. I am going to die but I do not regret it at all. I cannot help but wish for the prosperity and health of our family."

Mourners came to the office in the next hours. Mrs. Tanaka arrived and was impressively stoical in her acceptance of the death of her husband.

As she helped to change his uniform, badly stained with blood, a tall, bald-headed man stood to one side watching. General Gen Sugiyama, commander of the First Army, listened thoughtfully as Tanaka's aide explained his reasons for committing suicide. Since Sugiyama himself was undergoing a painful examination of his own philosophy in these emotional days after surrender, Tanaka's action came at a most crucial moment in his tortured thinking. Shortly thereafter the mustachioed Field Marshal paid his condolences to Mrs. Tanaka and left. Behind him the relatives and servants of Seiichi Tanaka placed his body in a wooden coffin.

Several hundred miles to the southwest of rainy Atsugi, another man was wondering exactly what conditions there were. He was particularly concerned because he was to be the first American soldier to set foot on Japan. He did not expect to live through the experience.

Charlie Tench, a colonel and West Point graduate, never thought of himself as a hero. As a member of MacArthur's staff in Manila, he had spent most of the war planning details of various invasions. When the atomic bomb fell, Tench found himself temporarily out of a job.

On the afternoon of August 19, he was sitting in his room reading old magazines when he received an unexpected summons to the office of General Stephen Chamberlain. The general laid before him a challenging assignment. Somebody had to lead a party of men into Japan before the main force landed. Communications had to be set up, the runways at Atsugi made serviceable, and order established at the airfield.

The general outlined the negotiations currently in progress with the Kawabe delegation in Manila, then asked, "How would you like to command the advance group into Japan?" Tench was flattered, though a bit staggered at the thought of being the first one into enemy territory. He recovered quickly, however, and said, "I wouldn't miss it for the world."

When the Kawabe delegation left, final plans were made for Tench's "invasion." He and his men would go to Okinawa on the twenty-fifth and leave for Japan at midnight that same day. The intervening period would be utilized by the Japanese to quell any disturbances by the kamikazes.

Tench was not very happy about the fact that rebels still roamed through Japan. At the colonel's mess in Manila, he endured the heavy humor of fellow officers who kept a betting pool on his chances for survival. Opinion was divided equally. Fifty percent thought his plane would be blown from the sky as it approached Atsugi. The others were sure that he would be murdered as he stepped from the plane. Tench was not amused. He was aware that General Kawabe had been worried about the unrest in his own country, and that he had implored the Americans to hold off occupation for at least ten days.

On the twenty-fifth, the advance party emplaned for Okinawa. It was buffeted by a typhoon, gaining strength in the area, and it did not reach Fifth Air Force Headquarters until noon of that day.

Tench went to the headquarters of General Whitehead and participated in a thorough briefing on the mission. Though no one openly suggested that the Japanese around Tokyo might resist the landing, everyone recognized that possibility. Tench was on edge but kept his thoughts to himself. As the afternoon progressed, the typhoon's fury increased. The rains became a deluge, and the area around Atsugi in Japan lay in the middle of the storm. While the Japanese labored desperately to make the airfield ready, the Americans debated the wisdom of sending Tench out into the bad weather. In the evening, the answer came from Manila. A forty-eight-hour postponement was ordered. The Japanese had two more days to bring sanity to the airstrip, to control the unmanageable elements, to repair the damage to the base. Everyone in Japan, and particularly Colonel Charles Tench on Okinawa, breathed deeply in relief.

Japan was growing tense with fear.

In Gifu City, the mayor ordered all girls aged fifteen to twenty-five to go into the mountains to avoid American soldiers.

Women workers at the Nakajima Aircraft Company plant in Utsonomiya asked the factory manager for poison to swallow in case American soldiers tried to rape them. They were given cyanide capsules.

At the Kanto Kyogo Company, similar capsules were distributed to one thousand women workers in order to help them "maintain their honor as Japanese ladies" in case of attack.

In Tokyo itself, newspapers published a series of articles advising the people how to act toward the advancing Americans. Women were warned to wear loose-fitting clothes in order to appear less attractive to soldiers. In case they were attacked, they must "maintain their dignity while crying loudly for help." Fathers and husbands were cautioned to remove their females to the countryside until the occupation was well underway. It was repeatedly stressed that women should not smile at strangers as they often did because Americans might misconstrue the basic Japanese friendliness as an invitation of another sort.

Above all, the citizens of Japan were reminded of the country's proud spirit which would lead them to a better life in the coming years. The Government was attempting to shore up the confidence of the people, to restore some semblance of self-respect to the nation.

FROM THE JAPANESE IMPERIAL G.H.Q.
TO THE SUPREME COMMANDER FOR THE ALLIED POWERS
RADIOGRAM NO. 13
SOME OFFICERS AND MEN OF THE ALLIED POWERS WITHOUT GIVING A PREVIOUS NOTICE CAME RY AIRPLANE TO SOME PLACES UNDER JAPANESE CONTROL FOR THE PURPOSE OF MAKING CONTACT WITH OR GIVING COMFORT TO PRISONERS OF WAR OR CIVILIAN INTERNEES. . . . WE EARNESTLY REQUEST YOU TO PREVENT THE RECURRENCE OF SUCH INCIDENTS. . . .

The Japanese were complaining about the mercy teams sent from Gus Krause's base at Hsian to various prison camps. They were afraid that such missions would cause bloodshed between Americans and still armed Japanese troops. So far, all of the parachute units dropped behind enemy lines had come through the ordeal unscathed, without suffering any killed or wounded. The fears of the officials at Chungking and Kunming had not materialized.

At Mukden, Hennessy's team survived an initial fright and effected a complete success.

At Weischien, parachutists found their biggest problem the civilian internees. Overjoyed at the sight of healthy-looking Americans, some of the women proved almost unmanageable in their affection.

At Keijo, Korea, the American team was greeted by a Japanese officer, who begged them to go home before any trouble erupted. He offered them gasoline, then put them under protective custody. The next day the Americans returned to base without getting to the nearby POW camp. The commanding officer of the parachute team was promptly relieved of his duties by angered American superiors.

At Peking, a team under Major Roy Nichols jumped in to find the Japanese-held city already "pacified" by Jim Kellis and his small band. While tending to the needs of POW's in the area, Nichols' group, code-named Operation Magpie, solved a mystery that had disturbed American officials for over three years. Guided by a released internee, Hector Duberriere, the team overcame Japanese efforts at concealment and found the last survivors of two American bomber crews missing since 1942.

In April of that year, a group of B-25's under General Jimmy Doolittle had been sent from the carrier Hornet to bomb Japan. On returning from the mission, eight airmen crash-landed in China and were trapped by the Japanese. Tried for "indiscriminate attacks on civilians," the Americans were sentenced to death. Three were actually executed.

On October 15, 1942, Lieutenant Dean Hallmark, Lieutenant William Farrow and Sergeant Harold Spatz were led out to a cemetery in Shanghai. They knew they were about to die. The day before, they had written last letters home.

Farrow told his mother: "Read Thanatopsis by Bryan if you want to know how I am taking this. My faith in God is complete, so I am unafraid." Spatz told his father that he loved him. Hallmark could not really believe he was going to be dead soon.

At the cemetery, the fliers were made to kneel before three wooden crosses to which their arms were tied. White cloths were wrapped around their foreheads. Black dots in the middle of each cloth marked the aiming point for the firing squad. The Americans died in a volley of rifle fire.

After the execution, Japanese soldiers placed the bodies in caskets and saluted the fallen warriors.

The sentences of the remaining crewmen were commuted to life imprisonment. Lieutenant Robert Meder lingered for over a year before dying of malnutrition, beri-beri and medical neglect. Of the surviving four, Sergeant James De Shazar became increasingly weak and was subject to visions. Lieutenants Robert Hite and Chase Nielsen remained in relatively fair condition, compared to George Barr, who was almost dead when he was rescued. Barr was hospitalized in China for months. The other three started for home immediately.

Elsewhere, the world was pleased by the announcement on August 24 of a peace pact. Chiang Kai-shek and Joseph Stalin, through their representatives T. V. Soong and V. M. Molotov, had agreed on a joint policy in the Far East, especially in the area of North China and Manchuria. Russia professed special interest in Port Arthur and Dairen, warm water ports on the Yellow Sea. China professed equal interest in Manchuria itself. Many points were thrashed out in the nine-part pact, but one in particular stood out. The Russians agreed "to render to China moral support and aid in military supplies and other material resources, such support and aid to be given entirely to the Nationalist Government and the Central Government of China."

Regarding the declaration, *The New York Times* reflected general feeling in the United States when it observed: "The clouds of civil war that have darkened China's horizon are already beginning to recede."

Some interested parties did not think so. State Department officials in Washington were not sure that Stalin had guaranteed China anything. Others, like Ambassador Averill Harriman in Moscow, were disturbed to realize that since Soviet armies were already in control of Manchuria, Russian adherence to any agreement was strictly at the whim of the Kremlin. Worried Americans could only hope that Stalin meant to keep his word, and to maintain, among other things, an Open Door policy in China. It was a forlorn hope.

Russia had already formulated a far-reaching scheme for the entire Far East. In July a Japanese espionage agent had gained access to a Soviet committee report prepared especially for the pending Potsdam Conference. This ambitious policy paper outlined both a long-range strategy and short-term tactics. Ultimately it called for (1) the union of Japanese leftists with disaffected Army and Navy officers after the war in order to thwart the growth of an "American" democracy in Japan; (2) combination of Japanese industry with Chinese agriculture in a Sino-Japanese Leftists Union, which would eventually control the propertied classes in both countries; (3) the organization of both Korea and Formosa into Communist states.

For the immediate future, it suggested support for the agrarian class in Northwest China, and envisioned this group as an anchor of strength for the Russians in the Far East.

The Soviets acted on this last objective in August of 1945.

FROM THE JAPANESE G.H.Q.
TO THE SUPREME COMMANDER FOR THE ALLIED POWERS
AUGUST 24, 1945
    . . . IN CERTAIN LOCALITIES DISARMED JAPANESE FORCES AND CIVILIANS ARE BEING MADE VICTIMS OF ILLEGITIMATE FIRING, LOOTING, ACTS OF VIOLENCE, RAPE AND OTHER OUTRAGES. . . . THE SITUATION IS CERTAIN TO GET OUT OF CONTROL. . . .

On the Asian mainland, the Communists had just begun to fight. Soviet forces were swarming over the countryside.

plundering like the Mongol hordes of the twelfth century. Already they had lanced through weakened Japanese fortifications along the Manchurian and Korean borders and were headed directly for the populous plains around Mukden and Port Arthur. Acting in concert with them, the long-besieged troops of Mao Tse-tung infiltrated from the caves of Yenan toward the big cities of North China in quest of guns and ammunition for the final battle to defeat Chiang Kai-shek. At Kalgan, near the Manchurian border, Russian soldiers captured a huge ammunition dump and turned it over to Communist guerrillas, an action specifically prohibited at the Yalta Conference. Stalin was beginning to break his agreements with the Chiang Kai-shek Government, with America, with all his wartime allies.

In North Korea, political officers of the Soviet Army agitated in the streets, exhorting the Korean civilians to expropriate all Japanese property. An "Executive Committee" of the Korean People was quickly formed as the Reds moved to set up a base for subversion of the masses. The discernible pattern was a familiar one; Russia had begun to seduce its newly won territories. Slowly a curtain of steel was being established around Stalin's Far Eastern gains.

In North China, American OSS units in the field were virtually surrounded by militant Chinese Reds. Major Gus Krause's prophecy of a new war was tragically accurate. In the countryside around the big cities, the Communists daily grew bolder. They blocked entrance to towns, they engaged in skirmishes with Nationalist and Japanese forces. They also killed their first American.

John M. Birch was a captain in the Air Force and a special agent attached to the OSS. From the main base at Hsian in North China, Birch operated in forays behind the Japanese lines. Fellow officers knew him as a quiet, unassuming person, devoid of any personality traits which would make him stand out in a crowd.

Later, in fact, some at Hsian were hard pressed to recall anything at all unusual about him.

When Emperor Hirohito broadcast the news of surrender to the Japanese people, Captain Birch was at Lingchuan, in Anhwei Province, positioned there to take advantage of any precipitate enemy collapse. Within days, Birch received instructions from Hsian to proceed toward the city of Suchow in an attempt to ascertain Chinese Communist intentions in the area. The OSS was concerned about the growing menace from the Reds, and had ordered several teams to reconnoiter their territories for further information to be passed on to Washington. Birch headed toward the danger zone at the head of a mixed band of American, Chinese and Korean agents.

The boyish-looking captain with the protruding ears was exceedingly well qualified for his job. The son of a Baptist missionary, he had spent much of his life among the Chinese people. He was amazingly fluent in the varied dialects of the countryside, and had also acquired a profound understanding of the Chinese. He was deeply disturbed by the rising power of the Communist army among the peasants and firmly convinced that the Reds posed a tremendous threat to the future of the country. Now at noon of August 24, Captain Birch embarked on a supposedly routine journey to Suchow.

The trip was not easy. The unit went on foot, by boat and by train. Communists were in evidence on all sides. In the vacuum left by the retreating Japanese, they had come out into the open to assume control of key points. Entire sections of railroads were being systematically ripped up by Red guerrillas, who occupied much of the rural landscape. Birch became increasingly dismayed.

As the OSS team neared Suchow, Birch and the others were forced to proceed by foot due to increasing interference with rail travel.

On August 25, he and his party had advanced to within thirty miles of their objective. At a rail depot, they ran right into a

Communist roadblock, set up to prevent access to the Japanese-held city.

Birch was furious. Already disturbed by the harassment imposed by the Reds during the arduous journey, he was incensed at this latest incident. He ordered his aide, a Nationalist officer named Tung, to find the Communist commander in charge and request permission to proceed into Suchow.

Tung found the man and repeated Birch's instructions. The officer listened for a moment, then turned to an aide and said, "Here come some more spies." He added that the Birch team should be disarmed.

Birch's aide was horrified at this prospect and rushed back to the American captain to warn him. Birch immediately confronted the Chinese commander who had voiced the threat. "So you intend to disarm us. Are you bandits? Are you the man responsible for this situation?" When the officer said that he was not, Birch insisted that he be taken directly to the Chinese officer's superior.

He told Tung, "I must find out who these soldiers belong to and who the commanding officer is." Fearful of the consequences, others in the Birch party cautioned him to be more subtle in dealing with the belligerent Communists who now escorted him along the rail line. One of the Nationalist officers in the OSS team whispered to Tung, "Tell the captain to be more polite to this group." Although Tung repeated the urgent message, Birch refused to change his attitude. He was disgusted with the hostile guerrillas and determined to have a showdown.

He spoke to Tung as they marched along: "I want to find out how they intend to treat Americans. I don't mind if they kill me, for if they do, their movement will be finished. The United States will use the atomic bomb to stop their banditry."

The Communists led the OSS team from one position to another, looking for the one officer Birch had requested permission to address. The American captain's temper was growing shorter by the minute as he was forced to walk around and around in the custody of the Red guerrillas. Finally he exploded. Seizing the nearest officer by the collar, he shouted, "You're worse than bandits." His aide, Tung, said quickly to the officer, "He is only joking."

In this tense atmosphere, a senior Communist officer appeared from a building and stood watching the two men shouting at each other. Suddenly he shouted, "Load your guns and disarm him." His finger pointed directly at Captain Birch. Tung saw that Birch was in no mood to be coerced, and pleaded, "Wait a minute. I'll get his gun for you." The Communist officer in charge looked at him coldly and said to his men, "Shoot him first."

A guerrilla cocked his gun and fired into Tung's right leg near the hip. As he fell to the ground, another soldier fired at John Birch. Tung heard a man say, "Bring him along," apparently in reference to Birch, who was lying in agony in the dust. Before Tung lapsed into unconsciousness, he heard Birch cry, "I can't walk."

The Communists dragged the OSS captain to another spot, where his hands were bound behind his back. He was then prodded into a kneeling position before his captors. A Communist officer stepped behind him, placed a pistol to his head and blasted a hole in his skull. The body sagged face down, blood spreading quickly from it. Then, perhaps to hinder identification, Birch's face was repeatedly slashed with bayonets.

Several days later, other OSS agents found him, his hands still tied behind his back, his G.I. fatigues caked with blood. He lay in the dirt, his face a festering mass without any recognizable features. The body was photographed, wrapped in a white shroud and placed in a pine box. Taken to Suchow, Birch's original destination, it was buried on the side of a hill overlooking the city. His murderers had long since vanished into the countryside.

The details of John Birch's death were brought back to OSS headquarters. Pictures of his mutilated body were displayed to shocked American officials who could do nothing more than

relay this latest symptom of Communist hostility and aggressiveness to Washington. They hoped that such evidence of Red tactics
in China might alert the United States Government to take a
more positive stance in the crucial weeks ahead.

NINETEEN

Lazarus

In Manchuria, General Jonathan Wainwright was still missing. In Washington and Chungking, alarmed officials continued to worry about his fate, and his rescue had assumed paramount importance. In the eyes of the American public, Wainwright was a martyred hero of the dark days of 1942. He symbolized the men who had paid the price for American unpreparedness before Pearl Harbor.

Wainwright was a professional soldier, a prototype of the men who led the American army during the tedium of peace before World War II. His family had a military heritage dating back before the Civil War. His grandfather had been a member of the first class to graduate from the Naval Academy in the 1840's. Killed at Galveston Bay in 1863, he had initiated a family tradition of duty to country. Wainwright's uncle had been killed in 1871 in a gun battle with a pirate ship off the coast of Mexico. In that same year his father had entered West Point.

In 1906, Jonathan himself graduated from the Academy and embarked on a career which included thirty-four long years of relatively uneventful service. He did fight against the Moros in the Philippines, and he served as a staff officer in World War I. But mostly he trained the small peacetime army. In 1938 he was made brigadier general.

In 1940, Wainwright received his most challenging assignment when he was sent to Manila to command the Philippines Division then being formed under a stepped-up program. There, General Douglas MacArthur directed the overall defense of the islands. Retired from the American Army in 1937, the famous soldier had gone to the Philippines at the request of that nation to help build up its fighting strength.

Neither MacArthur nor men like Wainwright could work a miracle in the brief time allotted. Though the Filipinos were given some semblance of training in the period of grace before Pearl Harbor, it was not enough. Equipment was practically nonexistent. Airpower was negligible. Ground troops had only a rudimentary knowledge of field strategy and tactics.

On the morning of December 8, 1941 (December 7, Hawaii time), General Wainwright rose in his darkened bedroom to answer the insistent phone. He learned that Pearl Harbor was devastated. At this point the general, in his thirty-sixth year of service, embarked upon the climactic assignment of his career—and perhaps the most cruel duty an American general endured during the entire war.

The Japanese struck boldly at the Philippines. On the first day they destroyed almost every bomber and fighter plane the United States had in the Far East. Within a week they invaded Luzon at several points and engaged the American and Filipino divisions in the first major land battle of the Pacific war. Wainwright fought a hopeless fight. Outnumbered, outgunned, his inexperienced men died on the trails in front of the onrushing enemy.

By December 23, just fifteen days after hostilities began, MacArthur saw that only one maneuver was left. He initiated War Plan Orange-3, the long-agreed-upon strategy of withdrawal to the Bataan Peninsula, on the northern side of Manila Bay. Here the Americans would stand and make a final effort. Wainwright was ordered to take his troops into this jungle fortress and assume predetermined positions.

As commander of the northern Luzon troops, Wainwright held the Japanese at bay while other elements from southern

Luzon moved up to and around Manila into the temporary sanctuary of Bataan. For over three months these men denied control of the peninsula to the Japanese. For over three months the thousands trapped on the steaming battleground managed to live, and challenge the enemy. During that time, MacArthur was ordered to Australia by President Roosevelt, and Wainwright assumed supreme command of all forces in the Philippines. Rarely has a man been given a more onerous responsibility.

War Plan Orange envisaged a six-months defense of the islands until help came from the United States. The forces on Bataan were holding fairly well to that concept. The only flaw was the lack of reinforcements from America. No armada was on its way. No fleet or concentration of air power was being readied at Pearl Harbor to bring relief to the beleaguered men on Bataan. They were isolated, without hope.

The soldiers had eaten the last horse and most were starving to death. Malaria had sapped their strength. Ammunition was very low. On April 9, guns stopped firing and an ominous silence came over the bay. On Corregidor, the island fortress at the entrance to the harbor, Wainwright looked across at the peninsula of Bataan and felt desperately alone.

The Japanese concentrated on Corregidor with ferocious intensity. Large-caliber shells rained on the Rock, where men trembled in tunnels. Over a thousand wounded lay helpless in the hospital deep inside the cavernous fortifications.

On the fifth of May, the Japanese landed on Corregidor and moved toward the main headquarters. Wainwright had to make a dreadful decision: to sacrifice the remaining survivors in a suicidal resistance, or to surrender in order to keep his men alive.

At 10:30 A.M. on May 6, the radio station on Corregidor came alive: "Message for General Homma . . . message for General Homma. . . ." A white flag went to the top of a pole at noon, and the Philippines command of General Jonathan Wainwright ceased to exist.

Wainwright went into captivity. When he heard the details of the Bataan Death March, he wondered if he was to blame for the horrible aftermath to surrender. Would it have been better to have ordered a fight to the last? He became a tortured man. For over three years his conscience nagged him. Wanting rescue badly, he nevertheless feared its consequences.

By the summer of 1945, Wainwright resembled a skeleton navigating under its own power. He weighed less than 130 pounds. The skin on his face was tightly drawn, and his clothes hung grotesquely on his six-foot-three-inch frame. His spirit had been sapped by the harsh treatment received in various Japanese camps, yet he had struggled manfully to stay alive until the day of freedom. The general was confined at Sian, a small waystop northeast of Mukden. Only thirty-five other prisoners were with him. Half of them were Allied general officers or high officials, such as the governor of Singapore and General Percival, the defender of that bastion when it fell in 1942.

They had come to this remote land only the previous fall from Formosa, where the bulk of the Bataan captives had been kept for over two years. During that time, many men had died and others had become living corpses. The enemy had been callous, calculatedly inhuman and vindictive. The worst treatment came from the Japanese privates and corporals—the beatings, the occasional punches in the face, the hours at attention in the freezing cold. Wainwright himself had been beaten badly on several occasions. What hurt him more, however, were the less direct torments. When Red Cross packages arrived at the camps the men would delight at the thought of food. Yet the packages seldom were distributed to the prisoners. Their hopes for this little extra supply of nourishment would rise and fall quickly as the commandants managed to "lose" the packages or pass them out to their own soldiers.

For over three years, Jonathan Wainwright managed to survive this life. He amused himself as best he could. He read *Northwest Passage* and *Oliver Wiswell* over and over till he could recite them almost word for word. He played solitaire by the hour and kept track of the times he won. He was the official sharpener of razors for the Allied personnel in the camp.

Though he picked up bits of information about the war by various means, he had no inkling that the Americans were even as close as Okinawa. He saw no planes, heard no bombings. For him, the war was still far enough away to make the future seem especially grim. Having barely survived the unbelievable cold of the Manchurian winter, he was despondent about his own life. He had nearly frozen to death in the barracks. Temperatures of 45 degrees below zero made the meager stove heat almost useless. Though he slept in all the clothing he could find, he shivered through the long, bitter nights and into a spring that was filled with a bleak sameness. The food was tasteless and barely palatable. There was cornmeal mush at breakfast, a thin gruel for lunch, and vegetables and soya curd for supper. Day in and day out, the monotonous, barren existence preyed on Wainwright and the others.

On August 16, after exactly twelve hundred days in captivity, General Wainwright was sitting in his room playing solitaire—game number 8,632. Corporal Willard, an orderly, knocked on the door, stuck his head in, and smiled: "I congratulate you, General."

"Really? For what?"

"The war is over."

Wainwright's mind reeled, "I don't believe it. Who told you?"

Willard told him that a Japanese interpreter at the camp had just explained that the Russians had invaded Manchuria and Japan had sued for peace.

Dazed, Wainwright said, "Was he drunk or sober?"

Willard answered, "Well, he'd had some sake."

Though not completely convinced, Wainwright could not sleep all night.

In the morning, the Japanese commandant, Lieutenant Marui, confirmed the prisoners' wild speculations. They were lined up in formation and told, "By order of the Emperor, the war has been amicably terminated." The phrasing of the speech struck the small group the same way at the same instant. They broke out into a spontaneous burst of laughter, which rose to an hysterical pitch. The years of imprisonment, the moments of torture, the sustained humiliation burst out of the mouths of the thirty-five emaciated soldiers and echoed among the foothills of the Manchurian mountains.

Major Robert Lamar arrived at the gates of Sian on August 19. While Sergeant Harold Leith remained outside, Lamar entered the commandant's office. Lieutenant Marui was quite gracious and promptly offered the doctor a cup of tea. When Lamar asked to see the prisoners, Marui said he would have to wait until the next day. The two men began to argue. After a prolonged discussion, the Japanese officer relented and sent for General Wainwright.

Several minutes later, the emaciated man appeared. He did not enter. Instead, he waited at the door. He stared at Lamar and whispered, "Are you really Americans?" Lamar nodded and identified himself.

Wainwright waited where he stood until Marui signaled him across the threshold. Then he took a few steps in, stopped again, and bowed from the waist to his captor.

Major Lamar quickly jumped up and offered the general a chair. Marui shouted, "He must remain standing." Wainwright said nothing. Lamar insisted that he be seated. Another argument began. During it Wainwright stood to one side, listening calmly.

Lamar won. Jonathan Wainwright sat down in the presence of his enemy. Lamar turned and said, "General, you are no longer a prisoner. You're going back to the States."

Wainwright thought a moment, then asked the one question that had plagued him for so many long days and nights: "What do the people in the States think of me?" His eyes bored into Lamar's as the major answered, "You're considered a hero there. Your picture is even in *Time* magazine."

Wainwright was not convinced. When he went back to his quarters, he was still not sure what awaited him on the outside.

Lamar and Leith stayed that night at Sian, and had breakfast the following morning with all of the Allied officers stationed there. The OSS men watched as the prisoners carefully counted out each bean for the soup so that no one would be cheated. They were impressed with the general lethargy that dulled the spirits of the men sitting at the table.

Lamar made a decision during the morning. Because his radio was out of order, he could not advise Hennessy at Mukden that Wainwright and the others were alive. Fearing that this special group of officers might possibly be used as hostages by Japanese or Russian forces in the area, Lamar left Leith behind and went back to Mukden that day to make arrangements for prompt transportation.

There, his plans for quick action were foiled by the entry of Russian troops. When he attempted to round up vehicles to accommodate the prisoners, he was met by indifference on the part of the Soviets, who had begun to drink up all the liquor in Mukden.

While Lamar fought his frustrating battle with the Russians, the wait seemed interminable to the prisoners at Sian. Three, four long, restless days passed without American troops appearing on the road from the south. Wainwright and the others moped around, deflated but at least free to go about the camp as they pleased.

Finally, on the morning of August 24, a commotion at the gate announced the arrival of strangers—not Americans, but a thirty-man squad of burly, vigorous Russian soldiers. Their leader, a ferocious-looking bearded lieutenant colonel walked up to Wainwright and said to him through Leith, who spoke Russian: "I'm headed for Mukden with my detachment and these jeeps. If you can furnish your own transportation and be ready in an hour, I'll take you with me." The colonel wanted no nonsense and brooked no delay by the Americans. He was still at war with Japanese units straggling through the fluid lines in Manchuria.

The Americans were only too glad to leave under any circumstances. Wainwright turned to Lieutenant Marui, his Japanese ruler for these many months, and asked that buses be provided for the prisoners. Marui, cowed by the sight of Russian troops cradling machine guns, quickly answered "Yes, sir." Wainwright savored the reply. It was the first time in years any Japanese had shown him that courtesy.

The contingent from Sian headed southwest in the midst of a convoy of American-built jeeps painted with the Red Star of the Soviet Union. The Russians promptly got lost. For almost a full day, the Americans endured the wanderings of the Soviet column as it drove up and down the roads of Manchuria looking for Mukden. Eventually they abandoned the jeeps for a train. When it broke down, they commandeered another one from a Japanese crew. In the meantime, American authorities had become frantic about Wainwright. Search planes scoured the countryside. Rumors circulated that the Russians had kidnapped the general and spirited him back into Siberia. He was alive, but where?

At 1:30 A.M. on the morning of August 27, a weary group arrived at the railroad yards in Mukden. The trip was over. As his coach car came to a stop, Wainwright slumped into an exhausted sleep. Leith went looking for Lamar, who soon came to Wainwright with exciting news. Not only was the general to fly to Chungking that morning but he had been invited to attend the surrender ceremonies on the *Missouri*. MacArthur had requested his presence. Wainwright was overjoyed. He waved the cane given to him years before by MacArthur, and stepped off the train and away from the past.

Nine men walked into a C-47 transport plane in the darkness of predawn China. Lights on the runway at the Kunming airstrip illuminated the parachutes on their backs and the American

flags sewn on their left sleeves. They were dressed in green fatigues and wore the jumpboots of the paratrooper. The nine
men were part of Mission Pigeon, a quick and skillful thrust
into the Japanese-held island of Hainan, off the coast of South
China. They were yet another OSS detachment intent on bringing relief to Allied prisoners still living in misery behind the
enemy lines.

There was reason to believe that the Japanese on Hainan, cut
off from normal communications with their headquarters, were
unaware that the war had been over for twelve days. The men
settling down in the C-47 for the long ride to the drop zone
expected trouble at the other end.

The leader of the team was a wiry, twenty-four-year-old blond
from California, Major John Singlaub. He had achieved that rank
within the last few hours and it was only temporary. It had been
decided that giving him such status would allow him more lever-
age in dealing with any Japanese officer who refused to concede
that the war was truly over. Singlaub would act as spokesman, and
on his actions might depend the fate of the entire group.

He had a radioman, Sergeant Tony Denneau; a medic, Corporal James Healey; Intelligence officers Charles Walker, John
Bradley, and Arnold Breakey; an adjutant, Captain Len Woods;
and interpreters, lieutenants Peter Fong and Ralph Yempuku, a
short, stocky Nisei from Hawaii. A veteran of OSS campaigns in
Thailand and Indochina, here Yempuku had a particularly tick-
lish job. It would be up to him to communicate quickly with possibly belligerent Japanese, to interpret for both sides, to smooth
over any rough spots.

None of the men had ever worked together before. They had
been called to Kunming from various assignments to fly as a unit
onto an enemy island. Singlaub had organized the many details
of the mission under great pressure, including a flood at Kunming
which had inundated the city. Now the C-47 gained speed down
the Kunming runway and took off into the night. Mission Pigeon
was airborne.

As the team flew southeast, it discussed the strategy to be used in meeting the Japanese. Singlaub knew that the first moments of the confrontation would be crucial to their fate. If the Japanese who saw the OSS men land were inclined to continue the war, Singlaub and his men might be quickly despatched. It all depended on that initial reaction.

In the early light of August 27, the C-47 droned over the South China Sea and came to its landfall, the Bakli Bay section of Hainan. Somewhere near this inlet, there was a prison camp housing remnants of Australian and Dutch armies that had been annihilated by the Japanese over three years ago in Java and other islands of the East Indies. Photographs taken recently showed a cluster of buildings about a mile or so in from the seashore. Without any other positive information, Singlaub could only assume that this compound was the target.

As the plane came down toward the island, he ordered the pilot to fly in very low over the terrain in order to pick a suitable landing place. Seeing a fairly clear field, he gave instructions to the men. They would jump from six hundred feet and quickly assemble the various supplies being dropped with them. When the Japanese appeared, Singlaub would talk to them through Yempuku.

The plane circled the designated landing area and nine men leaped out and floated down under billowing parachutes, followed by medical and food supplies.

Yempuku smashed his chin on landing and stood up with blood streaming from it. Captain Len Woods hit his head and was groggy as he reached for his camera to record the unfolding action. The others landed without mishap. Medic Jim Healey put a butterfly bandage on Yempuku's cut.

Singlaub looked about and saw in the distance a huge crowd of Chinese civilians, coming over the brow of a hill toward the group. From the other direction, he saw three trucks filled with Japanese troops speeding down a road from the general area of the prison camp. The OSS unit had reached its crisis almost immediately.

Affecting unconcern, the nine men went about picking up supplies and gathering them into a pile while the speeding trucks headed straight into the grassy meadow. When the trucks stopped, Singlaub turned to face the first man who got out and walked toward him. He was a lieutenant challenging the Americans at once:

"Who are you?"

Yempuku repeated the words to Singlaub, who shouted: "We have come to help the Allied prisoners now that the war is over. Send your soldiers to the far side of the field to protect my people and equipment from those civilians."

Prefacing his speech with "The major says," Yempuku translated for the Japanese. Obviously confused by Singlaub's abrupt command, the lieutenant hesitated. The two groups stood fifty feet apart, silent, alert and apprehensive. Singlaub and his men wore sidearms but kept their hands away from them. The Japanese troops, far outnumbering the Americans, held their rifles ready and waited for the lieutenant to make a move.

The Japanese officer's slow reaction lost him the initiative. Finally he spoke to his men, who quickly moved out across the field toward the Chinese bordering it. He had already committed himself to the Americans, and Singlaub followed up the advantage, saying, "Turn them around to face the Chinese."

The befuddled lieutenant turned his men and their weapons away from the Americans.

"Bring a truck over here to help load up the supplies."

The truck moved across the field to the supplies. By sheer nerve, Singlaub had won the first round.

The Americans sat in the back of a truck as it sped over the hills to a cluster of buildings where 356 soldiers and sailors lived in this August of 1945.

The OSS men were taken to a long barracks-like building which served as a mess hall for the Japanese. Their gear and supplies were brought inside and stacked up. At the moment they were still free men.

Singlaub would not discuss anything with the Japanese lieutenant, who appeared to have recovered his poise somewhat. Instead, he insisted on talking to the ranking officer at the camp, and told the lieutenant to get in touch with the colonel or general or whoever had authority to treat with the American unit. The Japanese, still compliant, went into the next room to telephone. Ralph Yempuku eavesdropped as he spoke excitedly to the person on the other end.

"Colonel, they jumped in here in broad daylight. . . . He says the war is over. . . . But they landed here in the middle of the day. . . . Yes, but the major says the war is over. . . . Yes, sir."

The lieutenant came back to his visitors and asked them to be patient. The colonel could not arrive until the next day, and until that time, they would be housed in the mess hall. They could also keep their guns.

The OSS men went into their new home and got settled. Unobtrusively, a full complement of Japanese troops took up positions around the perimeter of the building. The Japanese, still unsure of whether or not the Americans were telling the truth, had carefully balanced themselves on both sides of the issue. Though still armed, the team was under house arrest, and until the Japanese heard otherwise, the war was officially on.

As darkness settled over the compound on Hainan, Major John Singlaub did not know whether his bluff had worked or not. The guards outside were not a reassuring sign but at least his team was alive.

A Chinese cook came to the mess hall to cook dinner for the Americans. At first surprised and pleased by the friendly gesture, Singlaub and his weary, nervous men then began to consider the possibility of being poisoned. The Japanese could dispose of the bodies and claim that the Americans had met with foul play at the hands of the many bandits who infested the hills of Hainan.

The excellent food went down slowly and laboriously as the OSS men watched each other for spasms. None occurred. The last course was as good as the first.

During the night the nine men talked and dozed fitfully. The next morning, the guards were still outside the building. They offered no opposition to the Americans as they came and went, but obviously they were there in case an order came down from someone on the island to take action against the invaders.

The morning was nearly over before a procession of cars arrived at the gate. A colonel stepped out; at last Singlaub could deal with a ranking officer. They met across a long table, each surrounded by his own staff.

Major Singlaub was blunt: "We have come here to help the Allied prisoners under your control. The war is over and we want to get them medical treatment."

The colonel looked for a moment at the young American, who could gauge nothing from his reaction. Suddenly he smiled: "I have just learned about the ending of the war from headquarters."

The suspense was over. The American gamble had succeeded. The elated Singlaub launched into a discussion of the needs of the prisoners. He asked that a senior officer among the captives be brought to the conference to detail the most pressing problems. Reluctantly, the Japanese colonel agreed.

An Australian, Lieutenant Colonel William Scott, appeared. A tall, very lean military professional, Scott had endured the harsh years of captivity without breaking. Rather he had worked to maintain the morale of men gradually destroyed by disease and calculated privations. At the end, the Australians under his command were in far better condition than their Dutch counterparts.

When Scott stepped into the room, Singlaub immediately told the Japanese colonel to move and make room for him. The Japanese stiffened at the order. Singlaub repeated it in a harsh voice. The Japanese moved his chair to one side and Scott sat down as an equal.

He outlined the situation. Food was the main requirement. Medicine would come later. When the Americans adjourned the meeting, Scott passed Singlaub on his way out and furtively pressed upon him a worn collection of papers. It was a diary of his years of captivity and an indictment of the Japanese keepers.

The Japanese had stalled Singlaub overnight in order to do some housekeeping in the compound. An electric barbed wire fence had been removed but Singlaub saw holes in the ground where the poles had been. The prisoners' food had improved somewhat, but their cadaverous bodies testified to the systematic maltreatment given them for years. *Systematic* was the correct term, for a Japanese doctor had used the prisoners in a grim experiment. He had deliberately brought men to the edge of starvation to test his theories about nutrition. The staple food, rice, was frequently polished to rob it of its vitamin content. Though the men ate, they derived nothing from the diet. They had survived only by trapping and eating rats and other rodents.

When the American soldiers moved through the camp in the afternoon, captives wrapped their bony arms around them and cried with joy. For some it was too late. The rigors of prison life had sapped their strength too greatly and they died within days. For most, the arrival of the OSS saved them from certain death. The huge graveyard behind the prison testified to that fact.

In the Home Islands, American prisoners had begun to taste the heady wine of freedom. At a camp in Nagoya, 287 men pooled their meager supply of money and bought a bull that the Japanese had used to haul off each day's residue of human excrement. The bull was slaughtered and cooked. The prisoners gorged themselves for days on the carcass.

At other camps in Japan, captives had different designs. The Japanese Imperial General Headquarters advised Manila:

> ... THE PRISONERS HELD AT KOBE HAVE SINCE
> THE NIGHT OF AUGUST 19 BEGUN TO REFUSE TO
> LISTEN TO THE ORDERS OF THE CAMP AUTHORI-
> TIES; THEY RAN AWAY ... IN SMALL GROUPS, BROKE
> INTO STORE HOUSES IN THE NEIGHBORHOOD

AND STOLE CANNED FOODS, BEER, ETC., OR
ENTERED CIVILIANS' HOMES AND ANNOYED
WOMEN AND GIRLS . . .

The Japanese Government was concerned about possible violence between Americans and natives. They had good reason for
worry. Years of pent-up hatred festered in the minds of thousands
of Allied prisoners, who had wasted away under the acute conditions of Japanese detention. Hunger was the main complaint.
Medical treatment for the sick was almost nonexistent. At Shin-
igawa Hospital in Tokyo, more patients died of neglect than were
saved by care.

American Army and Navy planes had instituted relief measures immediately after the Emperor's broadcast. Drums of food
were dropped into prison compounds where starving men tore
them open and ate ravenously. As the day of occupation arrived,
thousands of skeletal human beings waited impatiently for the
sight of a friendly force at the camp gates. In the meantime, they
slowly adjusted to the prospect of freedom.

TWENTY

The Enemy Lands

Colonel Tench and 146 men left Okinawa at 3:00 A.M. on the morning of August 28. Forty-five C-47's formed a long trail to the northeast in the pre-dawn darkness. In the lead plane the colonel hid his own apprehensions by talking to his officers about details of the work to be done upon landing. None of the men spoke of danger ahead, but most were worried about being murdered.

As conversation petered out, men tried to catch some sleep in the cold, uncomfortable seats. At dawn, Tench and the others rose to look down on the conical slopes of Fujiyama. They were snow-less, causing one man to remark that the Japanese had purposely melted them down to annoy the Americans. More important and reassuring to the advance group was the sight of American war-ships and fighter planes under and around them as they headed in for a final approach to Atsugi.

When the C-47's appeared near the airfield, they caused con-sternation on the ground. General Seizo Arisue could not believe it when an aide told him that the Americans had been sighted, because Tench's party was not due for nearly an hour. He raced outside and looked toward the sound of motors. There they were, coming lower and lower, preparing to descend to the runway. Arisue was stunned. No one was ready to receive the enemy.

Orders were barked out. Uniforms were buttoned. Ties, swords, the paraphernalia of ceremony was sought for and found. The reception committee hastily formed a loose line in front of tents set up to accommodate the party. Arisue stood gazing anxiously at the planes circling for the final approach.

He was a nervous man that morning. Within a mile of the airstrip, sullen patriots lurked and brooded. On the airfield itself, hundreds of Japanese troops stood guard, protecting the enemy from danger without. Yet one of these men could easily forget himself and fire on the Tench party now arriving. If even one American was hurt or killed, the consequences could be severe for both the nation and himself. Arisue shuddered at the thought.

As the first transport put down its flaps, Arisue watched in horror. The pilot had misread the wind direction and was landing down-wind, in the one pattern calculated to cause disaster. The lead plane bounced five times on the runway before it settled down and churned across the field. Arisue was both furious and relieved.

Since the aircraft were coming in from the wrong angle, Arisue's carefully laid greeting plans were also upset. Tench and his group came to a stop far across the field from the reception committee. Other transports started touching down immediately after him.

While the motors of the first plane coughed and died, Colonel Charles Tench stood up to face his dubious future. Those behind him were as tense as he was, and no one spoke. As the bright sun streamed into the ship from an opened door, the colonel went out and down to the soil of Japan. He kicked his right heel once into the ground to mark the historic moment, then stared across the field to see what the Japanese had in store for him.

There was no one in sight. Nothing stirred. Tench stood flanked by his interpreter, Major Faubion Bowers, and by Major Charles Hutchison; both men carried carbines. Tench himself wore a .45-caliber pistol in a shoulder holster. He had ordered the rest of his men to stay in the shadow of the plane until the situation was clarified. As the small contingent waited for something to happen, Tench's nerves frayed just a little more. The silence was appalling.

The interpreter, Bowers, noticed the brown grass growing high on the field. He marveled at the brilliant sunlight that creased everyone's eyes. As he began to wonder where the Japanese were, he thought, "Just how the hell does one begin an occupation?" Then his heart jumped as he saw a surging, shouting group of Japanese heading hell-bent for the Americans.

Tench immediately imagined that he was the target of an all-out charge by a band of fanatics. His apprehension mounted as they came, some running, others hanging onto slow-moving cars. The convoy careened up to the unwavering figures in khaki. Then it halted, and from the group stepped a short, bemedaled figure who said, "I am Lieutenant General Seizo Arisue, in charge of the Atsugi reception committee."

Towering over the Japanese officer, Tench returned his salute and replied, "I am Colonel C. T. Tench, commanding the advance party for the Supreme Commander for the Allied Powers."

Bowers translated smoothly. There was no cordiality, no friendliness, just strict military protocol. The Americans looked especially grim to Arisue, who asked Tench to accompany him across the field to the reception area. While they walked, dozens of pictures were snapped by Japanese news cameramen and the Army Signal Corps photographers who had followed Tench to record the historic moment.

In the tent area, Arisue offered Tench a drink of orange punch. The colonel, thinking immediately of poison, paled at the suggestion, and refused. Arisue noticed his pallor, and wondered what was wrong with him. Then the Japanese general intuitively raised a glass and drained it. After a moment, Tench reconsidered and accepted a second proffered punch. As he gingerly tasted it and coaxed the liquid down his throat, Arisue watched him closely. His face was a study in determination. But the drink was cool and pleasant and Tench finally relaxed. He lit a cigarette and got down to business.

Arisue and he sat side by side in two overstuffed chairs under a tentpole and introduced their staffs. The Japanese general lit a huge cigar and sprawled comfortably. He, too, began to relax from the tension of the first moments.

In the middle of his discussions with the Japanese, Tench was baffled to see a white man in a strange uniform standing at the edge of the crowd. While he tried to figure out who he was, the stranger walked toward him and greeted him effusively: "I am Commander Anatoliy Rodionov, Naval Attaché of the Soviet Union in Japan. Welcome." Tench was dumbfounded at seeing the Russian, but recovered his poise and returned the greeting. He made a mental note to be wary of the Soviet delegation in the next days.

As the planes continued to land, the colonel sent a dispatch back to Okinawa signifying that operations were proceeding well and the situation appeared normal. Then he and his aides sat down to an elegant meal served on white tablecloths. The Japanese had provided the finest silverware, the choicest foods, and the most polite and efficient waiters. Tench's first hours at Atsugi passed quickly in a rapidly thawing atmosphere of cooperation and goodwill.

After lunch, Arisue himself mingled with American troops as they unloaded their supplies and prepared to set up camp. He was impressed by both their efficiency and their friendliness. As he passed one sweating sergeant, the soldier said, "Hey, General, how about some beer?" Arisue got some for him right away.

In the late afternoon, Tench found time to shave and shower from a bucket. As he sat down to dinner, an aide told him the Russian delegation waited to see him. It was obvious to him that the Soviets were determined to be a part of the American surrender ceremonies. He was correct. The group carried a letter from Jacob Malik, Ambassador to Japan. It asked that the Russians receive passes to the ceremonies when MacArthur arrived. It also requested that the arrival time be announced so that the Soviets could make their plans accordingly. Malik signed it "Faithfully yours."

Tench sent the message off to Manila where it received predictable treatment. The headquarters of the Supreme Commander ignored it. MacArthur wanted nothing to do with the Russians.

In the darkness of the twenty-eighth, Colonel Tench sprawled on a Japanese bed that was far too short for his six-foot frame. He had trouble unwinding from the exhausting strain of the day, and could not forget that he and his men were alone in the midst of an armed enemy who might revert at any moment to a hostile attitude. Beyond the airfield lived men filled with bitterness and capable of the most violent reactions.

Inside the compound, Japanese searchlights probed the darkness for any sign of danger. Finally Tench slept.

When he saw the dawn, he felt the simple relief of having survived the night. His apprehensions were still with him, but he knew it was important to show them to no one—neither to his own troops nor to the Japanese. He went outside to attend to the business of the day.

The Japanese labor battalions had begun improving the runways and taxi areas. Four thousand young men swarmed over the field, filling in potholes, tamping down dirt, smoothing the soil with an ancient roller. The primitive aspects of this confused assault on the Atsugi landscape struck Tench as both ridiculous and pathetic. One American bulldozer could have done the job better and more quickly.

After seeing General Arisue, Tench noticed that another Japanese officer lingered, hoping to talk with him. It was Lieutenant General Kamada, educated in the United States and once, in 1932, attached to the American First Division as an observer.

Kamada quickly found that he and Tench had mutual friends from the past. The Japanese attempted to ingratiate himself but Tench deliberately remained aloof. At last Kamada offered, "What

I'd really like to do is go back to America and—how do you call it?" He swung his arms as though delivering a bowling ball.

Tench asked, "Bowl?"

"Ah, yes, yes," Kamada replied. Tench walked away.

The American Navy landed at Atsugi that day too. Commander Harold Stassen came in by plane and told Tench that the Third Fleet under Bull Halsey was "right behind" the advance party. Someone standing close to Tench muttered, "Yeah, fifty miles behind us." Stassen seemed not to hear the remark and passed on.

Late in the day, excitement developed. Authorities in Tokyo reported that an American prisoner at Shinagawa Hospital was suffering from appendicitis and needed an operation quickly. The Americans wanted him taken to one of their ships riding at anchor in Sagami Bay. Tench discussed the case with Arisue, and decided to get a Japanese surgeon's report before taking action.

Still another crisis erupted right on the base. Junior American officers had commandeered the official Japanese cars brought to the field for use the following day, when the main American forces would arrive. The cars were to be driven in the MacArthur procession to Yokahama. Arisue went to Tench and explained that they represented the only transportation available for the occasion. Tench issued orders to find the cars. Arisue and the other Japanese were profoundly impressed with this mild but decisive man who moved quickly to solve a delicate problem.

At midnight, the Japanese again came to Tench, but this time they were furious. The sick prisoner in Tokyo had been spirited away by Commander Harold Stassen, who spent that day removing serious medical cases from the prison camps. To Arisue and his aides, the highly irregular tactics employed by the Naval party were outrageous. Protocol had been ignored. Yet efficient evacuation of the seriously ill had been achieved, and Tench was both pleased and amused by the American maneuver. He spent a half hour mollifying the Japanese anger. Then he went to bed.

At 7:00 A.M. the first elements of the Eleventh Airborne Division landed. The paratroopers jumped out and stood under the wings of the planes. They were fully armed, ready for any trouble. But only Japanese interpreters, committee members and other officials were in evidence.

The Japanese themselves were terrified. A number of the officers who greeted the American soldiers carried revolvers containing only one bullet. Thinking that they might be attacked by the "bloodthirsty" soldiers, they were prepared to kill themselves.

In one of the first planes, the commanding officer of the division, General Joe Swing, arrived to take over from Tench. An aggressive soldier, Swing landed prepared for a fight. His battle jacket was festooned with grenades, and he was willing to use them at the first sign of trouble.

Colonel Tench happily consigned the airfield to him. Pleased that his own forty-eight-hour reign over the Japanese people had ended without incident, he went looking for a bottle of cold beer. His actions had been carefully watched by the Japanese people in the first hours of the occupation and Charles Tench had passed all tests.

Shortly after General Swing assumed charge of the field, he went up to a bushy-browed American colonel and said plaintively, "Fred, there's a lousy Jap running around loose here and he keeps asking for you. He's wearing a big knife and is loaded with medals." The Japanese, unknown to Swing, was Arisue and the colonel was Fred Munson, an intelligence officer on MacArthur's staff. He and Arisue had first met in 1935 in the city of Himeji, Japan, where Munson, a second lieutenant, had been attached to a Japanese division. Arisue, a major at the time, had briefly befriended the young American. They met again in China in 1938 when Arisue was investigating the death of a Japanese soldier within American Embassy grounds in Peking. Then the war came.

When Arisue greeted his friend Munson-san at Atsugi in the summer of 1945, it was almost like old times, but not quite.

Arisue was now the suppliant serving the master. As the two men talked, the victors were pouring into Japan by the thousands.

The C-54's were landing every two minutes. An enormous fleet of aircraft was moving in with split-second precision in an awesome exhibition of coordination and strength. Hour after hour the huge four-engined transports circled and landed, circled and landed. The noise of the engines was deafening.

General Douglas MacArthur was due at two o'clock. He left Okinawa in the morning, surrounded by his aides, Sutherland, Willoughby, Whitney and others. He was in a jovial mood. Though some of his men feared for his safety during the first hours of occupation, the general seemed without worry. He walked up and down in the plane, pausing now and then to stab the air with his pipe as he spoke to his officers.

As the silver C-54, *Bataan*, descended over the fields and paddies of Japan, the fifty-foot-high bronze Buddha at Kamakura reared up underneath. Then the amazing hub of activity at Atsugi came into view. General Willoughby looked at the runway, which reminded him of a crazy quilt, broken by thousands of black cracks. It had seen more service this day than all during the war. And yet it held the huge weight of the C-54's without trouble.

At 2:19 P.M. MacArthur landed in Japan. At the door of the plane he stood gazing at the scene before him. His corncob pipe extending at a jaunty angle reflected his serene confidence.

At the foot of the ramp, General Bob Eichelberger welcomed him to Atsugi. MacArthur said simply, "Bob, this is the payoff." Three years before he had sent Eichelberger across the Owen Stanley Mountains in New Guinea to hold and defeat the Japanese advancing on Port Moresby. At the time, his instructions had been chilling and direct: "Win or don't come back." Thirty-six months later the two men were standing side by side on the runway eighteen miles southwest of Tokyo.

MacArthur moved toward the caravan of cars lined up to escort him into Yokohama. En route he reviewed soldiers of the Eleventh

Airborne Division. At one point, he paused to talk to some enlisted men. When the general was announced, one of them reached for his gun to present arms. By mistake he grabbed a bamboo pole. As MacArthur walked by, he stopped and said quietly, "Son, I think you're in the wrong army." The sergeant blanched and murmured, "Yes, sir." Chuckling, MacArthur moved on.

The procession got underway. It was a ridiculous yet quaintly charming sight. The Japanese had gathered a motley collection of private cars and trucks, most of which burned charcoal for fuel. These were led by a bright red fire engine, old and decrepit, whose siren wailed and screamed as the parade moved out of the base.

General Courtney Whitney, MacArthur's confidant, carefully scanned both sides of the road watching for possible snipers in the fields and homes dotting the route. MacArthur just sat back and enjoyed the view.

From the airport into Yokohama, fifteen miles away, thirty thousand Japanese soldiers stood at attention on both sides of the road. They did not look at the caravan, but instead kept their backs to the procession. Their posture signified deference to the new ruler of Japan, and at the same time enabled them to watch for trouble in the fields. They were like statues, mute and impressive in their rigidity. Civilians were almost totally absent. Once in a while, a face would appear at a window, then disappear.

It was a very hot day and the men riding were thirsty and sweaty. From time to time one of the old cars broke down. The fire engine backfired and snorted, stopped and started.

When the ludicrous procession reached Yokohama, the Americans could see the awesome results of the fire bombings. On May 29, B-29's had come and virtually wiped out the huge city in one day. Block after block was flat, just a jumble of masonry. A few refugees still lived in the remains.

At the front entrance of the New Grand Hotel, Yozo Nomura, an elderly Japanese dressed in a morning coat, waited nervously for the Supreme Commander. When MacArthur arrived, he bowed and welcomed him. The general asked, "How long have you been the manager of this hotel?"

Nomura hastened to correct him: "I am not a manager, I am the owner. Welcome. I wish to offer my respects to you. During your stay, we'll do our very best to service you and I hope you'll like the room I'm going to show you."

As the flustered Japanese spoke, he was thinking that his greeting to such a man was absurd. Nevertheless, he went through the motions of treating MacArthur like a guest instead of a conqueror. He showed him to Room 315 and the connecting rooms. The suite was the best available in the hotel though hardly sumptuous by American standards.

After Nomura departed, MacArthur tried to take a nap, isolating himself from the chaos in the lobby below. There, "brass" from the various services jockeyed for rooms. In all, 159 general officers from all Allied armies and navies found quarters in the hotel. Japanese waiters and waitresses were besieged by calls for food and drink. The waiters coolly supplied service but the waitresses were terrified by the influx of soldiers, and scurried about like flustered butterflies.

On a floor above, Colonel Fred Munson took off his shirt in a comfortable room and poured himself a Scotch. As he sat talking with Colonel Paul Craig, someone knocked. Standing in the doorway was a Japanese colonel in full uniform. Munson was startled and delighted to see Ichiji Sugita, another friend, a close one, from prewar days. The men embraced and asked for each other's family. The Japanese officer, a handsome, soft-spoken gentleman, had come to Atsugi as a representative of the Japanese Government, and would serve as a member of the liaison committee, working with the American forces to effect an orderly transfer of power around Tokyo. He had been brought from Korea for that purpose because of the contacts he had established within the American Army before the war. At one time, he too had lived with an American division and had taken orders from American officers.

During the war, Sugita had served as an aide to General Yamashita when that formidable soldier succeeded in outwitting British defenders at Singapore. It was Sugita who led the first Japanese soldiers down the streets of the city. Later he drew up plans for the Japanese evacuation of Guadalcanal. As he watched the piecemeal destruction of the Imperial Army during the next two years, Sugita, an astute soldier, repeatedly warned his superiors that the United States had somehow managed to break the Japanese codes, that every move was being monitored by American cryptoanalysts. They laughed at him and took no steps to correct the fatal flaw.

Now he stood in a hotel room in Yokohama and spoke to an American officer who had been like a brother to him for years. Since their last meeting his world had been destroyed.

Realizing what Sugita's feelings must be, the American colonel treated him with great compassion. Their friendship was above any temporary inequality in position. Sugita relaxed and had a drink.

As the New Grand Hotel echoed to the onslaught of hundreds of milling Allied military men, other Americans embarked on a forbidden trip into Tokyo. Strict orders had been issued that Tokyo was off limits except to those with passes, but foreign correspondents ignored the edict and rode trains or jeeps into the desolate city.

There, the Imperial Palace Hotel, famous for surviving the earthquake of 1923, became their base of operations. In its way, it was as isolated from the world as the Emperor's palace beyond the moat across the street. Damaged in the bombings, it nevertheless still functioned in an "elegant" manner. Americans recognized waiters and bellboys, barbers and maîtres d'hôtel, from the past. The hotel was an oasis in a wilderness of ruins. It retained an unhurried pace which denied that a war had ever occurred, and operated as though Pearl Harbor and Hiroshima were merely figments of the imagination.

Several reporters proceeded to toast each other into a stupor there, and then wander out through the streets, which were otherwise largely deserted.

At the Ministry of the Interior in downtown Tokyo, Japanese officials heard an uproar outside as a car sped up the street and screeched to a halt in front of the building. An American war correspondent stood up in the seat and fired his revolver into the air twice.

The Japanese cringed as they listened to the gunfire. One muttered, "Oh God, is this the way the Occupation is going to begin?" A young aide rushed down the steps to the reporter and asked if he could help.

"I want to see the Minister," the newsman shouted drunkenly. The official assured him that the Minister was not around and the correspondent listened to him, undecided what to do next. Then he lurched back into the jeep and drove off down the street. The aide took out a handkerchief and wiped his forehead as he mounted the steps back into the building.

Another Japanese official in Tokyo had a visit that day from American army officers. Kantaro Uemura, of the Metropolitan Police, received several counterintelligence men from the United States Army. They asked only two questions. The first was: "Where do the following live?" They named Government officials and military men who might possibly be held for war crimes trials. Uemura supplied the addresses. The other, more basic, question was of immediate importance: "Where is the red light district in Tokyo?" It was important to find out before the bulk of the American Army came into the city. The Intelligence people wanted to put it off limits right away.

The Yoshiwari district, world-famous prostitute quarter, had been burned down by fire raids, but the Government had quickly built a new one to buoy up the morale of thousands of Japanese men. When Uemura defined the section of the capital that now served as a brothel area, the Intelligence men departed with the vital information.

◆   ◆   ◆

As the Occupation began, the citizens of the Tokyo area were trapped in a classic situation. A conquering army was beginning to walk in the streets, and incidents between soldiers and civilians were bound to occur. Almost immediately, reports of looting and robbery on the streets of Yokohama and Yokosuka flooded in to alarmed Japanese and American officials. When, within the first forty-eight hours several instances of rape occurred, Japanese liaison committee members hastened to Allied Headquarters with the news. In one case in Yokosuka, three Americans had invaded the home of a man named Koizumi and assaulted his wife and daughter.

Supreme Headquarters ordered an immediate investigation of all such allegations. MacArthur reaffirmed the death penalty for convicted rapists. Senior American Army and Navy officers were warned to maintain discipline among their forces.

As a result, acts of extreme violence diminished markedly in the days that followed.

On August 30, at the Tokyo waterfront, prisoners from Camp Omori ran out to the shoreline to greet members of the Fourth Marine Regiment. As landing barges moved toward shore, battle-hardened Marines saw emaciated Americans wading out into the surf, crying hysterically, sobbing out inarticulate greetings. As they approached closer, the men in the boats wept, too.

Commander Harold Stassen walked up to the gates of Omori. He was stopped by the Japanese commandant, who blustered, "I have no authority to turn these men over to you." When the Japanese continued to fume Stassen kicked him squarely in the backside, then looked coldly at the officer and said, "You have no authority, period."

Among the prisoners freed that day at Omori was Lieutenant Marcus McDilda, the pilot who spread the rumor that Tokyo would be atom-bombed. Taken from Tokyo Kempei Tai headquarters to the camp just before the surrender on August 15, he joined men like Pappy Boyington, the Marine ace of South Pacific air combat fame, in watching the United States establish a beachhead on Tokyo Bay. McDilda's lie had actually saved his life. Because it caused him to be flown to Tokyo, he was spared the fate of other American prisoners detained at the Osaka secret police headquarters. Shortly after the Emperor broadcast the news of defeat, over fifty airmen there were beheaded by vengeful Japanese soldiers. McDilda's tale of nuclear bombs had won him a reprieve from that slaughter.

In early evening of August 31, Jonathan Wainwright came in from China to see his old boss.

MacArthur was at dinner when an aide announced Wainwright's presence in the hotel. The Supreme Commander jumped up and said, "Show him right in."

Suddenly the door opened and a spectral figure stood there leaning on his cane. MacArthur stared intently at the man who had taken his place on Corregidor and now bore the burden of having surrendered to the enemy. He noticed his sunken eyes and pitted cheeks; he was shocked by his snow-white hair and skin "like old shoe leather."

The two generals embraced. MacArthur held the bony man in his arms and called huskily, "Jim, Jim."

Wainwright could only cry, "General," before his voice broke.

In Nagasaki, at the site of the POW camp, Lt. Jacob Vink, a Dutch medical officer, was still caring for Allied casualties from the Fat Man. Four Dutch prisoners had died instantly on August 9. Three Dutchmen and one Englishman had succumbed to injuries in the days that followed. Thirty-eight other POW's were being treated for aftereffects. Vink hoped they would survive.

TWENTY-ONE

"These Proceedings Are Closed"

September 2, the day of retribution, dawned surprisingly cool. Under leaden skies, four black limousines drove at full speed down the shoreline of Tokyo Bay toward Yokohama. In the first car, General Yoshijiro Umezu sat back and reflected on his role this day. Against his wishes, he had been ordered by the Emperor to represent the armed forces of Japan on the battleship *Missouri*. Umezu was despondent. Though outwardly he mirrored the image of a samurai warrior, he was a bitter, chagrined man.

Beside him in the car was a frail, bespectacled veteran of the foreign service, Mamoru Shigemitsu. As the delegate of the Gaimusho, the Foreign Office, he too would sign the surrender document.

Shigemitsu shifted uncomfortably as the speeding limousine bounced over holes in the road. In 1932, his left leg had been blown off in China by a terrorist bomb. Because his wooden stump was both clumsy and ill-fitting, the statesman had since lived in constant pain.

The two men wore contrasting uniforms. Umezu was dressed in the olive garb of a general officer. Shiny cavalry boots and a dangling sword added to his military bearing. Shigemitsu was tailored in London style, with top hat, cutaway coat and striped trousers. Like a statesman going to court, he drove through the ruins of his country to meet the enemy.

Past the leveled dock area of Yokohama into the gutted heart of the seaport, the cars sped. At the Prefectural Office, Shigemitsu, Umezu and the nine other members of the delegation got out and stood mutely, waiting to be taken to a ship.

The Americans had provided one for them. Only the night before, Admiral Katsuhei Nakamura, charged with shepherding the Japanese to the ceremony, discovered that not one Japanese vessel in the vicinity was seaworthy. Not even a tugboat was available. His worries were relieved when the *Lansdowne* was designated as the official ship for the party. Three other destroyers were tied up at the pier to transport press, Allied representatives and MacArthur's group.

At 7:30 A.M., the Japanese boarded the destroyer, which headed out into the enormous bay for the sixteen-mile run to the *Missouri*. On every side they could see the truly awesome might of the American Navy, which had converged from all parts of the Pacific and now crowded Tokyo Bay.

Attention centered on Admiral William Halsey's flagship. The choice of the *Missouri* as the surrender site had its origins in Washington and reflected the intense rivalry between Army and Navy. Though James Forrestal had wanted Nimitz to conduct the ceremony, MacArthur as Supreme Commander got that assignment. The Navy Secretary then badgered James Byrnes into at least making a naval ship the setting for the drama. As an added lure, he suggested the one named for President Truman's home state. Thanks to this political horse trade back in America, Bull Halsey was to be host to the ceremony. Whatever the reason, no more fitting choice could have been made.

Halsey had fought the war from the first day. His task force had delivered the last fighters to Midway just before Pearl Harbor. In the dark days in the South Pacific, he had been a ferocious adversary, a combative leader whose profane, salty manner had endeared him to sailors and airmen. Though not a brilliant strategist, Halsey was a tactician of the highest order. In many ways he was the Patton of the Pacific, except that he was far more popular with the G.I.'s, who delighted in telling stories of the admiral's hatred of the Japanese.

Even after the cease-fire, Halsey was an implacable foe. When the *Missouri* had first entered Tokyo Bay on August 29, he stood on the bridge with his officers, one of whom pointed at the shore and a huge hospital festooned with red crosses. Halsey peered at it closely and snorted, "Hospital, that's no hospital. It's probably one of their biggest goddamn ammunition dumps." He added, "We ought to string 'em all up."

On September 2, Halsey was joined by old comrades and allies on the deck of his flagship. Admiral John McCain came aboard. Another man in the Halsey mold, McCain had fought beside Halsey from the beginning. His battered features had won him the nickname "Popeye," and his service during the war had added luster to his reputation. In the hours before the ceremony, he had a warm reunion with his friends. More relaxed than he had been in years, McCain went around buttonholing old classmates and acquaintances. His cup was full. Ten days later, Admiral John McCain was dead from a heart attack.

A boat came alongside the *Missouri* that morning carrying Jonathan Wainwright. As the gaunt man stood under the ladder, Halsey reached down and said, "Hi, Skinny." The general tried to reach up to shake hands. Their fingers touched and tears came to both men's eyes.

Halsey was enjoying himself tremendously as he presided over the festivities. His flagship was the center of world attention and he had embellished it with an appropriate historical symbol. In full view of the international audience was a faded American flag, vintage 1853, which had been flown by Matthew Perry when he entered Tokyo Bay ninety-two years earlier. It was now too brittle to be hoisted and was instead mounted on a bulkhead over the heads of the participants.

Getting it to Japan had not been easy. Only five days before, Halsey had wired the Naval Academy Museum at Annapolis, requesting immediate delivery of this relic. The young lieutenant who received Halsey's message saw his opportunity to witness a momentous event and arranged a Number One Priority to deliver the flag in person. From Washington to San Francisco to Pearl Harbor to Kwajalein to Guam to Iwo Jima, Lieutenant John Breymer never let Matthew Perry's flag out of his sight. Finally he arrived by sea plane at Sagami Bay, and from there carried the precious cloth to the *Missouri*. He was on hand to watch when the first Japanese pulled himself over the side at 8:55 A.M. on September 2.

That man was Mamoru Shigemitsu. Climbing the swaying rope ladder, behind Colonel Sidney Mashbir, his escort, he had to put unusual pressure on the painful stump of his amputated leg. As his countrymen watched Shigemitsu's agonizing ascent, several were struck with the similarity between this man's plight and the condition of their nation. Both were badly crippled, unable to stand.

Umezu followed, and then the others, and finally eleven Japanese were standing on the deck. They arranged themselves in three rows facing the table covered with a green cloth. Across it stood military men from nations still at war with Japan. Toshikazu Kase, Shigemitsu's aide in the Foreign Office, looked at the many representatives of the awesome coalition and wondered how Japan could ever have conceived of victory. Such madness was almost grimly humorous.

As movie cameras whirred and shutters clicked, the men tensed, waiting for the ceremony to begin. The American uniform of the day was suntans, no tie. They looked oddly casual in such a formal setting. The Japanese seemed stiff and uncomfortable in their ill-fitting, close-necked uniforms and diplomatic attire. Umezu and Shigemitsu stood in the front row of their country's delegation, staring straight ahead. Colonel Munson's old friend Ichiji Sugita, in the back row, glanced around and was amazed to see sailors perched precariously on the barrels of sixteen-inch guns to get a better view. Such informality would never be allowed in the Japanese Navy.

The British delegation were dressed in shorts and white knee stockings. The Russians were resplendent in red-epauletted uniforms. The elaborate outfits of the Chinese, French and Canadians contrasted sharply with the American suntans.

At exactly nine o'clock a small door swung open and General Douglas MacArthur, followed by Nimitz and Halsey, strode briskly to the table facing the Japanese. Almost immediately he began to read from the small white paper he carried:

"We are gathered here, representatives of the major warring powers, to conclude a solemn agreement whereby peace may be restored. The issues, involving divergent ideals and ideologies, have been determined on the battlefields of the world and hence are not for our discussion or debate. . . ."

Another of the Japanese representatives, Admiral Tomioka, glimpsed a familiar face behind MacArthur. For several years the admiral had kept a picture of that man in his office in Tokyo. Daily he had studied it, trying to fathom its owner's thinking. Regularly he had failed. Now, in September 1945, Tomioka, a naval strategist, stood on the deck of the *Missouri* and stared intently at Chester Nimitz, his enemy, his rival, his personal antagonist.

Across the deck, General Willoughby, MacArthur's intelligence chief, was annoyed. Anxious to be in a prominent place on this historic occasion, he had tried to stand as close as possible to his commanding officer. Now a huge Australian general blocked his view and kept him out of any photographs of the scene.

As the general read on, Colonel Sugita's eyes focused on General Sutherland, who stood behind MacArthur. Chief of Staff Sutherland was leaning over to whisper to British General Percival. Percival turned his head to stare at Sugita. They had met once before. Sugita had been on hand when the Japanese dictated surrender terms to Percival at Singapore in 1942. Both men remembered, and today their eyes met for a long moment.

MacArthur's hands trembled as he continued: ". . . The terms and conditions upon which the surrender of the Japanese Imperial Forces is here to be given and accepted are contained in the instrument of surrender now before you.

"As Supreme Commander of the Allied Powers, it is my firm purpose, in the tradition of the countries I represent, to proceed in the discharge of my responsibilities with justice and tolerance, while taking all necessary dispositions to insure that the terms of the surrender are fully, promptly, and faithfully complied with."

The general stepped back and motioned for the Japanese to sign. There was almost total silence on the great ship as Mamoru Shigemitsu clumped forward to the table. The wind whipped his hair over his forehead as he slowly eased himself into the chair. Placing his silk hat down, he nervously stripped off his yellow gloves and laid them on it. Kase, his aide, hovered at his left shoulder.

Shigemitsu took out a pen and gazed at the document. He seemed puzzled.

MacArthur spoke sharply: "Sutherland. Show him where to sign." The Chief of Staff went to the table and pointed to the correct line. The embarrassed Foreign Minister flushed, then bent his head as he scrawled his signature. It was 9:04 A.M.

Umezu, Japan's other signatory, came to the table. Without reading any part of the document, he quickly slashed his name under that of Shigemitsu. Then, his face impassive, he turned away without looking right or left and marched back to his group. Some of the officers in his delegation had tears on their cheeks.

MacArthur then sat down to sign. As he wrote his name in fragments, the first pen went to Wainwright. Percival got the next one. Another was for West Point, then one for the Archives. The fifth was for his aide, Gen. Courtney Whitney. The last was a red-barreled one and it was for his wife, Jean, and his son Arthur, back in Manila. He finished with a flourish, put the red pen in his shirt pocket, and rose.

Admiral Chester Nimitz sat down and signed for the Navy. The other nations followed. When the last signature was inscribed, MacArthur stepped forward and solemnly declared: "Let us pray that peace be now restored to the world and that God will preserve it always. These proceedings are closed."

When the Japanese delegates went to pick up their copy of the surrender document, a problem arose. The Canadian representative had inadvertently signed on the wrong line. General Sutherland promptly sat down and made appropriate corrections on the paper. The Japanese headed back toward the gangway. As they passed through a cordon of Allied officers, they received very proper salutes. Umezu stared stonily ahead but returned the gesture. His aides gratefully followed suit.

The Japanese filed down the ladder and entered the small boat for the trip back to Tokyo. They were generally pleased at the tone of MacArthur's remarks. Foreign Office representative Kase scribbled down his impressions to repeat to Hirohito while others questioned him closely about the exact meaning of the message from the Supreme Commander.

Overhead, a massed flight of B-29's and carrier planes paraded in a final exhibition of the strength that brought an end to an empire, while the sun shone for the first time that day.

Later that day, soldiers of the First Cavalry Division came ashore from transports and formed up on the docks at Yokohama. The Eleventh Airborne Division Band, which had already been in Japan for three days, serenaded the new arrivals with "The Old Gray Mare, She Ain't What She Used to Be."

Twenty-four hours before the ceremony on the *Missouri* ended, far south of Tokyo Bay, a heavy-set man had walked about on a mountainside and brooded about his future. He was not optimistic. Wearily he gazed around his campsite where emaciated men cooked rats over fires and shivered in the summer heat from malaria.

The figure moved toward the center of the clearing. His wrinkled uniform was that of a Japanese general. Tomoyuki Yamashita surveyed the remnants of his army and sighed softly. Three years ago he had commanded a victorious drive that astounded the world. Now he commanded only a dismal retreat. His army was a rabble, existing on vermin while rotting away in the jungles.

The mountain he stood on was called Prog and it rose in the north central highlands of Luzon in the Philippines. There Yamashita had managed to hold off several American divisions closing in on him.

His ordeal had begun the previous October when MacArthur landed at Leyte. At that time Yamashita was brought to the Philippines to stem the irresistible flow of the enemy toward Japan. Though the Japanese had an impressive army in the area, they were woefully deficient in airpower and practically impotent on the sea. Yamashita brought with him an unquestioned talent as a military leader and a fierce determination to bring about a miracle.

His history was impressive. Like many Japanese officers, he was an ardent student of the German military system. In 1940, as head of a military mission, he had gone to Germany to observe at close range the methods employed in Hitler's lightning conquest of the continent. In 1941 and 1942 he adapted some of these practices to inflict the most stunning defeat the British Empire suffered in the entire war. Miracles were not strange to him; he accomplished one in the jungles of Malaya.

When hostilities began in December 1941, the Japanese war machine needed the resources of the Dutch East Indies in order to survive. The naval bastion of Singapore, at the tip of the Malay peninsula, was a strategic Allied strongpoint that denied access to that area. Yamashita was told to conquer it.

The Japanese who landed on the torturous trails of the Malay peninsula brought a secret weapon with them: the bicycle. Columns of soldiers sped down the trails on wheels while tanks followed and lent their firepower at critical moments. Allied defenders were completely demoralized by the unorthodox tactics.

Yamashita also instituted the first large-scale usage of amphibious landings behind enemy lines. Time after time he cut off enemy divisions holding tenaciously to the narrow peninsula. Repeatedly the defenders were dislodged by such maneuvers.

Inside the British lines, a weary and discouraged General Percival made a fatal mistake. He badly overestimated Yamashita's strength. Because his own forces had been driven into a disastrous retreat, he could only conclude that the Japanese maintained tremendous reserves of manpower and supplies. Nothing else seemed to account for the pathetic state of his army.

Percival was wrong. At the gates of Singapore, the Japanese halted, concealing a glaring weakness. The British forces actually outnumbered the Japanese by three to one. Yamashita had only thirty thousand men and was almost out of ammunition and food. His supply lines were badly clogged and stretched back hundreds of miles. Japanese troops, already living on two bowls of rice a day, faced starvation unless the fortress surrendered promptly.

Yamashita prepared for one all-out attack. He was convinced that further delay would allow the British time to receive reinforcements by sea and eventually drive back the Japanese.

The first assault troops came across the straits separating Malaya from the island of Singapore, and managed to secure a foothold against a raw and disorganized Australian division. With this beachhead established, the outcome was assured. The British began blowing up their tremendous oil tanks while the Japanese pressed the attack.

On the fourteenth of February, three English officers approached the Japanese lines carrying white flags. The opposing generals met at 7:00 P.M. at the Ford factory on the outskirts of the city. Percival was nervous, shaking and rather pitiable. Yamashita was relaxed, almost serene. His only problem at the moment was his interpreter, who could not seem to translate the technical aspects of the surrender terms. Yamashita finally asked for a yes-or-no answer. Correspondents and soldiers alike assumed he was being belligerent in his statement. Such was not the case. He actually felt sorry for the British general and even wanted to say something consoling to him in his moment of shame. However, he thought better of it and left. When the Japanese Army marched into the city the next day, General Yamashita became a household word in Japan.

His success was short-lived. Apparently afraid of the publicity his subordinate was getting, General Tojo transferred him quickly to the Manchurian border. The Tiger of Malaya disappeared into that quiet backwater of war, watching the Siberian hills and plains for any sign of Russian hostility. His name disappeared from the newspapers in Japan and his image among the people dimmed.

For over two years the uncomplaining soldier remained in oblivion while the war went badly. After Tojo fell from power in 1944, he emerged once more. In Tokyo military strategists correctly foresaw a huge American thrust against the Philippines and chose Yamashita to blunt the attack. In September of 1944 he left Japan for the last time.

His instincts warned his that the decisive battle would be fought on Luzon, the largest island in the Philippines. He planned to concentrate his troops there and wage a stubborn defensive action which would tie up the Americans for many months. His strategy was almost immediately overruled by superiors in Tokyo, who insisted on sending reinforcements to Leyte where Douglas MacArthur had returned to the scene of the greatest disaster in his career.

On October 20, the Americans came in on the beaches of Leyte and MacArthur sat under a palm tree and talked with correspondents about the long road back from Australia. Thirty-one months before he had furtively stolen away from a dock at Corregidor. Behind him he had left the "battling bastards of Bataan." Since MacArthur had never known defeat in his life, the bitter memory of the debacle on Luzon rankled in him for over two years. On the beach at Leyte, he partially fulfilled his debt to return. The final payment would come later on Luzon.

Disillusioned at the stupid waste of manpower dictated by higher authorities in Japan, Yamashita continued to funnel troops into the maelstrom at Leyte and, in doing so, played right into the hands of the Americans. One infantry general likened the island to a butcher's market, where the Americans set up shop and waited for the enemy to come in to get killed. Many of the reserves Yamashita had counted on for the ultimate fight on Luzon were lost to him forever.

On January 9, when the Sixth United States Army waded ashore at Lingayen Gulf on Luzon, the last struggle for the Philippines began. Once the massive strength of the Americans was unloaded, the outcome was never in doubt. It was only a question of time. Yamashita withdrew, stopped and fought, retreated, turned and attacked. Slowly the Americans forced him into the mountains. The city of Manila lay open. Yamashita was content to go into the hills, for there he planned to hold out for a long time. He had no intention of fighting for the capital and, though he did not declare it an open city, he took his men away from it and retreated skillfully.

MacArthur himself expected that Manila would be left untouched. He reasoned that it would be too much of an effort for the enemy to maintain an adequate defense within the limits of the city. One million Filipino civilians would act as a dead weight on Japanese supply channels. They had enough trouble feeding themselves without being concerned about the fate of the natives. MacArthur thought the enemy would leave a small rear guard to destroy military objectives such as harbor facilities. Then they would retreat to the south and east and set up another defense line.

His estimate of the situation coincided with Yamashita's. The Japanese general's orders were explicit. The installations would be blown up, all supplies removed or destroyed, and a new line established outside the city.

When MacArthur's troops arrived on the outskirts, it appeared that the Japanese had truly withdrawn. A communiqué was sent out to the world announcing the capture of the city. A triumphal parade was planned. The First Cavalry Division was accorded the honor of leading the procession into the capital. Uniforms were pressed. Speeches were prepared.

Then observation planes flying over the peaceful streets noted large fires burning in the center of the city. Manila was in flames. The Japanese were staying to fight.

American officers were appalled at the news. No one wanted to see the beautiful city become a battlefield. Many of the men around MacArthur had spent years in the Far East and looked upon Manila as one would a home town. To some it was a romantic mistress, to others an adventurous oasis from a former life. The Sixth Army went into battle with heavy hearts.

Up in the mountains, Yamashita assumed that his soldiers had left the capital. Cut off from the rest of his army, he could not know that a naval landing force had entrenched itself inside the walls and erected barricades on the streets in defiance of expressed orders. As usual in Japanese military circles, the Army and Navy seldom agreed on anything. Admiral Okochi, in charge of naval personnel, decided that Manila should be defended and sent Rear Admiral Iwabuchi into the still unmarked city with a vague plan to delay the Americans as long as possible. Iwabuchi and his desperate rear guard did a formidable job.

For nearly one month, into late February, Manila was a slaughterhouse, the scene of multiple atrocities, as Japanese marines fought insanely to defend the strategically unimportant city. In the hills of Luzon, Yamashita could know nothing of the extent of the carnage, but he was advised of the ridiculous rear guard action and ordered the Navy to leave. He even sent an Army relief column to help Iwabuchi's forces to withdraw. It failed to make contact, but the situation could hardly have been altered anyway.

Meanwhile, harried by advancing American troops, the general strove only to keep his army together. His troops were scattered, but still potent. They occupied the attention of three American divisions which painfully flushed out the survivors in the tangled undergrowth. Yamashita had done an excellent job in tying down the enemy and giving his homeland time to prepare for the inevitable invasion. He could do nothing more. For six more months, Yamashita held out.

On August 13, the shortwave radio from Tokyo carried the controversial Army speech urging Japanese soldiers to "crush the enemy." Yamashita grimaced as he heard it; his men were dying of starvation before his eyes.

When the radio brought the word of the Emperor's decision to surrender, the tired general retired to his hut and stared at the ceiling. Akira Muto, his chief of staff, watched him carefully to make sure that he would not commit suicide. Yamashita quickly allayed his fears by telling him that it was his duty to return all the soldiers in the Philippines to their homes in Japan. Then he went to bed.

On the second day of September, in bright, warm sunlight, a column of men walked away from the last headquarters of the Japanese Army in the Philippines. Yamashita was going to meet the enemy and he had no illusions about his future. His nation had lost a war and the conqueror would exact tribute. Behind him, Muto was filled with fear. He sensed that the Americans would hold Yamashita responsible for what had happened in Manila months before. Muto urged the general not to go into the enemy camp but to retreat further into the mountains and live as a guerrilla chieftain. Yamashita brushed his fears aside.

The procession continued down slopes wild with the beautiful lushness of a tropical summer. A tall, heavy-set man, Yamashita wore riding pants below his jacket. Puttees were wrapped about his legs. His clothes were badly wrinkled and sagged on his thin frame. On his head he wore a standard garrison cap. The general's eyes were badly pouched, and he carried a heavy cane to support himself on the long walk. The column stopped frequently to eat and rest. Only the birds sounded above them in the stillness. For a brief time the awful war receded.

At Kiangan, several miles away from his final command post, Yamashita stopped in front of Item Company, Thirty-second United States Infantry Division, and entered into captivity. Within hours, he and his party were taken to Baguio and their first ordeal before the victors.

There, on September 3, in the former home of the High Commissioner to the Philippines, a long table was the focal point of a ceremony. In an ornate room, in finely carved chairs, American officers sat waiting. Across from them, Yamashita, Muto and Admiral Okochi stood stiffly for ten long minutes. Then the door opened and the Japanese watched as several more men entered the room. Yamashita's right eyebrow rose perceptibly as he suddenly recognized a ghost from the past. It was General Percival, just flown in from Tokyo to witness the signing. Yamashita quickly recovered his composure and never again looked at the emaciated British officer. With Percival was Jonathan Wainwright, who watched closely as General William Styer accepted Yamashita's capitulation in a formal manner.

Then the American general spoke sharply: "General Yamashita, Vice Admiral Okochi and the others shall be held as prisoners of war."

A burly American MP poked a finger in Yamashita's shoulder and pointed to the door. As the general turned to leave, Wainwright noticed tears in his eyes. Then the Japanese went through the door and into bondage.

After the ceremony, Wainwright went up to General Styer and asked that Yamashita be treated fairly. Styer looked at him and muttered: "He'll be given everything he's entitled to under the Geneva Convention. We don't want to be accused of doing to him what they did to you." Wainwright thanked him and walked away.

Yamashita was driven that day to the outskirts of Manila and the New Bilibid Prison. Within days he would be charged with 123 separate counts of war crimes and put on trial for his life. General Muto's prediction had been correct.

Yamashita, the loser, was the first man to go on trial before his accusers. Some Americans later described his judges as a lynch mob seeking vengeance. Behind the walls of Bilidid, Yamashita, dressed in G.I. fatigues, sat down to prepare his defense. It was hopeless.

On the eighth of September, the First Cavalry Division led the way into Tokyo. Japanese General Gen Sugiyama had skillfully withdrawn all Japanese troops north of the capital in compliance with Eichelberger's orders. Now MacArthur was on his way to the American Embassy to raise the flag over the heart of the Japanese Empire.

Admiral Bull Halsey was with him. He was not riding the Emperor's white horse as he had threatened to do, but he was present in the procession, beside the Supreme Commander.

General William Chase rode at the head of his division, which had fought the Japanese for three years through jungles into the scorched and broken city of Manila. At the sign marking the city limits of Tokyo, Chase ordered his car stopped. He stepped down, walked across the line into the capital, then returned to his jeep for the uneventful trip to the ceremony at the Embassy.

His men were impeccably clad, their boots shining, their helmets gleaming. Mile after mile of trucks, guns and men moved into the center of Tokyo, into the last bastion of the Land of the Rising Sun. The Emperor's own palace was virtually surrounded by legions of a foreign power.

In the grass courtyard of the white-walled Embassy, MacArthur enjoyed another dramatic moment in his illustrious career. Standing with Eichelberger and Halsey in front of a drained lily pond, he listened as "The Star-Spangled Banner" resounded off the walls of the compound. Fully conscious of the importance and irony of the moment, MacArthur turned to Eichelberger and said firmly: "Let our country's flag be unfurled, and in Tokyo's sun let it wave in its full glory as a symbol of hope for the oppressed and as a harbinger of victory for the right."

Old Glory rose above the rubble of Tokyo.

TWENTY-TWO

The Last Recourse

Tokyo was occupied. Only thirty days after the bomb fell on Nagasaki, troopers of the First Cavalry Division patrolled the streets of the capital. The folly begun in Manchuria and compounded at Pearl Harbor had come to its inevitable end.

For the Japanese survivors the situation was desperate. Soldiers of the Imperial Army had no jobs and faced a purge by the Occupation authorities. Sailors had no navy and little hope. The thoughts in many minds centered around the possibility of suicide.

Already General Anami had offered his life to atone for the crimes perpetrated by the military. Admiral Onishi had died in expiation for defeat. Tanaka had done the same.

In the suburb of Setagaya, the most famous general of all pondered a difficult choice. Hideki Tojo, the "architect" of the Pacific War, had lived in relative seclusion for over a year. Deposed in July of 1944, he had retired to an unfamiliar role as adviser to the Throne. Younger men acceded to his authority while he watched the war go even more badly for his nation. When the surrender came, the sixty-three-year-old former Premier felt that he would be held responsible for the war and made his plans accordingly.

It was expected by every Japanese that he would kill himself. As a mastermind in the planning for the war, he would have to atone for the unfortunate state of affairs at the end of hostilities. As Japan's situation had worsened, so had Tojo's public reputation. Even his family received telephone calls urging that he commit hara-kiri. Tojo was torn between the traditional way out and another obligation. He wanted to accept full blame for the war and divert any possible onus of responsibility from the Imperial House. If he lived, he could testify to his own role in the planning of strategy. If he died, he would be taking the easiest way out.

He compromised. Just before the surrender, he went to his doctor and had him mark on his chest the exact location of his heart in case he decided to shoot himself. As an alternative, he also prepared his kimono and knives for a possible hara-kiri ceremony. In his study he arranged these implements and wrote several last statements, one of which absolved the Emperor of any guilt for the war.

When his wife begged him not to do anything rash, he promised her that he would keep himself ready for testifying to the American authorities. Yet the days went by and no one appeared from MacArthur's headquarters. It was rumored that the Japanese leaders were being given time to kill themselves and save the Allies the trouble of dealing with them.

On September 10, reporters visited the old man in his garden. They sat and talked with him of the war and his plans for the future. At first he was rather curt, but then became quite friendly. After complaining about Allied bombers' damage to his property—specifically his pine trees—he told them that he alone was responsible for the conflict and would accept full blame. He made it clear, however, that he did not think that he was a war criminal, explaining: "There is a difference between leading a nation in a war which it believes right and just and being a war criminal." When the correspondents left, Tojo was in a pleasant mood, and examined their jeep with great interest. He had never seen one before. As they drove off he waved goodbye to them.

The next day Tojo's time ran out. When orders were cut at Eighth Army Headquarters in Yokohama to pick up men deemed responsible for the war, his name was on the list. A throng of correspondents rushed out to Setagaya to be on hand for his arrest; the first of them arrived at about 1:00 P.M.

Tojo's house was in an expensive neighborhood. Placed on a grassy slope, it was flanked on one side by open fields used for farming. To the rear, Fujiyama could be seen some fifty miles to the west. Bombing raids had caused some damage to the area, and an outbuilding on the property had gone up in flames months before.

Tojo was at home with his wife and a contingent of Kempei Tai policemen who were there to protect him from Japanese attempts on his life. As correspondents swarmed over the grass outside, Tojo remained behind his study window, to the left of the front door, and ignored them.

They were waiting for a Counterintelligence Corps unit to arrive from Yokohama. As they stood in the hot sun, some of the reporters got thirsty and asked Tojo's servants to find some beer or something stronger to drink. Still Tojo remained out of sight. Presently he called for his wife and told her to get away from the house. Despite her apprehensions, Mrs. Tojo respected his wish and left by the back door for a neighbor's property. Tojo locked his study door and continued to wait.

At four o'clock a six-man CIC team, led by Major Paul Kraus, arrived at the house. Kraus pounded on the locked front door and demanded to see Tojo. A Kempei Tai man inside gave the message to the general, who answered that he would speak only to those in charge. When they were told this, Kraus and his men stood at the front door waiting, undecided as to the next step.

Tojo himself took it. He opened the study window, leaned out, and said, "I am General Tojo." A photographer snapped his picture. The flash infuriated him. Incensed, Tojo slammed the window shut. Kraus swore. Minutes later, Tojo again opened the window. On the lawn, a reporter looked up and said, "This is beginning to look like a balcony scene from *Romeo and Juliet*." Tojo asked if Kraus had the authority to arrest him. Kraus told the interpreter to tell Tojo that he was there to take him into Yokohama. That was enough for Tojo, who disappeared from view. He quickly picked up a .32 pistol which his son-in-law, Hidemasa Koga, had used to kill himself on the day the war ended. Tojo knelt in a chair and aimed the gun at the mark on his chest.

At 4:17 P.M., those outside the house were startled by a gunshot. Kraus and his men broke down the front door and then the door to the study. Furniture piled against it was shoved aside as the mob crowded in.

Tojo, still held the revolver in his right hand. It was pointed at Kraus, who said, "Drop it." Tojo then slumped into the chair behind him, and the revolver fell to the floor. His shirt was open and a gaping wound showed just below the left nipple. His eyes closed and he began to sweat. At 4:29, still conscious, he asked for water and was given some by an aide. When he wanted more, an American officer refused because of his condition.

The bullet had inflicted a sucking wound. As Tojo breathed, air was taken in and discharged through the hole in his chest. While the correspondents shouted and pushed, an enormous gush of blood shot out from the wound and flew across the room. The boisterous journalists, many of whom had landed at beachheads and seen the fury of the Pacific war, showed little sympathy. The reporters vied with each other for stories. It was as though Tojo were already dead.

"Look at that yellow bastard. He didn't even have the guts to use a knife."

"Tojo has earned himself a Purple Heart."

Souvenir hunters went right to work. Someone cut a piece out of the general's riding breeches as he lay in them. Others dipped handkerchiefs in the flowing blood to keep as mementos. One reporter took his cigarette case. The cigarettes inside, of Japanese make, bore the brand name "Hope." Tojo never moved. He was still conscious but did not speak. As the bedlam increased, he groaned once or twice but that was all. His face was turning gray.

Across the street, Mrs. Tojo had watched the scene from her neighbor's lawn. Dressed in gardener's clothes and wearing a sun hat, she had been peering through the hedges at the reporters. When the gunshot sounded, she got on her knees and prayed that her husband would not suffer before he died. She cried softly in the grass for over a half hour, then went away from the street and from the horror in her own house.

At about the same time, CIC Major Kraus went out to get an American doctor. While he was gone, a Japanese physician appeared and had the general lifted from the chair to a sofa bed in the same room. He was covered with a homemade patch quilt and examined. At this point another souvenir was taken. The bullet that had passed through Tojo's body was dug out of the back of the red armchair and went into the pocket of one of the reporters, Harry Brundidge.

The doctor was immediately convinced that the general was beyond help, and he simply placed two bandages over the wounds, front and back. The CIC agents insisted that he do whatever he could to help the victim. While the physician fought to save Tojo's life, correspondents fought to release the story. There was only one telephone, in a hall in the back of the house. One reporter got it and held it while others fired information at him.

Little things were being flashed to the world. A fly trapped in the room was fascinated by Tojo's sweaty bald head. It settled on his brow and walked up and down, over and back. It stopped to consider the terrain, then marched again through the wrinkles and folds. Everyone in the room was fascinated. Now and then it would take off and circle the room, but inexorably it would glide back onto the shiny pate and walk through the wet surface. The fly achieved instant fame.

An enterprising American newsman ran a quarter of a mile down the road to another phone and had reports on Tojo's condition relayed to him by a Japanese messenger. By mistake he flashed word to the wire service that Tojo was dead. Fortunately, he was able to rescind the story before it was released to the world.

Inside the house one man cared very much for the stricken figure. Tojo's secretary burst through the crowd of men and cradled the general's head in his arms. He moaned softly as he gazed down into the ashen face. The American reporters looked at him curiously but were not moved. The mad scramble continued.

At 6:24 P.M., an American physician attached to the First Cavalry Division walked into the bedlam and took charge. Dr. James Johnson consulted briefly with his Japanese counterpart, then went to work. General Tojo spoke to him through the interpreter and asked that he be left alone to die. Johnson refused. As he began administering plasma, Tojo's pulse quickened.

Cigarette smoke hung in bluish gray layers over the head of the wounded man. People watched his chest heaving and falling and made bets on whether he would draw another breath. While the crowd milled and shouted, an enterprising photographer for *Yank* magazine stood outside the house and looked in through the side window. He furtively reached his right arm into the room and clutched an object from a table. It was a shiny sword, one of Tojo's own. The cameraman stuffed it quickly down the front of his pants and hobbled off toward the road and freedom. A bored CIC man let him get just so far, then ambled over and asked for the souvenir sticking stiffly inside his trousers. The embarrassed thief pulled out the sword and surrendered it.

More photographers had arrived, and they created more chaos. Flash bulbs popped, stepladders were brought in to get better shooting angles, requests were made to shift the body of the victim lying helplessly under the multicolored quilt. Some asked that Tojo's head be moved for better angle shots. His legs were crossed and recrossed as the insatiable cameras recorded the scene. His body was just a limp doll to position, an object to photograph.

Correspondents took turns being photographed taking Tojo's pulse. The confusion grew. One cameraman, on hearing that the wounded man was Tojo the "archfiend," had to be restrained from punching him.

Dr. Johnson labored on in the eye of this human hurricane. He gave the general morphine, sutured the wound front and back, bandaged him again, and let the plasma drain into his arm. Tojo's condition improved noticeably and Johnson decided to take him to better medical facilities.

He ordered him driven to a clearing station for more care. First he talked for nearly fifteen minutes to the newsmen, who wanted to know if the old bastard would make it. Then they rushed out to file the biggest story of the Occupation. Tojo left his home for the last time on a stretcher.

General Eichelberger, the leader of the Eighth Army, went to observe him later that night. Tojo tried to raise his head, but fell back and whispered, "I am dying. I'm sorry to have given you so much trouble."

Eichelberger retorted, "Do you mean tonight or for the last few years?"

Tojo mumbled, "Tonight." Then he offered to turn over his sword to Eichelberger. The American general already had it.

Eichelberger issued orders for Tojo to receive the best possible treatment. It was his responsibility to keep the Japanese leader alive for whatever trials were being planned for the war criminals.

A call went out for blood type B. Whole blood was needed since Tojo had already lost nearly half his own. A mess sergeant named John Archinal was tapped for transfusion. Archinal was pleased at the chance: "I'd like to see him live so he gets his just due when he is tried. It would be too easy for him to come in here and pass out comfortably." Archinal echoed the sentiments of most G.I.'s.

In Tokyo that night, while Hideki Tojo lay ashen-faced in a United States Army hospital in Yokohama, his own people mocked him for the bungled suicide. As reports of his recovery were issued, they were greeted by a mixture of shame and derision from his countrymen.

◆   ◆   ◆

While Tojo fought to die and surgeons refused to let him, three
people sat down to dinner in another suburb of Tokyo. One was a
general, Field Marshal Gen Sugiyama, Army Chief of Staff at the
time of Pearl Harbor. Though bald and afflicted with a perma-
nently dropping right eyelid, he was a strikingly impressive figure.
His wife of over thirty years sat near him. The other member of
the group was Colonel Shinaji Kobayashi, the general's devoted
secretary. They conversed animatedly about the events of the last
few days.

For Sugiyama and his wife, it was a last meal together after a
long and mutually enjoyable life. He planned to die the next day by
his own hand. She was pleased. Though she loved him deeply, she
felt that her husband, a senior member of the Imperial Army, owed
it to the nation to atone for the defeat of Japan. She believed there
was no other way to prove to the people that Sugiyama, an honorable man, felt sufficient remorse for the tragedy he helped cause.

As they sipped sake wine and ate heartily from the table
before them, the couple spoke of more pleasant days. Colonel
Kobayashi, almost a member of the family, shared their recollec-
tions. The colonel was miserable at the thought that his superior
would end his life within hours. As a confidant to the general, he
knew the mental struggle Sugiyama had gone through in the past
weeks. He also knew the tremendous pressures put upon the old
man by his wife, who felt so strongly about personal honor.

Kobayashi had watched sadly as the devoted couple clashed
over the subject of suicide. The contest of minds had started on the
day the Emperor broadcast his solemn declaration of surrender.

Mrs. Sugiyama was visiting relatives to the south of Tokyo
when she heard the dreaded news. She immediately rushed back
to the capital to be with her husband. She fully anticipated that
the general would kill himself and she wanted to be with him in
his last hour.

When she reached the city, Sugiyama greeted her warmly
and told her that he had been admonished by the Emperor to do

everything he could to speed demobilization of the troops around the city. After General Anami's death, the Emperor had asked the senior officers to forget their personal feelings and devote themselves to the nation in the difficult days ahead.

His wife was shocked. For two days she brooded. A normally pleasant, even-dispositioned lady, she usually radiated a genuine warmth to those around her. Plump and small, she reminded everyone of a smiling Buddha. But the woman who greeted her husband when he came home on the night of the seventeenth of August was far from even-tempered. She was almost hysterical as she berated him.

"When are you going to commit suicide?" she asked in a shrill voice. The general looked closely at her. Her eyes were wide with excitement, her features flushed with anger. He was dumbfounded.

"I have a responsibility to the Emperor right now. It's important that I stay alive to serve him."

"It is more important that you atone for the surrender," she cried.

The couple argued heatedly over the question of his death, and later went to bed in a strained atmosphere.

Each night thereafter the argument continued. After the servants had gone to bed, the woman pressed her husband for an answer, and he put off the question. Neighbors noticed that Mrs. Sugiyama was becoming more distraught, more wild-eyed. She no longer smiled. She pouted in frustration.

On the seventh day, she confronted the general once more in his bedroom.

"When are you going to commit hara-kiri?" she repeated. The general braced for another tirade as she continued, "I'll die before you if you don't go through with it."

Sugiyama was shattered. His wife was goading him, taunting him with the prospect of her own suicide. It was the last blow. He gazed steadily at her, then spoke softly: "All right, I'll do it, but you must promise not to think of doing the same thing."

Mrs. Sugiyama smiled at him for the first time in days and then bowed deeply. They went to sleep beside each other.

On the next day, Sugiyama was a witness to the death of General Seiichi Tanaka, and his resolve to die was strengthened by his friend's suicide. With his mind firmly made up, he approached his last military task with great fervor. The First Army around Tokyo was completely equipped with weapons, and it was imperative to withdraw the units from the area to be occupied by the Americans in a few short days. Sugiyama plunged gratefully into the assignment.

A thought kept nagging at him. A few days before, he had seen his wife sewing material for two white ceremonial kimonos, normally used only in suicide rituals. Though he remembered her recent threat, he hesitated to believe that she would follow through with it. Still it bothered him. The general tried to put it out of his mind, but the memory of the two kimonos returned constantly.

On the fifth of September, General Sugiyama went to a most important appointment. After the Americans landed at Atsugi and Yokosuka, he was summoned to the headquarters of Lieutenant General Robert Eichelberger, commander of the Eighth United States Army. There he would formally surrender his army.

His first reaction was to refuse, not because he balked at turning over his command, but rather because Eichelberger was beneath him in rank. Sugiyama considered it an insult to have to treat with a junior officer. Only the cahn persuasion of his secretary, Kobayashi, prevented a major incident. The colonel told him repeatedly that it was not intended as a slur against him that Eichelberger was in fact the legitimate representative of the American forces in the Tokyo area.

Even on the way to Yokohama, Sugiyama grumbled about the alleged slight. But he went into the conference room and bowed to the inevitable.

Eichelberger was a courtly man, a gentleman in a cruel business. Realizing the turmoil that Sugiyama must be suffering, he treated him with courtesy and dignity. The Japanese was charmed and grateful. Eichelberger's generous conduct earned him Sugiyama's almost slavish loyalty in the days ahead.

As the two ended their discussions of the steps to be taken in withdrawing Japanese forces away from Tokyo, Eichelberger observed, "I'm sorry we have to meet under such circumstances." Sugiyama nodded gratefully and withdrew.

The next six days were pleasant ones for him. Kept busy by the delicate task of moving his men out of the path of advancing occupation troops, he worked diligently to cooperate with the Americans. His home life had returned to normal. His wife was again pleasant and thoughtful. Their last days together were serene. They spoke no more of suicide.

By the eleventh of September, the last of the Japanese forces had gone north of the Tone River. No incidents had been reported between the opposing armies. Sugiyama had helped finish a most difficult task and now his work was ended.

That evening he invited Kobayashi to dinner. The news of Tojo's attempted suicide had filtered in and the three deplored the bungled attempt. They also talked about the list of war criminals issued that day by MacArthur's headquarters.

Sugiyama wondered if he was included. His career had mirrored the rise of the Imperial Japanese Army to dominance in Japanese governmental affairs. As a leader of the conservative section of the General Staff, he embraced and sometimes advocated policies which had led the nation down the road to war. Sugiyama had been a strong proponent of the "pacification" of China. It was rumored that the Emperor had lost faith in him in that period because the general assured him that the China situation would be resolved quickly.

Though the Field Marshal was far from being a fanatical exponent of expanding Japanese hegemony over vast areas of the Pacific, he knew that he might be indicted by the Allies, if only for one incident in his career. In April 1942 he and others in the military had been shocked at the daring raid on Tokyo by the

Doolittle fliers. When eight of them were captured after crash-landing in China, Sugiyama had concurred in a decision that resulted in the execution of three of the imprisoned men. He had even gone to Tojo and demanded that punitive measures be taken against them. Now, three years later, the Americans would probably remember the part he played in that affair. But Sugiyama had no intention of waiting for a summons.

On the next morning, September 12, 1945, General Sugiyama appeared at his office on Ichigaya Heights. At 10:00 A.M. he called Kobayashi to him.

"I want you to do me one last favor. Please go to my wife and find out what she plans to do. I have been so worried that she might kill herself and I want to make sure that she has no such intention."

Kobayashi promised to go right away and shortly thereafter drove to the Sugiyama home. There he confided the general's fears to his wife. She laughed gaily and said: "Don't worry. I can't commit suicide because I'm an old woman and much too weak to do such a thing. I know General Sugiyama will do it and that is enough."

The colonel rushed back to Ichigaya and repeated these words to the general who sat back in his chair and sighed contentedly. She had been his only concern and now his mind was at rest. "Thank you, Kobayashi. Everything is all right now."

The colonel went to his office and sat thinking of the two people he loved so deeply. Fifteen minutes later he heard a gunshot and rushed out into the corridor. The door to Sugiyama's office was open and Kobayashi ran to it.

After taking off his officer's tunic, the general had seated himself in a comfortable chair. Then he had pressed a service revolver to his white shirt and fired into his chest. Unlike Hideki Tojo, Sugiyama had found the mark and fallen unconscious.

Kobayashi was overcome by grief as he stood beside the dying man. Noting that the general was perspiring greatly, he brought out a handkerchief and tenderly wiped his brow. The secretary whispered, "This is Kobayashi. This is Kobayashi." Sugiyama's head rolled upward slightly and nodded several times as he tried to recognize the presence of his aide. Then he slumped further into a coma. Other officers came to the room and watched the Field Marshal as he labored for final breaths.

One of them told Kobayashi that he had just called Mrs. Sugiyama to give her the sad news. She had asked only one question: "Is he really dead?" When the officer said that he was, Mrs. Sugiyama had hung up.

As this information was given to the saddened Kobayashi, he was suddenly alarmed and sensed that he should go immediately to the Sugiyama home. He drove quickly to the suburbs and hastened into the house. The general's adopted daughter stood in the reception hall, her face lined with horror. Kobayashi brushed by her and went to the bedroom. As he opened the door he realized that he was too late.

Mrs. Sugiyama had put down the telephone and gone to her room. There she knelt before a Buddhist temple and prayed. Taking a small ceremonial knife in her hand, she pressed it to the front of her kimono. Then she picked up a cup and drained its contents. She fell forward onto the tiny knife, which pricked her chest and drew a small amount of blood. The dagger did not inflict the mortal wound. The cyanide in the cup did.

Kobayashi called and called her name but she could not answer. As he looked on helplessly, she died on the floor.

EPILOGUE

In Mukden, Manchuria, where the Japanese Army had first defied its Government in 1931 by staging a coup, new armies walked the streets. Russian and Chinese Communist soldiers controlled the city. Merchants flew the flags of the USSR and Mao Tse-tung in their shopwindows. Chinese peasants looted the factories so laboriously built up by Japanese industrialists. Soviet trains pulled up to sidings and were loaded with heavy equipment and machine tools for shipment to Russia.

American OSS agents strolled casually about, snapping pictures of the virtual brick-by-brick dismemberment of the industry of Manchuria. They sent this evidence of Communist duplicity back to headquarters, which told them to stay where they were as long as possible, until the Russians threw them out. That would happen within days.

In the Home Islands of Japan, the enemy had come and taken control of the major cities. So far the occupation had been peaceful. Though scattered instances of rape, robbery and murder had occurred, both sides were amazed at the manner in which the two former foes had managed to adjust. Japan was under the control of a conquering army, but the ruling hand was quite restrained.

In countless towns and hamlets, the first sight of the invader was frightening but the fear was short-lived. The Americans were businesslike and peaceful.

In the city of Nagasaki, three men walked down still-cluttered streets. The lonely trio were Chuck Sweeney, Kermit Beahan and Don Albury from the crew of *Bock's Car*. Little more than a month before, they had come to Nagasaki, but at a height of twenty-nine thousand feet. From their plane had come the ugly, bulbous Fat Man which blew down buildings, roasted bodies and invaded bloodstreams. The three airmen had come back with the first American medical team into the stricken area. The night before they had stopped just outside town at a place called Mogi. After a pleasant meal, the fliers had talked awhile, then gone to bed. For the first time in his life, pilot Chuck Sweeney took out his pistol and belt and hung them on the bedpost. He felt uneasy—some Japanese might already have discovered the identity of the three men on the outskirts of Nagasaki.

The next morning they rode through the wreckage and walked the streets. It was only a little more than a month since the bomb had fallen, and some of the bodies had not yet been removed. Skulls lay on both sides of the road. In holes that had been scooped out as air-raid shelters, skeletons were piled on top of each other. The stench made it hard to breathe. It assailed the nostrils and caused an involuntary sucking in of breath.

In a cavity off the road, fire engines lay squashed down like bugs. At the medical center on the hill, the main building was still standing, but its interior had been burned out. From it doctors and nurses had run up to safety. In it patients who screamed for rescue from the approaching flames had been ignored.

The three strangers walked through the blackened rooms and saw bones lying in beds. They had been there for over a month, sightless skulls staring at the ceilings over which the great light had shone weeks before.

In one of the operating rooms, a patient lay on the operating table where he had been when the bomb burst. The skeleton waited as though hoping to be repaired. Around the room the remains of doctors and nurses sprawled in the positions they assumed at death. The room was a dreadful tableau, suspended in time by that awful brilliance which had touched everyone in Nagasaki.

They walked through the devastation, through the numbed and sullen survivors who acted differently from the people in Tokyo and other cities. These people were hurt beyond repair, warped forever by an unearthly power. They were indifferent to strangers, withdrawn from each other. Many were still dying from the insidious illness which had crept into their bloodstreams. They lived in lean-tos, thrown up to protect them from the cold nights and the burning sun, thrown up to bring some privacy to bodies stripped of pretensions to normalcy by the bomb. They ignored the men walking through the Urakami Valley in September of 1945.

The three Americans thought it was just as well.

IMAGE GALLERY

Kamikaze pilots preparing for take-off—as painted by
Japanese war artist. *(U.S. Army)*

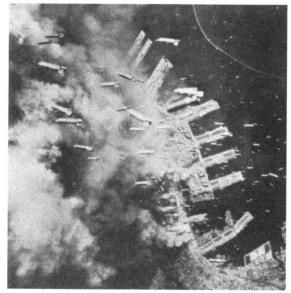

Kobe, Japan, under air attack by B-29s. *(U.S. Air Force)*

The Big Three at Potsdam. *(U.S. Army)*

The Little Boy. *(inset, Atomic Energy Commission)*; The *Enola Gay* home from bombing Hiroshima. *(U.S. Air Force)*

The Genie over Nagasaki. *(U.S. Air Force)*

The Fat Man. *(Atomic Energy Commission)*

Crew 15. Rear, from left to right: Kermit Beahan, Jim Van Pelt, Don Albury, Fred Olivi, Chuck Sweeney. Front, left to right: Ed Buckley, John Kuharek, Ray Gallagher, "Pappy" Dehart, Abe Spitzer. *(U.S. Air Force)*

Lieutenant Marcus McDilda. His fantastic lie caused
consternation in Tokyo. *(Courtesy of Marcus McDilda)*

General Korechika Anami.
(Courtesy of Mrs. Korechika Anami)

Lieutenant Colonel Masahiko Takeshita.
(Courtesy of Lt. Col. Takeshita)

Major Kenji Hatanaka.
(Courtesy of the Hatanaka family)

Kawabe mission lands at Ie Shima. Green crosses on bomber were painted on orders from MacArthur. *(U.S. Army)*

Kawabe and staff transfer to American plane for flight to Manila. *(U.S. Army)*

OSS agents jump behind Japanese lines in North China. *(U.S. Army)*

General Jonathan Wainwright and fellow prisoners have breakfast with their rescuers in Mukden, Manchuria. Left to right: General George Moore, Major Robert Lamar, Major James Hennessy, Governor General of the Dutch East Indies, Tjarda Van Starkenborgh Stachouwer, and General Wainwright. *(U.S. Army)*

General Jonathan Wainwright on his way home after three years in captivity. Major Gus Krause welcomes him to Hsian, China. *(U.S. Army)*

Major John Singlaub, Commander of Mission Pigeon, stands in drop zone on northwest coast of Hainan Island, Aug. 27, 1945. *(U.S. Army)*

Australian and Dutch survivors rescued by Singlaub team; traps on the ground were used to catch rats for extra food. *(U.S. Army)*

A grim Colonel Charles Tench takes command of Atsugi Airbase from General Seizo Arisue. Interpreter, Major Faubion Bowers, is at Tench's left. *(U.S. Army)*

Tench and Bowers walk resolutely across the field quite aware that they may be murdered. *(U.S. Army)*

Top-hatted Mamoru Shigemitsu, followed by General Umezu,
stands on deck of U.S.S. *Missouri. (U.S. Army)*

General Umezu surrenders the Imperial Japanese Army
to the enemy. *(U.S. Army)*

General Tomoyuki Yamashita surrounded by his accusers in
Manila. He was later hanged for war crimes. *(U.S. Army)*

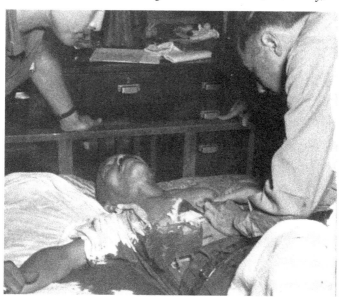

General Hideki Tojo near death after attempted suicide. An
American doctor saved him for the gallows. *(U.S. Army)*

ACKNOWLEDGMENTS

During the past two years, many people have contributed their knowledge to this book. They have also shown much hospitality and kindness to a stranger. My sincere gratitude is extended to the following:

IN THE UNITED STATES: Charles D. Albury, John Auxier, Kenneth Bainbridge, William Barney, Kermit Beahan, Jacob Beser, Faubion Bowers, John Bradley, Arnold Breakey, General Clovis Byers, John Cantlon, Patricia Carey, Ralph Curry, L. J. Deal, Allen Dulles, David Dunne, Myron Faryna, Raymond Gallagher, Leonard Godfrey, General Leslie Groves, James Healey, James Hennessy, Roger Hilsman, Colonel Joseph Jackson, James Kellis, Mr. and Mrs. Gustave Krause, Robert Lamar, William Laurence, Harold Leith, George MacPherson, John Madison, Sidney Mashbir, Marcus McDilda, General Frederick Munson, General George Olmstead, General William R. Peers, Mrs. Earl Ricks, Alexander Sachs, Robert Serber, Colonel John Singlaub, Edward Starz, Stanley Steinke, General Charles Sweeney, Charles Tench, General Paul Tibbets, General Albert Wedemeyer, General Charles Willoughby.

IN EUROPE: Vice Admiral Frederick Ashworth, Commander, United States Sixth Fleet.

IN JAPAN: Genichi Akatani, Mrs. Korechika Anami, Okikatsu Arao, General Seizo Arisue, Yoshiro Fujimura, Hiroshi Fuwa, Saburo Hayashi, Zenshiro Hoshina, Masao Inaba, Tadao Inoue, Masao Ishii, Masataka Iwata, Naomichi Jin, Shinaji Kobayashi, Toru Kumamoto, Masao Matsuda, Yoshio Manaka, Katsuhei Nakamura, Setsuzo Nishiura, Toshikazu Ohmae, Atsushi Oi, Hisatsune Sakomizu, Ichiji Sugita, Masahiko Takeshita, Rikihei Takuma, Morio Tateno, Mrs. Hideki Tojo, Sadatoshi Tomioka, Makoto Tsukamoto, Kantaro Uemura, Mrs. Mitsuru Ushijima, Professor Kei Wakaizumi, H. Yoshioka.

Of great help were the following archives and archivists: IN THE WASHINGTON, D.C., area: Federal Records Center, Alexandria, Va.—Wilbur Nigh, Thomas Hohmann, Joseph Avery, Robert Krauskopf, Lois Aldridge; Office of the Chief of Military History—Mr. Charles Romanus and Miss Hannah Zeidlik; The National Archives—Mr. Charles Taylor; U.S. Navy Historical Records Division—Mr. Dean Allard and Miss Florence Mayhew; Department of the Navy, Bureau of Medicine and Surgery—Mr. Quinton Sanger.

ALSO: Office of the Assistant Secretary of Defense—Major Robert Webb, Major B. J. Smith; U.S. Marine Corps Library, Henderson Hall; Library of Congress, Japanese Research Room; Japanese Embassy.

IN THE NEW YORK, NEW JERSEY, NEW ENGLAND AREA: U.S. Signal Corps Museum, Fort Monmouth, New Jersey; New York City Public Library, Main Branch; Columbia University Law Library and East Asian Library; Yale University, Sterling Memorial Library, New Haven, Conn.; Harvard University, Widener Library, Cambridge, Mass.; Norwalk and Westport, Conn., public libraries.

ALSO: Military Personnel Records Center, St. Louis, Mo.—Mr. Herman Gross and Mrs. S. Levy, in particular; Department of the Air Force, Headquarters, Fifth Air Force—Colonel Milton Frank and William Vizzard.

IN JAPAN: In Tokyo—The staffs of the Diet Library, Foreign Office and Japanese Defense Agency, who were so helpful to my research associates and myself during the past months. In Hiroshima—the Atomic Bomb Casualty Commission, which supplied case histories of survivors of the Little Boy and Fat Man.

ALSO, SPECIAL THANKS TO THE FOLLOWING:

Congressman Don Irwin, 4th District, Connecticut, who repeatedly snipped reams of red tape; his assistant, Ronay Arlt, who never refused to help with my research problems; Robert Travers and Richard Goldhurst, who lent encouragement at crucial moments; David Jones, Pan American Airways, who opened many doors in Tokyo; his assistant, Mrs. T. Saito, whose phone calls saved me hours of frustration; Edwin Kiester, who introduced me to David Jones; Robert Trumbull, Emerson Chapin and Junnosuke Ofusa, *New York Times*, Tokyo, who were most courteous and kind to me; Messrs. Fujita and Yokokawa of the Mainichi Newspapers for unfailing hospitality.

To Michael Magzis, who acted as counselor and critic; to Margaret Cameron, who suggested many helpful changes; to Mrs. Kiyoko Ishii, whose extraordinary enthusiasm and devotion to research problems contributed so much to the final manuscript. Besides those attributes, her warm personality has endeared her to the entire Craig family, which, incidentally, deserves a medal for courage in the face of the enemy, the author.

Lastly, may I thank the people of The Dial Press; especially E. L. Doctorow, Editor-in-Chief, and Richard Baron, President; their original faith in me made possible *THE FALL OF JAPAN*.

NOTES AND SOURCES

Certain books and documents proved extremely helpful as reference material for nearly every chapter. To avoid needless repetition, I will mention these works only once; this is not to minimize their value to me.

Diplomatic History

Robert J. C. Butow's *Japan's Decision to Surrender*; Herbert Feis' *Between War and Peace: The Potsdam Conference*, and *Japan Subdued: The Atomic Bomb and the End of the War in the Pacific*; Len Giovanitti and Fred Freed's *The Decision to Drop the Bomb*; The Japanese Foreign Office publication *Shusen Shiroku*; Shigenori Togo's *The Cause of Japan*; Koichi Kido's *Nikki*.

Military Affairs

Samuel Eliot Morison's *History of Naval Operations in World War II*, especially Vols. XIII and XIV; Walter Karig's *Battle Report*, Vol. V; Masanori Ito's *Gumbatsu Koboshi* (3 vols.), and *Teikoku Kaigun No Saigo*; Wesley Craven and James Cate's *The Army Air Forces in World War II:* Vol. V, *The Pacific: Matterhorn to Nagasaki*; Takushiro Hattori's *Daitoa Senso Zenshi* (4 vols.); Saburo Hayashi's *Kogun*.

Documents, Records

U.S. Strategic Bombing Survey: Interrogations (2 vols.). Japanese Research Division, U.S. Army Far East, Military History Section: Interrogation of Japanese Officials (2 vols.); Statements of Japanese Officials on World War II (4 vols.); Translation of Japanese Documents (7 vols.). International Military Tribunal for the Far East: selected interrogations and statements of witnesses and defendants.

In the following notes on individual chapters, the term *Statements by* almost always refers to those made to the Japanese Research Division, U.S. Army Far East, by Japanese officers and statesmen.

CHAPTER ONE: *The Tactics of Despair*

On Admiral Onishi and the Founding of the Kamikazes

From interviews with naval officers Zenshiro Hoshina, Rikihei Inoguchi (Takuma), Toshikazu Ohmae, Atsushi Oi.

From logs of U.S. ships *St. Lo, Kitkun Bay, Santee*.

Also: Inoguchi and Nakajima's *Divine Wind*; Yoshio Kodama's *I Was Defeated*.

On Okinawa

From interviews with Naomichi Jin, the widow of General Ushijima, Rikihei Inoguchi, Okikatsu Arao.

From U.S. Army interrogations of Japanese officers Jin, Yahara, Shimada (32nd Army), and Setsuzo Nishiura.

Also: After action reports and histories of U.S. 1st and 6th Marine Divisions, and 7th, 77th and 96th Army divisions; daily reports of U.S. 10th Army and XXIV Corps.

From logs of U.S. ships *Bush, Colhoun.*

From books: *Okinawa: The Last Battle*, a most informative official U.S. history; Japanese works *P. W. Doctor, Senkan Tomato No Saigo* and *Okinawa Senshi*, which reflect the precipitate decline of Japanese power and morale both on land and sea.

Also: Japanese Army Monographs Number 53 and Number 83, on Okinawa campaign.

On Suzuki Cabinet Formation

From interview with Hisatsune Sakomizu.

From statements of Koiso, Suzuki, Hiranuma, Kido, Sakomizu, Togo, Saonji.

CHAPTER TWO: *Meetinghouse*

On Raid

From interviews with 35 Japanese civilians who lived in Tokyo and witnessed the raid on March 9 and later ones.

From memoirs of Curtis Lemay (see Bibliography).

From operations and debriefing reports of the 20th Air Force Headquarters, Guam, 73rd, 313th and 314th Bomb Wings.

Also: Martin Caidin's *A Torch to the Enemy*; Gene Gurney's *Journey of the Giants*; Masuo Kato's *The Lost War*; and the *Saturday Evening Post* (Jan. 12, 1946). These books capture the terrible tragedy of Japan aflame.

CHAPTER THREE: *The Diplomacy of Defeat*

On Switzerland

From interviews with Yoshiro Fujimura, Allen Dulles, Zenshiro Hoshina.

From statements of Fujimura, Hoshina, Sadatoshi Tomioka, Soemu Toyoda.

On U.S. Radio Broadcasts, etc.

From conversations with Sidney Mashbir.

Also: Microfilm copies of Mashbir broadcasts to Japan.

From books: Ellis Zacharias' *Secret Missions*; Sidney Mashbir's *I Was an American Spy*; Ladislas Farago's *Burn After Reading*.

Also: Federal Communications Commission records on broadcasts from Japan in 1945.

On Tokyo-Moscow Interlude

From interviews with Hisatsune Sakomizu.

From statements of Togo, Sato, Hirota, Kido, Suzuki, and others.

Also: Copies of cables between Togo and Sato.

On Japanese-American Battle Plans (Ketsu Go vs. Downfall)

From interviews with Seizo Arisue, Charles Willoughby.

From statements of Arisue, Ohmae, Amano, Haba, Fuwa, among many others.

From U.S. Operational Plan as described in "Downfall" document published in May 1945.

CHAPTER FOUR: *The Project*

On Manhattan Project

From interviews with Leslie Groves and crew members of 509th Group and the *509th Pictorial Album*.

Also: Grove's *Now It Can Be Told*; William Laurence's *Dawn Over Zero*; Arthur H. Compton's *Atomic Quest*; Hewlett and Anderson's *The New World, 1939–1946*; Lamont's *Day of Trinity*; Knebel and Bailey's *No High Ground*; and others (see Bibliography).

On Potsdam

From interviews with Allen Dulles.

From the diary of Henry Stimson at Yale University (unpublished).

From memoirs of Truman, Churchill, Eden, Byrnes, Forrestal, Leahy, King, Stimson, Lord Alanbrooke.

Also: Defense Department publication: *The Entry of the Soviet Union into the War against Japan, Military Plans, 1941–1945*; U.S. State Department: *Potsdam Papers* (2 vols.); John Ehrman's *Grand Strategy: October 1944–August 1945*.

On Tokyo Reaction to Declaration

From interviews with Sakomizu, Takeshita.

Also: statements of Suzuki, Kido, Toyoda, Sakomizu, Yoshizumi.

CHAPTER FIVE: *The Little Boy*

On 509th: Tinian and Hiroshima

From interviews and/or correspondence with Leslie Groves, Paul Tibbets, Charles Sweeney, Frederick Ashworth, Kermit Beahan, Don Albury, Raymond Gallagher, and others.

From *The Atomic Bombings of Hiroshima and Nagasaki*, The Manhattan Engineering District. Washington, D.C., 1947.

Also: Atomic Energy Commission files at Germantown, Md., which were made available to me by Mr. L. J. Deal. The files dealt primarily with Little Boy, its design, etc.; with messages between Tinian and Los Alamos and Washington; with observations of the blast. The figure of 13,500 tons for the energy yield of Little Boy has only recently been computed after years of analysis. The Fat Man's yield at Nagasaki has been placed at slightly over 22,000 tons.

Also: Knebel and Bailey's *No High Ground*, a superb re-creation of the Hiroshima drop.

On McDilda

From conversation and correspondence with Marcus McDilda; from interview with Hisatsune Sakomizu.

From operations reports, 21st Fighter Group, Iwo Jima, August 1945.

Also: Curious friends in Japan who had heard of the American pilot's story but could not remember his name.

CHAPTER SIX: *The Genie*

On Nagasaki

From interviews and/or correspondence with Leslie Groves, Paul Tibbets, Charles Sweeney, Frederick Ashworth, Kermit

Beahan, Don Albury, Jacob Beser, Raymond Gallagher, John Cantlon, Stanley Steinke, Myron Faryna, Leonard Godfrey, Ralph Curry, William Barney, Edward Buckley, reporter William L. Laurence, scientists Robert Serber and Norman Ramsey, and others.

From diaries and unpublished notes of Raymond Gallagher, Don Albury, James Van Pelt.

Also: Spitzer and Miller's, *We Dropped the A-Bomb*; Laurence's *Dawn Over Zero*; Knebel and Bailey's *No High Ground*.

On Ground Damage, etc.

From conversations with John Madison, a survivor.

From nearly 200 reports among thousands that Japanese survivors filed, after the war, with the Atomic Bomb Casualty Commission.

From Atomic Energy Commission volumes on medical effects of bombs (1951).

From U.S. Strategic Bombing Survey publications on medical effects, blast damage, etc. caused by Fat Man.

Also: Nagai's *We of Nagasaki*; Trumbull's *Nine Who Survived Hiroshima and Nagasaki*.

The letter to Professor Sagane was recovered by Japanese military personnel and delivered to him, but only after the war had ended.

CHAPTER SEVEN: *The Air-Raid Shelter*

On Conference

From interviews with participants Sakomizu, Hoshina.

From statements by Suzuki, Togo, Yonai, Hiranuma, Toyoda, Ikeda, Hoshina, Yoshizumi, Sakomizu, Kido.

Also: Memoirs of Togo, Toyoda, Sakomizu, Toshikazu Kase (see Bibliography).

CHAPTER EIGHT: *Reaction in Washington*

Washington Conference

From memoirs of participants in White House meeting: Truman, Byrnes, Forrestal, Stimson, Leahy.

On China

From interviews with Albert Wedemeyer, George Olmstead.

Also: Memoirs of General Stilwell, General Chennault, General Wedemeyer; Romanus and Sunderland's book on China-Burma-India Theater (see Bibliography); White and Jacoby's *Thunder Out of China*.

CHAPTER NINE: *August 11—The Conspiracy Begins*

On Ominous Developments in Tokyo

From interviews with Japanese officers Arao, Hoshina, Hayashi, Ida, Inaba, Inoue, Kobayashi, Ohmae, Oi, Takeshita, Makoto Tsukamoto.

From statement by Taihei Oshima.

On Previous Rebellions

From the *Transcript of Proceedings* of International Military Tribunal Far East: testimony of Okada, Ando, and others.

Also: Sakomizu, Grew books (see Bibliography).

On OSS in China

From interviews with Gustave Krause, Raymond Peers, Joseph Jackson, James Kellis, Albert Wedemeyer, George Olmstead.

From Elizabeth McDonald's *Undercover Girl.*

On Fukuoka Atrocity

From transcript of testimony by witnesses at the Yokohama war crimes trials.

CHAPTER TEN: *August 12—Day of Crisis*

On Tokyo Intrigues

From interviews with Sakomizu, Kobayashi, Ohmae, Oi, Takeshita, Inaba, Ida (Iwata), Fuwa, Arao, Hayashi.

Also: statements by Toyoda, Hiranuma, Hayashi, Kido, Takeshita, Togo, Matsumoto, Sakomizu.

CHAPTER ELEVEN: *The Mounting Peril*

On Anami

From interviews with the two men closest to Anami: Hayashi, his secretary, and Takeshita, his brother-in-law.

From correspondence with Hayashi.

Also: statements by Hayashi, Kido, Takeshita.

On Yonai

From interviews with Yonai's aide, Zenshiro Hoshina.

Also: statement by Hoshina.

On Rebels

From interviews with rebels Arao, Ida, Inaba, Takeshita; also with Hayashi. Also correspondence with Hayashi.

Also: from statements by these men.

CHAPTER TWELVE: *August 14—The Final Word*

On Conference and Its Effects

From interviews with Arao, Fuwa, Hayashi, Ida, Inaba, Inoguchi, Ohmae, Oi, Sakomizu, Takeshita, Tsukamoto

Also: statements by Hayashi, Kawabe, Kido, Suzuki, Takeshita, Togo, Toyoda.

From Niwa's *Nihon Yaburetari*; Shimomura's *Shusen Hishi.* (Used also in Chapter 13.)

CHAPTER THIRTEEN: *The Rebellion*

On Rebellion and Anami's Death

From interviews with Arao, Fuwa, Hayashi, Ida, Inaba, Tadao Inoue, Shinaji Kobayashi, Sakomizu, Takeshita, Morio Tateno, Mrs. Katsuko Tojo, Makoto Tsukamoto.

Also: statements by Arao, Fuwa, Ida, Ishiwata, Kido, Takeshita, Tokugawa, Kiyoshi Tsukamoto.

From Soichi Oya's *Nihon No Ichiban Nagaihi*.

I visited the grounds of the Imperial Palace and walked through the woods where the rebels camped; the building where Mori died still stands; so does the Imperial Household Agency in which Kido hid in great fear.

The rebel who killed Colonel Shiraishi is still known only as Mister X because of a pact between Inaba, Takeshita and Ida to protect him from possible vengeance by relatives of the slain victim. Mister X lives near Tokyo and sees his comrades from the *coup d'état* infrequently.

CHAPTER FOURTEEN: *Peace on Earth*

V-J Day

From The New York Times, San Francisco Chronicle, Washington Post, Pacific Stars and Stripes, Yank, logs of ships in Task Force 38 off Japan.

Also Japanese Secret Police reports.

CHAPTER FIFTEEN: *The Emperor Speaks*

On Reaction to Surrender

From interviews with police official Kantaro Uemura.

From U.S. Strategic Bombing Survey case studies on Japanese attitudes toward defeat.

From: Japanese Secret Police reports on disturbances in Tokyo.

Also: Sakai's *Samurai*.

On Anami's Cremation

From interviews with Anami's widow, Anami's brother-in-law, Takeshita, and Shinaji Kobayashi.

On Ugaki's Death

From interviews with Inoguchi, Ohmae.
Also: Inoguchi and Nakajima's *Divine Wind*.

CHAPTER SIXTEEN: *Delayed Reactions*

On Delayed Reactions in Capital

From interviews with Ida, Inoue, Inoguchi, Masao Matsuda, Makoto Tsukamoto, Oi, Ohmae, Uemura.
Also: Yoshio Kodama's *I Was Defeated*; Ammyo Kosono's reminiscences in *Bungei Shunju*.

On Mukden Jump

From interviews and correspondence with James Hennessy, Roger Hilsman, Robert Lamar, Harold Leith, Edward Starz.
Also: diaries, letters, photographs supplied by members of Mission Cardinal.

CHAPTER SEVENTEEN: *An Order from MacArthur*

On Kawabe Flight

From interviews with Mashbir, Willoughby, Faubion Bowers, Ohmae, Matsuda.
From statements by Kawabe, Okazaki, Terai, Yokoyama.
Also: Mashbir's *I Was an American Spy*; *Life*.

CHAPTER EIGHTEEN: *Violent Interlude*

On Incidents in Tokyo Area

From interviews with Fuwa, Uemura
Also: Microfilm copies of Tokyo police reports for that period;

Japanese newspaper accounts for August 15–August 31, 1945; Yoshio Kodama's *I Was Defeated*.

On Atsugi

From interviews with Seizo Arisue.

Also: statements by Yoshizumi; Masuo Kato's *The Lost War*.

On Tanaka

From interview with Fuwa.

From Kiyoshi Tsukamoto's *Ah Kogun Saigo No Hi*.

On American Advance Party

From interviews with Charles Tench, Faubion Bowers, David Dunne.

(An Air Force pilot, Lieutenant Colonel Clay Tice, had landed at Nittigahara Airfield on Kyushu, to be the first American on Japanese soil. He was greeted with candy and flowers, then given fuel for his return trip to Okinawa.)

On OSS in China

From interviews with Raymond Peers, Gustave Krause, James Kellis, Joseph Jackson, Robert Lamar, Howard Leith.

Also: Wedemeyer's memoirs; White and Jacoby's *Thunder Out of China*; Herbert Feis' *The China Tangle*, all excellent analyses of the chaotic situation on the Asian mainland.

John Birch's death was described to me by several men who knew him in China but asked not to be identified. I was also shown photographs of his mutilated body taken just before burial. *Life's* May 1961 story, "How John Birch Died," is the most accurate description of the event and was relied on heavily by the author.

CHAPTER NINETEEN: *Lazarus*

On Wainwright

From interviews with Robert Lamar and Harold Leith, who rescued Wainwright.

From interviews with Gustave Krause, who spent some very pleasant hours with Wainwright shortly after the General's return to freedom.

Also: correspondence with General Wedemeyer; Wainwright's *General Wainwright's Story*.

On Mission Pigeon

From interviews with John Singlaub, Arnold Breakey, John Bradley, James Healey.

From documents, letters, photographs given me by Colonel Singlaub.

Also: John Bradley's diary.

CHAPTER TWENTY: *The Enemy Lands*

On Atsugi, Yokohama Landings, etc.

From interviews with Charles Tench, Faubion Bowers, David Dunne, Sidney Mashbir, Frederick Munson, Clovis Byers, Charles Willoughby, Seizo Arisue, Ichiji Sugita, Genichi Akatani, Kantaro Uemura.

From Japanese Secret Police files.

From memoirs of Douglas MacArthur, Courtney Whitney, George Kenney, Robert Eichelberger, William Halsey.

From daily reports of 11th Airborne Division, 4th Marine Regiment.

From books by correspondents Brines, Lee, Kelley and Ryan (see Bibliography).

CHAPTER TWENTY-ONE: *"These Proceedings Are Closed"*

On the Ceremony

From interviews with participants Sugita, Tomioka, Naka-mura, Willoughby, Mashbir.

From memoirs cited in previous chapter, plus those of Wainwright, Percival, Kase, Shigemitsu.

Also: *Life*; *Yank*; *Bungei Shunju*.

On Yamashita

From diary of General Akira Muto.

From Wainwright and Percival autobiographies.

Also: daily reports of U.S. 32nd Infantry Division.

Also: John Dean Potter's *The Life and Death of a Japanese General*; Masanobu Tsuji's *Singapore: The Japanese Version*.

On American Embassy

From interviews with Bowers, Mashbir.

Also: memoirs of Halsey, MacArthur, Eichelberger, Whitney.

CHAPTER TWENTY-TWO: *The Last Recourse*

On Tojo

From interviews with Mrs. Katsuko Tojo, Clovis Byers.

From newspaper accounts by George Jones, *The New York Times;* Frank Kelley, *New York Herald Tribune*; Frank Bartholomew and Frank Tremaine, *Washington Post*; Robert Trumbull, *The New York Times*.

From CIC report by Paul Kraus.

Also: article by Harry Brundidge in *American Mercury*, August 1953.

From books by Clark Lee; by Frank Kelley and Cornelius Ryan (see Bibliography).

Also: Yukio Hasegawa's article in *Bungei Shunju*, August 1956.

On Sugiyama

From interviews with Fuwa, Hayashi, Kobayashi.

EPILOGUE

On Mukden

From interviews with OSS personnel James Hennessy, Joseph Jackson, Gustave Krause, Robert Lamar, Harold Leith.

OSS agents took photographs of Russian depredations and wrote reports on the activities of the Chinese Communist forces in Manchuria. All Americans were forced to leave by the Russian authorities in Mukden. Hennessy in particular remembers being told by Field Marshal Rodion Malinovsky that he had twenty-four hours in which to leave.

By October 1945, the last American left Manchuria under threat of death.

On the Walk through Nagasaki

From interviews with Charles Sweeney, Don Albury, Kermit Beahan.

SELECTED BIBLIOGRAPHY

BOOKS

AMRINE, Michael. *The Great Decision*. New York: G. P. Putnam's Sons, 1959.

ARNOLD, Henry. *Global Mission*. New York: Harper & Bros., 1949.

BAXTER, James Phinney. *Scientists Against Time*. Boston: Little, Brown and Co., 1952.

BOYINGTON, Gregory. *Baa Baa Black Sheep*. New York: G. P. Putnam's Sons, 1958.

BRINES, Russell. *MacArthur's Japan*. Philadelphia: Lippincott, 1948.

BRYANT, Arthur. *Triumph in the West*. New York: Doubleday & Co. Inc., 1959.

BUTOW, Robert J. C. *Japan's Decision to Surrender*. Stanford, California: Stanford University Press, 1954.

—— *Tojo and the Coming of the War*. Princeton, New Jersey: Princeton University Press, 1961.

BYRNES, James F. *Speaking Frankly*. New York: Harper & Bros., 1947.

—— *All in One Lifetime*. New York: Harper & Bros., 1958.

CAIDIN, Martin. *A Torch to the Enemy*. New York: Ballantine Books, 1960.

CHENNAULT, Claire. *Way of a Fighter*. New York: G. P. Putnam's Sons, 1949.

CHIANG KAI-SHEK. *Soviet Russia in China: A Summing-Up at Seventy*. New York: Farrar, Straus and Cudahy, 1957.

CHURCHILL, Winston S. *Triumph and Tragedy*. Boston: Houghton, Mifflin Co., 1953.

COMPTON, A. H. *Atomic Quest*. New York: Oxford University Press, 1956.

CRAVEN, Wesley, and CATE, James. *The Army Air Forces in World War II, Vol. V, The Pacific: Matterhorn to Nagasaki, June 1944 to August 1945*. Chicago: University of Chicago Press, 1953.

CUNNINGHAM, Winfield Scott. *Wake Island Command*. Boston: Little, Brown & Co., 1961.

DAVIS, Kenneth S. *Experience of War*. New York: Doubleday and Co. Inc., 1965.

DEANE, John R. *The Strange Alliance*. New York: Viking Press, 1947.

EDEN, Anthony. *The Reckoning*. Boston: Houghton, Mifflin Co., 1965.

ERHMAN, John. *Grand Strategy: October 1944–August 1945*. London: Her Majesty's Stationery Office, 1956.

EICHELBERGER, Robert L. *Our Jungle Road to Tokyo*. New York: Viking Press, 1950.

FARAGO, Ladislas. *Burn After Reading*. New York: Walker and Co., 1961.

FEIS, Herbert. *The China Tangle*. Princeton, New Jersey: Princeton University Press, 1953.

—— *Between War and Peace: The Potsdam Conference*. Princeton, New Jersey, Princeton University Press, 1960.

—— *Japan Subdued: The Atomic Bomb and the End of the War in the Pacific*. Princeton, New Jersey: Princeton University Press, 1961.

FERMI, Laura. *Atoms in the Family*. Chicago: University of Chicago Press, 1954.

FORRESTAL, James. *The Forrestal Diaries*. Edited by Walter Millis with E. S. Duffield, New York: Viking Press, 1951.

GAYN, Mark. *Japan Diary*. New York: Sloan, 1948.

GIOVANNITTI, Len, and FREED, Fred. *The Decision to Drop the Bomb*. New York: Coward-McCann, Inc., 1965.

GLINES, Carroll V. *Doolittle's Tokyo Raiders*. Princeton, New Jersey: D. Van Nostrand Co. Inc., 1964.

GREW, Joseph C. *Turbulent Era* (2 vols.). Boston: Houghton, Mifflin Co., 1952.

GROVES, Leslie R. *Now It Can Be Told*. New York: Harper & Bros., 1962.

GURNEY, Gene. *Journey of the Giants*. New York: Coward-McCann, Inc., 1961.

HACHIYA, Michihiko. *Hiroshima Diary*. Chapel Hill, North Carolina: University of North Carolina Press, 1955.

HALSEY, William F., and BRYAN, J., III. *Admiral Halsey's Story*. New York: McGraw-Hill, Inc., 1947.

HASHIMOTO, Mochitsura. *Sunk! The Story of the Japanese Submarine Fleet*. New York: Henry Holt & Co., 1954.

HATTORI, Takushiro. *Daitoa Senso Zenshi* (4 vols.). Tokyo: Masu Shobo, 1953.

HAYASHI, Saburo with Coox, Alvin D. *Kogun: The Japanese Army in the Pacific War*. Quantico, Virginia: Marine Corps Association, 1959.

HAYASHI, Shigeru, editor. *Nihon Shusen Shi*. Tokyo: Yomiuri Shimbun, 1962.

HELM, Thomas. *Ordeal by Sea*. New York: Dodd, Mead and Co., 1963.

HERSEY, John. *Hiroshima*. New York: Alfred A. Knopf, 1946.

HEWLETT, Richard, and ANDERSON, Oscar E., Jr. *The New World, 1939–1946*. University Park, Pennsylvania: Pennsylvania State University Press, 1962.

HIGASHUCUNI, Naruhiko. *Ichi Kozoku No Senso Nikki.* Tokyo: Nihon Shuhosha, 1957.

—— *Watakushi No Kiroku.* Tokyo: Toho Shobo, 1947.

HULL, Cordell. *The Memoirs of Cordell Hull*, Vol. II. New York: Macmillan Co., 1948.

INOGUCHI, Rikihei, and NAKAJIMA, Tadashi. *The Divine Wind.* Annapolis, Maryland: United States Naval Institute, 1958.

ITO, Masanori. *Gumbatsu Koboshi* (3 vols.). Tokyo: Bungei Shunju, 1957–1958.

—— *Teikoku Kaigun No Saigo.* Tokyo: Bungei Shunju, 1961.

—— TOMIOKA, Masatoshi, and INADA, Masazumi, editors. *Jitsuroku Taiheiyo Senso*, Vols. V–VI. Tokyo: Chuo Koron, 1960.

JAMES, David A. *The Rise and Fall of the Japanese Empire.* London: Allen and Unwin, 1951.

JONES, F. C. *Japan's New Order in East Asia: Its Rise and Fall, 1937–1945.* London: Oxford University Press, 1954.

KARIG, Walter, with HARRIS, Russell L., and MANSON, Frank A. *Battle Report*, Vol. V, *Victory in the Pacific.* New York: Rinehart & Co. Inc., 1949.

KASE, Toshikazu. *Journey to the Missouri.* New Haven: Yale University Press, 1950.

KATO, Masuo. *The Lost War.* New York: Alfred A. Knopf, 1946.

KELLEY, Frank, and RYAN, Cornelius. *Star-Spangled Mikado.* New York: McBride, 1947.

KENNEY, George C. *General Kenney Reports.* New York: Duell, Sloan & Pearce, 1949.

KIMURA, Hachiro. *Nihon Kaigun*, Vols. I–III. Tokyo: Kawade Shobo Shinsha, 1961.

KING, Ernest, and WHITEHILL, Walter Muir. *Fleet Admiral King.* New York: Norton, 1952.

KNEBEL, Fletcher, and BAILEY, Charles W., II. *No High Ground.* New York: Harper & Bros., 1960.

KODAMA, Yoshio. *I Was Defeated.* Tokyo: Booth and Fukuda, 1951.

KONOE, Fumimaro. *Saigo No Gozenkaigi.* Tokyo: Jikyoku Geppo Sha, 1946.

KRUEGER, Walter. *Down Under to Nippon.* Washington: Combat Forces Press, 1953.

KURIHARA, Ken. *Tenno: Showa-Shi Oboegaki.* Tokyo: Yushindo, 1955.

LAMONT, Lansing. *Day of Trinity.* New York: Atheneum Publishers, 1965.

LAURENCE, William L. *Dawn Over Zero.* New York: Alfred A. Knopf, 1946.

LEAHY, William D. *I Was There.* New York: Whittlesey House, 1950.

LEE, Clark. *One Last Look Around.* New York: Duell, Sloan and Pearce, 1947.

LEMAY, Curtis. *Mission with Lemay.* Garden City, New York: Doubleday & Co. Inc., 1966.

LOCKWOOD, Charles A. *Sink 'Em All.* New York: E. P. Dutton and Co., 1951.

MACARTHUR, Douglas. *Reminiscences.* New York: McGraw-Hill, Inc., 1964.

MACDONALD, Elizabeth P. *Undercover Girl.* New York: Macmillan Co., 1947.

MANAKA, Yoshio. *P. W. Doctor.* Tokyo: Kongo Sha, 1962.

MASHBIR, Sidney F. *I Was an American Spy.* New York: Vantage Press, 1953.

MORISON, Samuel Eliot. *History of the United States Naval Operations in World War II*, Vol. XIV. Boston: Little, Brown and Co., 1960.

—— *The Two-Ocean War.* Boston: Little, Brown and Co., 1963.

MOSLEY, Leonard. *Hirohito, Emperor of Japan.* Englewood Cliffs, New Jersey: Prentice-Hall, Inc., 1966.

NAGAI, Takashi. *We of Nagasaki.* New York: Duell, Sloan and Pearce, 1951.

NEWCOMB, Richard. *Abandon Ship.* New York: Henry Holt & Co., Inc., 1958.

NIWA, Fumio. *Nihon Yaburetari.* Tokyo: Ginza Shuppan Sha, 1948.

OBATA, Taketora. *Ichi Gunjin No Shogai.* Tokyo: Bungei Shunju, 1956.

OSSIP, Jerome J., ed. *509th Pictorial Album,* written and published by and for the members of the 509th Composite Group. Marianas Islands: Tinian, 1945.

OYA, Soichi. *Nihon No Ichiban Nagaihi.* Tokyo: Bungei Shunju, 1965.

PEERS, William R., and BRELIS, Dean. *Behind the Burma Road.* Boston: Little, Brown and Co., 1963.

PERCIVAL, A. E. *The War in Malaya.* London: Eyre and Spottiswoode, Ltd., 1949.

PHILLIPS, Cabell. *The Truman Presidency.* New York: Macmillan Co., 1966.

POTTER, E. B., and NIMITZ, Chester W. *The Great Sea War.* Englewood Cliffs, New Jersey, Prentice-Hall, Inc., 1960.

POTTER, John Deane. *Yamamoto.* New York: Viking Press, 1965.

—— *The Life and Death of a Japanese General.* New York: New American Library, 1962.

ROMANUS, Charles F., and SUNDERLAND, Riley. U.S. *Army in World War II. China-Burma-India Theater, Stilwell's Command Problems.* Washington, D.C.: U.S. Government Printing Office, 1956.

—— *U.S. Army in World War II: Time Runs Out.* Washington, D.C.: U.S. Government Printing Office, 1958.

SAKAI, Saburo. *Samurai.* New York: Ballantine Books, 1957.

SAKOMIZU, Hisatsune. *Kikanjuka No Shusho Kantei.* Tokyo: Kobun Sha, 1964.

SHERWOOD, Robert E. *Roosevelt and Hopkins: An Intimate History.* New York: Harper & Bros., 1948.

SHIGEMTTSU, Mamoru. *Showa: No Doran* (2 vols.). Tokyo: Chuo Koronsha, 1952.

SHIMOMURA, Hiroshi. *Shusen Hishi.* Tokyo: Kodan Sha, 1950.

SLIM, William. *Defeat into Victory.* London: Cassell and Company, Ltd., 1956.

SMITH, Gaddis. *American Diplomacy During the Second World War, 1941–45*. New York: John Wiley and Sons, Inc., 1965.

SMITH, Henry D. *Atomic Energy for Military Purposes*. Princeton, New Jersey: Princeton University Press, 1948.

STIMSON, Henry, and BUNDY, McGeorge. *On Active Service in Peace and War*. New York: Harper & Bros., 1948.

TAKAGI, Soldchi. *Shusen Oboegaki*. Tokyo: Kobundo, 1948.

TAKAMI, Jun. *Haisen Nikki*. Tokyo: Fuji Shoen, 1953.

TANEMURA, Sako. *Daihonei Kimitsu Nisshi*. Tokyo: Diamond Sha, 1952.

TERESAKI, Gwen. *Bridge to the Sun*. Chapel Hill: University of North Carolina Press, 1957.

TOGO, Shigenori. *The Cause of Japan*. New York: Simon and Schuster, 1956.

TOYODA, Soemu. *Saigo No Teikoku Kaigun*. Tokyo: Sekai No Nihon Sha, 1950.

TRUMAN, Harry S. *Memoirs, Vol. I. Year of Decisions*. Garden City, New York: Doubleday and Co., Inc., 1955.

TRUMBULL, Robert. *Nine Who Survived Hiroshima and Nagasaki*. New York: E. P. Dutton and Co., 1957.

TSUJI, Masanobu. *Singapore: The Japanese Version*. New York: St. Martins' Press, Inc., 1961.

TSUKAMOTO, Kiyoshi. *Ah Kogun Saigo No Hi*. Tokyo: Koyo Sha, 1953.

UECHI, Kazufumi. *Okinawa Senshi*. Tokyo: Jiji Tsushin Sha, 1959.

UYEHARA, Cecil H., compiler. *Checklist of Archives in the Japanese Ministry of Foreign Affairs, Tokyo, Japan, 1868–1945*. Washington, D.C.: Library of Congress, 1954.

WAINWRIGHT, Jonathan M. *General Wainwright's Story*. Garden City, New York: Doubleday and Co. Inc., 1946.

WATERMAN, Alan, editor. *Combat Scientists*. Boston: Atlantic-Little, Brown, 1947.

WEDEMEYER, Albert C. *Wedemeyer Reports!* New York: Henry Holt & Co., Inc., 1958.

WHITNEY, Courtney. *MacArthur: His Rendezvous with Destiny.* New York: Alfred A. Knopf, 1956.

WILLOUGHBY, C. A., and CHAMBERLAIN, J. R. *MacArthur 1941–1951.* New York: McGraw-Hill, Inc., 1954.

YOKOTA, Yutaka, and HARRINGTON, Joseph D. *The Kaiten Weapon.* New York: Ballantine Books, 1962.

YOSHIDA, Mitsuru. *Senkan Yamato No Saigo.* Tokyo: Sogen Sha, 1952.

YOSHIDA, Shigeru. *Kaiso Junen* (4 vols.). Tokyo: Shincho Sha, 1957–1958.

YOUNG, John, compiler. *Checklist of Microfilm of Selected Archives of the Japanese Army, Navy and Other Government Agencies, 1868–1945.* Washington, D.C.: Georgetown University Press, 1959.

ZACHARIAS, Ellis M. *Secret Missions.* New York: G. P. Putnam's Sons, 1946.

DOCUMENTS, REPORTS, STATEMENTS, INTERROGATIONS

Atomic Energy Commission: Selected documents pertaining to the atomic bombings of Hiroshima and Nagasaki—survivor reports, messages, blast effects, Tinian-Washington-Los Alamos messages, etc. (unpublished).

Dull, Paul S., and Umemura, Michael: *The Tokyo Trials: A Functional Index to the Proceedings,* Ann Arbor, Michigan, University of Michigan Press, 1957.

Gaimusho (Japanese Foreign Office): *Shusen Shiroku,* Tokyo, Shimbun Gekkan Sha, 1952.

Gaimusho: Selected documents related to period January–September 1945 (unpublished).

International Military Tribunal for the Far East: *Transcript of Proceedings* (48, 412 pp.): Miscellaneous statements, interrogations, documents, evidence.

Japanese Defense Agency, Historical Division, Tokyo, Japan: Selected records and documents related to military and naval activities in period March–September 1945 (unpublished).

Japanese Research Division (ATIS), U.S. Army Far East, Military History Section: Japanese Monographs: Number 7: *Philippines Operations Record Phase III (January–August 1945).* Number 45: *History of Imperial General Headquarters, Army Section (1941–1945)* Number 53: *32nd Army Operations in Okinawa (March–June 1945).* Number 72: *Army Operations in China (January 1944–August 1945).* Number 83: *Okinawa Area Naval Operations (January–June 1945).* Number 119: *Outline of Operations prior to the Termination of War and Activities Connected with the Cessation of Hostilities (July–August 1945).* Number 154: *Record of Operations against Soviet Russian Eastern Front (August 1945).* Number 155: *Record of Operations against Soviet Russia, Northern and Western Fronts (August–September 1945).*

Japanese Research Division (ATIS), U.S. Army Far East Military History Section: *Interrogations of Japanese Officials* (2 vols.) (unpublished); Memo on the Course of the War, by Sokichi Takagi (unpublished); *Personal History Statements* (2 vols.) (unpublished); *Special Studies* (4 vols.) (unpublished); *Statement of Japanese Officials on World War II (4* vols.) (unpublished); *Translation of Japanese Documents* (7 vols.) (unpublished).

Office of Strategic Services: Selected reports and intelligence data (unpublished).

U.S. Army, Supreme Commander for the Allied Powers, Counter Intelligence Section: *The Brocade Banner: The Story of Japanese Nationalism.*

U.S. Department of Defense: *The Entry of the Soviet Union into the War Against Japan, Military Plans, 1941–1945,* Washington, D.C., U.S. Government Printing Office, 1955.

U.S. Department of State: *Potsdam Papers* (2 vols.).

U.S. Department of State Publication No. 3573: *United States Relations with China, with Special Reference to the Period 1944–1949,* Washington, August, 1949.

U.S. Federal Communications Commission: Selected Far East radio reports monitored in 1945.

U.S. 79th Congress Hearings, S.R. 179, Part One.

U.S. Strategic Bombing Survey: *Interrogation of Japanese Officials* (2 vols.), Washington, D.C., U.S. Government Printing Office, 1946.

U.S. Strategic Bombing Survey: Selected interrogations, documents, reports, analyses related to wartime conditions in Japan (unpublished).

MISCELLANEOUS

Magazines: Bungei Shunju, Chuo Koron, Collier's, Life, Newsweek, Saturday Evening Post, Time, Yank.

Newspapers: Asahi Shimbun, Mainichi Shimbun, New York Herald Tribune, The New York Times, San Francisco Chronicle, Stars and Stripes, Washington Post.

Other: Facts on File Yearbook, United States Signal Corps; Audio-Visual Division, Who's Who in Japan.

INDEX OF NAMES

INDEX BY SUBJECT

ABOUT THE AUTHOR

William Craig (1929–1997) was an American historian and novelist. Born and raised in Concord, Massachusetts, he interrupted his career as an advertising salesman to appear on the quiz show *Tic-Tac-Dough* in 1958. With his $42,000 in winnings—a record-breaking amount at the time—Craig enrolled at Columbia University and earned both an undergraduate and a master's degree in history. He published his first book, *The Fall of Japan*, in 1967. A narrative history of the final weeks of World War II in the Pacific, it reached the top ten on the *New York Times* bestseller list and was deemed "virtually flawless" by the *New York Times Book Review*. In order to write *Enemy at the Gates* (1973), a documentary account of the Battle of Stalingrad, Craig travelled to three continents and interviewed hundreds of military and civilian survivors. A *New York Times* bestseller, the book inspired a film of the same name starring Jude Law and Joseph Fiennes. In addition to his histories of World War II, Craig wrote two acclaimed espionage thrillers: *The Tashkent Crisis* (1971) and *The Strasbourg Legacy* (1975).

WILLIAM CRAIG

FROM OPEN ROAD MEDIA

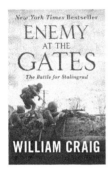

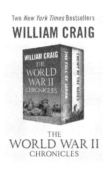

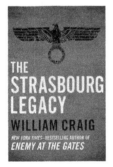

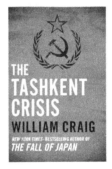

OPEN ROAD

INTEGRATED MEDIA

Find a full list of our authors and
titles at www.openroadmedia.com

FOLLOW US
@OpenRoadMedia

CPSIA information can be obtained
at www.ICGtesting.com
Printed in the USA
JSHW030541090222
22667JS00002B/2

9 781504 046893